D1792948

AN EIGHTEENTH-CENTURY SHOPKEEPER
ABRAHAM DENT OF KIRKBY STEPHEN

An
Eighteenth-Century Shopkeeper

ABRAHAM DENT
of
KIRKBY STEPHEN

by
T. S. WILLAN

MANCHESTER UNIVERSITY PRESS

Printed in Great Britain by Butler & Tanner Ltd., Frome and London

Preface

THIS book is based very largely on Abraham Dent's business records, only part of which has survived. I have not thought it necessary to give footnote references to these records or to other records in my possession or to parish registers. Thus where statements are made for which no source is given, it must be assumed that the source is either the business records or other records in my possession or a parish register. Some additional information has been found in local record offices. Visits to these record offices are one of the great pleasures of this sort of research. On such visits I have always met with unfailing courtesy and helpfulness from the archivists and their staffs. I would like to thank the archivists of the Record Offices of Westmorland, Cumberland, the North Riding and Lancashire, and of the Archives Department of Leeds City Library, and of the Borthwick Institute at York. I am especially grateful to Miss S. J. MacPherson, the archivist of the Westmorland Record Office, for searching out material and for the loan of a microfilm of the bishops' transcripts of Kirkby Stephen parish registers. My colleague Mr. B. L. Anderson kindly read the typescript of this book and made very helpful suggestions. Any errors that have survived his scrutiny are all my own. Finally I am indebted to Mr. W. John Smith of Alkrington for drawing the pedigrees and the map.

Manchester, 1969   T. S. W.

Contents

Illustrations

Chapter I

The Setting

EIGHTEENTH-CENTURY Kirkby Stephen was a small market town with a long and uneventful history. At the census of 1801 there were 2,515 inhabitants in the parish, but of these only 1,141 were in the township of Kirkby Stephen; the remainder were in the surrounding hamlets and villages and in Mallerstang. The district was primarily agricultural, and the majority of the men buried in the churchyard at Kirkby Stephen in the decade 1772–81 were described as yeoman, husbandman or farmer. The majority, but only a bare majority, were so described. It is easy to exaggerate the proportion of people directly engaged in agriculture for any period before the nineteenth century. No doubt most people in Kirkby Stephen were dependent either directly or indirectly on agriculture for their livelihoods, but many of them were neither farmers nor farm labourers. When the parish registers begin to record occupations in the 1770s and 1780s, they show a wide range of callings. There were the usual craftsmen: carpenters, masons, plasterers and slaters; tailors, shoemakers and cloggers; saddlers, tanners and curriers; millers, maltsters and tallow chandlers; blacksmiths and plumbers. Such occupations were not confined to the town itself; Winton had its clogger, shoemaker, tailor and carpenter, Wharton its carpenter, Hartley its miller and carpenter, Soulby its rope maker and basket maker and carpenter, and Kaber its stone cutter.

Of other industrial occupations there is not much trace. Some mining of lead and coal was carried out in the district. In 1772 David Harker of Hartley, a boy of 13, was killed by falling 'down a shaft at the lead mines upon Hartley fell'. The following year Hugh MacFarson was described as a miner, Matthew Magee as a coal miner and Thomas Waller as a collier; all were of Kirkby Stephen. There was also a sprinkling of miners in the smaller places, in Hartley, Winton and Nateby. Even if the county historians were right in claiming in 1777 that both coal and lead mining had ceased on Hartley fell,[1] there was clearly some mining going on, though it does not seem to have been very important. There was also some manufacture of cloth, though it too may not have been important. In the 1770s and 1780s there were weavers at Kirkby Stephen and at Soulby, which also had a fuller. Kirkby Stephen had its comb makers too, but their combs may have been used on wool that went, not into cloth, but into knitted stockings, which were the most important manufactured product of the whole region.

Kirkby Stephen itself was 'a considerable market town; noted for the sale of a great number of stockings, knit there and in the neighbourhood'.[2] It had an ancient parish church, an Elizabethan grammar school endowed by Thomas Lord Wharton in 1566, a market on Mondays and two fairs a year. By the 1770s it was linked by turnpike roads southwards to Kendal and Sedbergh, and northwards to Brough and Appleby.[3] As a shopping and commercial centre Kirkby Stephen served an area wider than the parish itself, though that covered nearly 28,000 acres. This role as a commercial and shopping centre is reflected not only in the number of carriers and innkeepers which the parish registers reveal, but also in the professional and commercial occupations of the inhabitants, or some of them. In 1784 the town had two attorneys at law, James Fawcett and John Harrison, two surgeons, apothecaries and men midwives, Thomas Harrison and John Jackson, two brewers, John Dickinson and the partnership of Dent, Portees and Mason, and a wine and brandy merchant, Christopher Alderson. There were three comb makers, all called Merril, three curriers, all called Bradley, two skinners, both called Mason, and two tanners, Thomas Bradley and Miles Mason: all reflecting the pastoral agriculture of the district. Finally there were two tallow chandlers, two clock makers, a saddler and ten

---

[1] J. Nicolson and R. Burn, *The History and Antiquities of the Counties of Westmorland and Cumberland*, i, p. 547.

[2] Ibid., i, p. 544.

[3] J. F. Curwen, *Records relating to the Barony of Kendale*, iii, pp. 1–20.

shopkeepers. Of the shopkeepers two were described as milliners, one as a hardwareman, one as a grocer and hardwareman, and the rest as grocers or linen and woollen drapers and grocers.

It is doubtful whether this list, drawn from the Directory of 1784, is exhaustive.[1] The Directory obviously drew the line at tailors and shoemakers, but why exclude William Barnett and John Shaw, both described as butchers in the parish registers for 1783–84, or John Bird described as a barber? Useful as they are, these early directories obviously have their limitations; perhaps they give the truth but not the whole truth. As a market town Kirkby Stephen could be expected to have its attorneys and surgeons and shopkeepers. It had also its parson and schoolmaster, and in the 1770s its dancing master, Thomas Inman, and its itinerant musician, John Lamb, who claimed that 'he was married in Scotland to Eleanor Eubank of this place', but as he could produce no certificate of the marriage, his successive children were registered as illegitimate. By the 1780s there was a tobacconist and a bookbinder and Thomas Breaks, mathematician, who died in 1789 and was in fact a schoolmaster.

This community showed some mobility in a geographical sense. Abraham Dent himself finally went to live at Sedbusk in Wensleydale, one of his daughters lived in London after her marriage, and his kinsman, John Waller, went south to Plymouth as a naval purser. There were others who sought their fortunes or their livelihoods elsewhere. Thomas Eubank was a gunner in the East India service when he married Isabella Parkins in 1773. Joseph Cowper of Kaber was a 'waiter at a coffee house in London' when his son John was baptized in 1782. In the reverse direction were the 'incomers' like Zorayda Anna, a Blackamoor girl, who was baptized on 1 January 1766, and Christopher Wartenburdg, 'a Pensioner but formerly a gunsmith in the Tower of London', who was buried on 18 July 1772. These were hardly typical. Most incomers were probably brides drawn largely from the courting catchment area. They certainly came on occasion from upper Wensleydale, Swaledale, Sedbergh, Brough and elsewhere, despite

---

[1] W. Bailey, *British Directory* (1784), iii, p. 605. Kirkby Stephen is not included in Bailey's *Northern Directory* of 1781.

the fact the census of 1801 showed 1,140 males and 1,375 females in the parish.

It is not always easy to trace geographical mobility in this period, but it is still more difficult to trace social mobility in the sense of people moving up and down the social scale. Clearly there were such movements. John Waller, the naval purser, was the son of a carpenter; one of Abraham Dent's sons became an army officer and so a gentleman, a title only given to his father late in life. Such movement was easier for the sons than for the fathers, partly because the sons were more mobile and could move both outwards and upwards. And easier for the daughters than for the mothers, for the daughters could better or worsen themselves by marriage. John Waller's wife seems to have been the daughter of a butcher. There was plenty of room, if not plenty of opportunity, to move, for even small town society showed wide gradations. There was a big gap, both social and economic, between Charles Kinsey, esquire, of Smardale Hall, and William Sayer, collier and pauper, who died in 1784, or between Abraham Dent and one of his customers, James Petty, 'labourer in town'.

It was in this community of a northern market town that Abraham Dent lived and worked for most, but not all, of his life. There were many Dents in and around Kirkby Stephen in the eighteenth century, and their exact relationship cannot now be disentangled. There were Dents in Mallerstang and at Wharton, Hartley, Kaber, Winton and Soulby. Most of them were farmers, though Francis Dent of Hartley who died in 1781 was a tailor, as was Joshua Dent of Soulby who died in 1774 aged 23. In Kirkby Stephen itself the name was common and was held by a number of families who may or may not have been related. The evidence suggests poorer and richer families of Dents in the town. John Dent, who died in 1763, was described as 'poor', Agnes Dent, who died eight years later at the age of 23, was 'a servant', and Isabel Dent, who bought goods from Abraham Dent in the 1760s, was described as 'our servant'. Finally Henry Dent, who died in 1814 at the age of 61, was described starkly as 'pauper', but he seems to have been born outside the town and may have come in to die in the workhouse. On the richer side may have been James Dent, a churchwarden in 1770, Joseph Dent, a husbandman who died in 1801 aged 76, and William Dent, a butcher who was killed in 1805 'by the overturning of a cart upon him'.

The shopkeeping Dents undoubtedly belonged to the better off section of the Dents, though their pedigree remains obscure. William Dent, Abraham's father, was born in 1698 and died in 1774. His parents are not known, nor is it certain when or whom he married. He seems to have had only two children, Abraham and a daughter, Isabel, baptized in 1732. William Dent was variously described as a mercer, a merchant and a wine merchant. He was in fact a shopkeeper and wine merchant in company with, and perhaps in partnership with, his son Abraham. In the 1750s he held some property as a customary tenant of the manor of Kirkby Stephen. This consisted of a messuage and tenement, a close, inclosure or parcel of ground called Fowl or Fool Pool, and another parcel of ground with the appurtenances. The parcel with appurtenances was in fact three 'beastgates, pasture gates or cattle-gates' in the common pasture called Kirkby Stephen Intack, which Dent had bought from John Moore of Kirkby Stephen in 1742 for £13. The total rent of this property, payable to the Lord of the Manor, Sir James Lowther, was 5s. 10½d., but the total fines payable in 1757 on the death of Lowther's father, Robert Lowther, were £2 18s. 9d., which was ten times the rent. The entire holding hardly suggests that William was a farmer as well as a shopkeeper; it was not more than any country shopkeeper might need for his horse or horses.

Abraham Dent, apparently William's only son, was baptized on 4 February 1729. Nothing is known of his upbringing, but he wrote a good hand which may have been acquired at the local grammar school. The business of a shopkeeper and wine merchant he presumably learned from his father, but this is mere conjecture. Even the details of his successive marriages remain obscure. On 19 August 1754 he married Elizabeth Grainger of Kirkby Stephen. There seems no doubt about this marriage, as a Mr. Grainger is referred to as Abraham's father-in-law. A son, William, was born and died in 1755 and a second William, born in 1759, died the following year. In 1761 a daughter, Betty or

Elizabeth, was born. One of her exercise books, in which she practised handwriting, has survived. In it she wrote, in an enormous copperplate hand, such improving maxims as 'Knowledge procures general Esteem', 'Labour improves Wealth', 'Missfortunes are a kind of Discipline', 'Quarrelsome Persons are dangrous', and 'Youth is the best time for learning'. That was in 1775 and 1776. In 1778 at the age of 17, Elizabeth married William Dobson, who was 20 years old, and she and her husband seem to have gone to live in London.

Elizabeth was followed by a son, Thomas, baptized on 10 April 1765, a year in which his father was churchwarden. Thomas married Ann Rudd on 21 April 1790. She was aged 23 and was the daughter of Richard Rudd, an apothecary in Kirkby Stephen. She bore Thomas at least eight children. Finally Abraham Dent's last child, called Abraham after his father, was born in 1767. He married Ann Brathwaite of Warcop in 1796. They appear to have had only one child, a daughter Isabella, born in 1797.

All these children of Abraham Dent senior seem to have been born to his first wife Elizabeth, but even this is not quite certain. On 17 February 1781 there was buried at Kirkby Stephen Ann, wife of Abraham Dent of Kirkby Stephen, wine merchant, aged 42. Ann's age makes it virtually impossible that Ann should be a mistake for Elizabeth, and it is highly unlikely that there were two wine merchants called Abraham Dent in 1781. It can only be concluded that Elizabeth had died and that Abraham had re-married, though there is no record of these events. Nor is it certain who Ann was. It is probable that she was either a Waller or a Barnett, for Isabella Barnett, who married John Waller, referred to Abraham Dent as her brother. Two years after Ann's death Abraham married a widow of Sedbusk in Wensleydale, where he eventually went to live.

Abraham Dent was a man of many activities. He was a shopkeeper and a wine merchant as his father had been. He was also a brewer and a considerable dealer in, and perhaps manufacturer of, knitted stockings. He owned some land; for example on 14 March 1771 he paid £3 17s. 10d. for the 'great tithes of corn' on three closes which he owned in the township of Kirkby Stephen. The closes were known as North Waitby Thorns and consisted of 5 acres 3 roods and 38 perches of land adjoining the highway leading between Crosby Garrett and Kirkby Stephen. There is no evidence that Dent farmed this land, but it may have provided fodder for the horse or horses which he must have used. It was business in various forms, and not farming, that occupied most of his life, and it is his business activities which merit examination.

Chapter II

The Shopkeeper: Goods and Customers

THE history of shopping has been written,[1] but not the history of shops. This may be the result of a persistent belief that people, before the nineteenth century, obtained their goods at fairs and markets or from pedlars. People did buy goods at fairs and markets and from pedlars, who may themselves have got their supplies from shopkeepers, but shops were more numerous and more important than is commonly realized. Thus Kendal, which had a population of 6,892 in 1801, had at least 29 shops in 1784, when Appleby had at least eight and Penrith at least 15.[2] In the same year Kirkby Stephen had at least 12 shops, if the butchers are included. Of these, three were described as grocers, three as linen and woollen drapers and grocers, and one as hardwareman and grocer. Obviously the number of specialized shops increased with the size of the town. Most of the shopkeepers in Kendal were described simply as grocers or mercers or ironmongers or linen drapers, but they may have sold a wider range of goods than these descriptions imply. Both William and Abraham Dent were sometimes described as mercers, but their trade was not confined to mercery if any reasonable definition is given to that elastic term. In 1781 the hamlet of Soulby had a stationer, but it is difficult to believe that he lived solely by selling stationery.

This retail trade is elusive partly because of the paucity of sources. If shopkeepers kept accounts, few of those accounts seem to have survived. If shopkeepers were more articulate and kept diaries, few of those too seem to have survived, and when they have, they can be tantalizingly uninformative. Young Strother, who worked in a draper's shop in Hull, kept a Journal from 1784 to 1785, but it says little of his activities as a shopkeeper, which he

---

[1] D. Davis, *A History of Shopping* (1966).
[2] W. Bailey, *British Directory* (1784), iii, pp. 554–7; iv, pp. 811, 878–9.

regarded as rather beneath him.[1] The Dents do not seem to have kept diaries, but they certainly kept accounts, parts of which have survived. Those relating to the shop fall within the period 1756 to 1777. For most of this period Abraham Dent's father was still alive and certainly during the earlier years he was actively engaged in shopkeeping. It is not clear what the business relationship between father and son was. Their suppliers sometimes referred to them as Messrs. W. Dent & Son, which suggests a partnership. Certainly Abraham was active in the shop throughout this period, and the evidence suggests an increasing activity as his father grew older. He seems also to have carried on the shop for some time after his father's death. It seems convenient, therefore, and not grossly misleading, to refer on occasion to Abraham as the shopkeeper during this period, though bearing in mind that for part of the time he shared that position with his father.

Among the records relating to the shop is a day book in which were entered goods sold, but not paid for at the time of sale. When the goods were finally paid for, the entry was crossed through. These entries of credit sales give the quantity and price of the goods and the customer's name. They extend from May 1762 to September 1765, though there are a few entries of later date. Obviously these credit sales do not give a complete picture of the trade during those years, but they do give a very detailed picture of what was sold in the shop and to whom. They show clearly that the Dents were grocers, mercers and stationers, though it is interesting to note that they were never described as grocers or stationers, which shows the limitations of contemporary descriptions. Most of the goods sold in the shop could be loosely classified as grocery, mercery and stationery.

Of the groceries, three items were especially prominent: tea, sugar and flour. Green and black tea was sold, and both sorts were expensive. Green tea of unspecified type cost 10*s*. to 10*s*. 6*d*. lb., but Hyson cost 16*s*. to 19*s*. lb. Of the black teas, Bohea was much the cheapest at 4*s*. 8*d*. to 6*s*. lb., compared with Souchong at 9*s*. to

---

[1] C. Caine, ed. *Strother's Journal*. The original Journal is B. M. Egerton MSS. 2479; it is fuller than the printed version, but even so it does not throw any more light on Strother as a shopkeeper.

B

12s. lb. A fine Congou cost 11s. 4d. lb. These high prices were due less to the cost of production or the cost of bringing the tea from China than to the high duty. Whatever its other attractions Kirkby Stephen was hardly a good centre for smuggling. It is not surprising that tea was often sold in very small quantities and that tea caddies had locks. Despite its high price tea seems to have been fairly widely consumed, as Arthur Young was always noting with disapproval. Coffee, on the other hand, rarely appeared; when it did the price ranged from 4s. to 6s. lb. The Rev. Mr. Knowsley of Musgrave apparently preferred to grind his own for he bought the beans at 2s. lb. Cocoa was even rarer than coffee, though Jonathan Ewbanke paid 1s. for a pound of 'coccoa' in December 1763. Alcoholic drinks do not figure much in the day book, perhaps because the Dents did not often sell them on credit or perhaps because, as wine merchants, they kept separate accounts of them which have not survived. Some rum and brandy were sold with the groceries, the former at 6s. and 7s. a gallon, the latter at 6s. and 6s. 6d. a gallon; Jonathan Ewbanke on Stainmore bought 6 quarts of rum for 9s. and a bottle of brandy for 1s. 6d., which must have been a quart bottle. There is no mention of wine, but The Rev. Mr. Knowsley bought a dozen 'cyder' in 1764 for 6s. 6d. Kirkby Stephen was in a beer and not a cider region, and this may be reflected in the sales of barley and is certainly reflected in the sales of hops. Barley ranged in price from 1s. 7d. to 2s. 0½d. a stone, but the latter was exceptional. It was sometimes delivered 'with our leather bagg' by the mealman. Hops ranged even more widely in price, from 7½d. to as much as 2s. 8d. lb. The figures show a fairly steady increase from 1763 to 1765. Hops were sold widely and often in small quantities, which suggests considerable home brewing.

Sugar, like tea, was widely bought although it was rather expensive. When described simply as sugar the price ranged from 4d. to 6½d. lb. Loaf sugar was dearer, ranging from 7½d. to 11d. lb., and there was a double refined loaf sugar at 12d. lb. The sugar loaf, which was only suitable for those who bought in quantity, cost 8½d. or 9d. lb. Leonard Barnett bought a sugar loaf of 24½ lb. for 18s. 4½d. in August 1763 and Dr. Richard Rudd one of 23 lb. for 16s. 3½d. on 18 December 1763, well in time for Christmas. Candy, sometimes described as sugar candy, cost $9\frac{1}{4}d.$ to 10*d.* lb. Matthew Thompson 'in town' bought 38 lb. of it on 9 May 1763, which suggests that he either had a sweet tooth or kept a sweet shop or was going to have a sweet stall at the fair later in the month. Sugar was not the only sweetening on sale, for large quantities of treacle were sold. At 16*s.* 6*d.* to 20*s.* cwt., treacle was much cheaper than sugar. It was sold by the pound, the runlet, the hogshead and the hundredweight. The quantities sold were sometimes so large that they must surely have been bought for resale. Thus John Cockbain of Sedbergh bought 22 cwt. 3 qr. $14\frac{3}{4}$ lb. of treacle between May and November 1763. What could he do with more than a ton of treacle except retail it?

Flour was more essential than tea or sugar and was widely sold for home baking, though in the 1770s, if not before, Kirkby Stephen had a bread baker. Flour ranged in price from 1*s.* 7*d.* to 2*s.* 5*d.* a stone. It was wheaten flour and was bought by all classes of customers, including James Petty, 'a labourer in town'. The county historians maintained that 'persons of condition' ate wheaten bread while the common people ate oaten bread,[1] but the Dents seem to have sold very little oats or oatmeal, though they did very occasionally sell a rye loaf at $5\frac{1}{2}d.$ to the Merrils, who were comb makers. They also sold considerable quantities of wheat at 11*s.* 4*d.* to 12*s.* a bushel. Most of this went to a single customer, Ann Jack in town, who bought by the boll (of one bushel) and by the load (of two bushels). It is not known what she did with the wheat, for she bought far more than she could possibly have consumed. Perhaps she had it ground and then sold the flour, for as Sir John Clapham once remarked, men do not live by chewing wheat.

Obviously grocers dealt in tea and sugar and treacle and flour, but outside these staples, what sort of a stock was a country grocer expected to carry? If the Dents are any guide, he was expected to offer a considerable range of goods, which almost defies classification. The Dents sold household goods: soap, hard and soft, at $6\frac{1}{2}d.$ to 7*d.* lb., powder blue at 1*s.* 2*d.* to 2*s.* lb., Spanish white at 1*d.* lb., ivory black at 1*d.* oz., lamp black at 1*s.* lb., pearl ashes at

[1] Nicolson and Burn, op. cit., i, p. 11.

10*d*. lb., starch at 5¼*d* to 6*d*. lb., and bees wax at 1*s*. 4*d*. lb. They sold a little tallow at 4*s*. 8*d*. cwt. and some candles at 6*d*. to 6½*d*. lb., but these were probably more often bought direct from the tallow chandlers. Their tobacco cost from 1*s*. 1½*d*. to 1*s*. 4*d*. lb., but it was possible to get twist at 11½*d*. lb.; snuff was 1*s*. 4*d*. lb.

Among eatables, rice at 3*d*. lb. and split peas at 3*d*. to 4*d*. a quart were more common and much cheaper than sago at 2*s*. 4*d*. lb. No fresh fruit was sold except lemons at 2*d*. each and a single pannier of apples for 1*s*. 6*d*., and no nuts except almonds at 2*s*. lb. On the other hand the shop sold a good deal of dried fruit: figs at 3½*d*. to 4*d*. lb., prunes at 3½*d*. to 5*d*. lb., currants, sometimes described as Smyrna currants, at 3*d*. to 7*d*. lb., and raisins, sometimes described as Malaga raisins, at 3*d*. to 8*d*. lb. On occasion currants and raisins were bought in surprising quantities; on 6 February 1764 Mr. Leonard Barnett in town bought 76 lb. Malaga raisins and 56 lb. Smyrna currants, all at 3*d*. lb. Finally among the groceries sold in the shop were the usual condiments and spices: mustard at 1*s*. to 1*s*. 6*d*. lb., vinegar at 4*d*. a quart, pepper at 1¼*d*. to 1½*d*. oz., nutmegs at 1*d*. each, aniseeds at 9*d*. to 10*d*. lb., mace at 1*s*. 4*d*. oz., and cloves at 1*s*. 2*d*. to 1*s*. 4*d*. oz.

The Dents clearly kept a good range of groceries, most of them originally imported, but there are interesting omissions from their stock. The absence of butter, cheese and eggs may perhaps be explained by the fact that people either produced these themselves or bought them in the market direct from the farmers or their wives. In that case shop and market were complementary. The shop sold exotic products, the market sold local produce. No doubt there might be some competition between the two, but it should be remembered that people came to town on market day to buy as well as to sell. The Lancaster shopkeeper, William Stout, got additional help in his shop 'on the market and fair days'.[1] The weekly market may explain the absence of butter, cheese and eggs from the Dents' stock, but the absence of salt is curious and not so easily explained. It is not likely that the sale of salt was monopolized by some other grocer or that people always paid cash for

[1] J. D. Marshall, ed., *The Autobiography of William Stout of Lancaster, 1665–1752*, p. 162.

their salt. It is likely that a good deal of salt was used, even if the autumn holocausts of slaughtering and salting are no longer believed in. Even so, the Dents do not seem to have sold salt. The groceries they did sell, they sold at retail prices, and one of the interesting things about those prices is the wide variation in price of the same commodity. There are many possible explanations of this. The evidence relates to credit sales, and the Dents may have varied the price according to the credit standing of the customer, but this seems unlikely. Again prices may have varied because small quantities were sold at relatively higher prices than large quantities, but this does not seem to have been the case. Or again, within a three-year period the price of identical goods could vary because of general price movements, and this seems to have been true of things like flour, wheat and hops, which are subject to seasonal fluctuations. Finally goods are not necessarily identical even when they bear the same names, and some of the variations in prices reflect variations in quality. This seems to have been true of such things as tea, sugar, currants and raisins. These variations in prices show how difficult it would be to compile a satisfactory price index, still more a satisfactory cost-of-living index, even for a limited area and a limited time.

Although the Dents were never described as grocers, they were certainly described as mercers. But what did a country mercer sell in the 1760s? The term mercer was no longer confined, if it ever had been, to dealers in silks and other costly fabrics, but cloth seems to have remained the basis of the trade. As mercers the Dents did not normally sell clothes, though on one occasion they sold a silk cloak for 15*s.* and a scarlet cardinal, also a cloak, for 15*s.* 6*d.* Nor did they normally sell hats, though again they sold a single satin hat for 3*s.* 6*d.* and a cotton cap for 1*s.* Black stockings at 2*s.* to 3*s.* a pair and scarlet garters at 6*d.* a pair were other rare items, as were gloves, though in March 1764 The Rev. Mr. Wilson bought 5 pairs of women's gloves at 1*s.* 1*d.* a pair and 11 pairs of men's at 1*s.* a pair, which must surely have been a mourning order. Handkerchiefs were much more common and were sold in a variety of fabrics and colours: silk at 4*s.* 4*d.* to 5*s.* each, red linen at 2*s.*, muslin at 4*s.* 6*d.* and Barcelona at 5*s.*

All these were incidental to the main mercery trade, which consisted of things necessary for the making of clothes. These included a little silk at 2s. to 2s. 6d. the ounce and a good deal of lint or flax ready for spinning at 8d. to 1s. 4d. lb. They included, obviously, thread, pins, hooks and eyes, stay hooks, whale bone (at 6s. to 8s. lb.), and a variety of braids, ribbons and tapes. The greatest variety among these small items was in buttons: horn, shell, glass, gilt, twist, pearl, metal and filigree, at anything from 2d. to 2s. a dozen, though the most usual prices were from 3d. to 8d. a dozen. But the greatest variety of all was in cloth, of which at least forty sorts were sold. They ranged in price from 6d. yd. for harden to 16s. yd. for superfine black cloth bought by the clergy. A good deal of the cloth sold was linen, sometimes further defined as glazed, unwet, bleached or unbleached. The Dents got some of their linen and harden bleached by Robert Bradshaw of Black Sike, 'the bleatcher', who charged 6s. 10d. for bleaching $36\frac{1}{2}$ yds. harden and the same sum for bleaching 42 yds. linen in 1764. Linen ranged in price from 10d. to 1s. 4d. a yard. Other popular cloths were shalloon (11d. to 1s. 4d. a yd.), flannel (11d. to 1s. 2d. yd.), everlasting (2s. to 2s. 8d. yd.), drill, often described as Russia drill (1s. to 1s. 5d. yd.), calamanco (11d. to 1s. 2d. yd., but a specially fine calamanco cost 2s. yd.), tammy, some described as Yorkshire and some as Coventry (11d. to 1s. 4d. yd.), thick-set (1s. 7d. to 2s. 6d. yd.), buckram (1s. yd.) and fustian (9d. to 1s. 8d. yd.). One variety of fustian was described as 'Bulls Lug fustian', which sounds like a bucolic jest. Some of the cloths were more esoteric, for it is not clear what types of cloth were represented by blushown, allopen and dorsetteen, though dimothy was presumably a variant of dimity. Of the very expensive cloths, velvet was on one occasion sold by the nail of $2\frac{1}{4}$ inches, 3 nails costing 2s. 9d.

Much of this cloth was sold for making clothes, and it was often sold in lengths of from 3 to 5 or 6 yards, but the width is not stated. It would be rash to assume from this that the buyers necessarily made up the clothes themselves. In March 1764 The Rev. Mr. Wilson bought 3 yards superfine black cloth, 6 yards of shalloon, 3 yards dimothy, 1 yard buckram, some pocket fustian and 'canvis', 3 dozen coat buttons and 3 dozen breast buttons, and some thread, tape and twist. This may have been an almost standard collection of materials for a clerical outfit, for in December of the same year The Rev. Mr. Richardson of Huddersfield bought the same items though not always in the same quantities. It is not likely that either of these parsons made up the material himself or even got his servants to do it. Again and again people bought a collection of cloths, together with buttons, thread and tapes, which must have been in anticipation of a visit to or a visit from the tailor. There is a popular belief that people made their own clothes before the nineteenth century, but in that case how did the numerous tailors get a living?

At least people did not make their own paper though they may have made their own pens. They could have bought both from the Dents' stationery department, if that anachronistic term may be used. As stationers the Dents sold a considerable variety of paper, some of it described as gilt, blue, brown, ruled, at prices ranging from 3*d*. to 1*s*. a quire. Single sheets cost more, and the stamped paper for deeds and indentures usually cost 2*s*. 8*d*. a sheet, but this of course included the stamp duty. Some paper was sold in book form: two quires 'paper bound for turnpike' cost 2*s*. 6*d*. A shop book of 5 quires bound and ruled cost 6*s*. and its alphabet or index 6*d*. Other shop books cost 4*s*. and 4*s*. 6*d*., and a memorandum book 1*s*. 6*d*. To use with the paper there were quills at 3*d*. to 3½*d*. for 50, pencils at ½*d*. each, ink and inkhorns and sand and wax and wafers. As an alternative a slate could be bought for 1*s*. and slate pencils for 1½*d*. each. For pleasure there were packs of cards at a shilling a pack.

These items are less interesting than the almanacs, magazines and books that the Dents sold. A sheet almanac could be bought for 6*d*., but that perennial source of rural culture, *Old Moore*, cost 9*d*. A Rider almanac, if bought in December or January, cost 2*s*.9*d*., but if the buyer waited until May, as Mathew Thomson did in 1764, he could get it for 2*s*. 6*d*. It may have been difficult to gauge the almanac market for in April 1763 the Dents returned to their supplier '24 Moor Almanaks, 4 Partridge, 3 Ladies, 2 Saunders, 1 Andrews, in all 34 at 8*d*.', which implies that the wholesale price of an almanac, or at least of *Old Moore*, was a penny less than the retail price. Five different magazines were sold, the *London, Universal, Royal, Gentleman's,* and *The Beauties of all the Magazines selected,* though the last was less popular than the others. There is some evidence of how many copies of these magazines the Dents sold. In 1759 it seems to have been 125, of which the wholesale price was $5\frac{1}{4}d.$ a copy. In 1762 they sold 26 *Gentleman's,* 28 *Universal,* 39 *London* and 24 *Royal,* and in 1763 26 *Gentleman's,* 28 *Universal,* 13 *London* and 24 *Beauties.* As these were monthly magazines, 26 *Gentleman's* could represent two annual subscriptions and two odd copies. No doubt copies would circulate among families and friends, for the *London* cost 6s. 6d. for a year. Bound magazines, presumably no longer current, were much cheaper. Dr. Wilson of Redgill bought 5 volumes of bound magazines at 8d. a volume in 1763.

Bound magazines should perhaps be classed with books in which the Dents had a considerable trade. Very occasionally the books were described as second-hand: Anthony Simpson bought a second-hand grammar in 1762 for a shilling, which seems to have been two-thirds of the price of a new copy. But most of the books were new, and they are difficult to classify. Many of them were educational, ranging from the most elementary instruction to classical texts. A Royal Primer cost 3d., a spelling book 6d. (but Markham's spelling book cost 8d.), an Accidence 8d., and a spelling dictionary 1s. (though Young's *Dictionary* cost 7s.). The most popular of these works was undoubtedly Weild's *Reading made quite easy,* which sold at 6d. and which the Dents sometimes bought by the dozen from the supplier, and sometimes returned to him by the dozen when unsold. This return of unsold books rather suggests that the Dents worked on a sale or return basis, but it would be difficult to prove this. The classical works were more varied and more expensive. They included Joseph Warton's edition of Virgil in 4 volumes at 13s. and Joseph Trapp's edition of the same author in 2 volumes at 6s.; John Stirling's edition of Terence, 'with . . . the words of the author . . . placed in their natural and grammatical order' for 5s. and Christopher Smart's Horace in 2 volumes at 6s. Other authors were Justinian, if that is what 'Latin Justin' at 1*s*. 1*d*. means, Cicero, Ovid, Juvenal, Florus, Sallust, Xenophon and Dionysius. Latin clearly predominated over Greek, though an occasional Greek grammar and Greek Testament were sold.

Other books that were sold in the shop seem to have been mainly religious. They included Testaments at 11*d*. and 1*s*., Prayer Books at 1*s*. 6*d*. and 2*s*. 8*d*., Tillotson's *Sermons*, Hervey's *Meditations among the Tombs*, and King's *Heathen Gods*. On a more secular plane were Salmon's *Geography* and Leadbetter's *Dialling*.

It is not possible to discover the full range of books which the Dents sold. The surviving titles, often in cryptic form, are to be found in the day book of credit sales, supplemented by a few references in the accounts of the wholesalers. As far as it goes, the evidence suggests a reading public that was either involuntary, as in the case of educational books for children, or was rather austere. Lighter books are conspicuously absent; there are no novels, no Richardson, Sterne or Smollett. Perhaps such books were always bought for cash, or perhaps they were bought elsewhere. It is difficult to believe that some of them were not read, or that the magazines were an adequate substitute for them.

In the eighteenth century country printers sold patent medicines. The Dents were not printers, but their business as stationers brought them into contact with the Kendal printers, Thomas and James Ashburner, and it was probably from this contact that their trade in patent medicines arose. Some of the goods they sold, though not patent medicines, had a medicinal use: the 'flour of brimstone' at 1*d*. oz., the Spanish juice or liquorice at 1*d*. to 1½*d*. oz., and the bottle of eye water for 6*d*. Of patent medicines properly so called, the Dents seem to have sold only two kinds. One was Anderson's pills, which cost 1*s*. a box, though it was possible to buy sixpenny worth or even threepenny worth. The other was Daffy's Elixir. This famous eighteenth-century remedy was 'a certain Cure (under God) in most Distempers, viz The Gout and Rheumatism, with all those torturing Pains attending them; it takes away the Scurvy Root and Branch . . . Is wonderful in the Stone, and Gravel in the Kidneys'. According to a broadsheet, still in the Dents' day book, the Original Daffy's Elixir was 'appointed to be Sold by Mr. Ashburnar, Bookseller and Stationer in Kendal, Wholesale and Retail, and by no other Person in this Town'. It exceeded 'all the Medicines ever Prepared' and was 'the Only Family Medicine in Great Britain'. The public was warned 'not to buy a Spurious Sort, made by various Pretenders, who know nothing of the Preparation, and who, to make their rubbish Elixir go off, have counterfeited this Seal and Bill of Cures'. A 'Daffy Bottle' cost 1s. 3d., and it was undoubtedly popular. In September 1762 Thomas Yeats in town got a bottle on the 14th, sent the maid for another bottle on the 18th and his daughter for yet another on the 27th. Thomas Pearson bought 12 bottles between March and December 1764, which suggests great faith or hypochondria or both.

Though most of the goods sold in the shop can be loosely classified as grocery, mercery or stationery wares, a few do not fall into these categories. The most important of these was, rather surprisingly, gunpowder. Some of this was bought for sporting purposes: John Yeats bought $4\frac{1}{2}d$. worth of powder and shot in 1763 and in the same year Mrs. Jane Brecan bought 2 lb. fine powder and 6 lb. shot for 3s. $5\frac{1}{2}d$. But most of the gunpowder was obviously used for industrial purposes, that is for blasting in quarries or mines. The biggest buyers were at Awgill,[1] where a variety of partnerships or companies seems to have operated. In October 1762 George Harker, John Coat and Company at Awgill bought 20 lb. powder, and 38 lb. the following month. The following spring they were buying at the rate of 4 lb. a week. About the same time Robert Wharton and Company at Awgill were buying 12 lb. powder a month and Matthew Bell, senior, was buying 6 lb. a month. In the autumn of 1762 Samuel Peacock and Company at Riggs were buying between 4 lb. and 8 lb. of powder a month. The price was nearly always 1s. 1d. lb. Gunpowder was not produced locally at that time, for the first mills in Westmorland were built by John Wakefield at Sedgwick in 1764.[2]

There was a regular sale for gunpowder and an irregular sale

[1] Perhaps Augill near Brough.
[2] P. N. Wilson, 'The gunpowder mills of Westmorland and Furness', *Trans. Newcomen Soc.*, xxxvi (1963–4), pp. 47–65.

Just Arrived, from *Jackson* and Co's. Great Original.
Wholesale DAFFY's ELIXIR Warehouse,
Fleet-Market, LONDON: A FRESH PARCEL of the

Original DAFFY's *Elixir,*

Which is Appointed to be Sold by
Mr. *Ashburnar,* Bookseller and Stationer in *Kendal,*
Wholesale and Retail, and by no other Person in this Town.
Where this Original *DAFFY's* ELIXIR has been sold many Years, with great Success.
☞ *This Original* ELIXIR *exceeds all the Medicines ever Prepared, and is the Only.*
FAMILY MEDICINE *in* GREAT BRITAIN.

The following CURES, *amongst many Hundreds, have lately been.*
performed by this Noble ELIXIR.

THE following is a Copy of a Letter, sent by Mr. *John Taylor,* Grocer in *Saltash,* to Messrs. *Jackson* and Co. at their Wholesale Original DAFFY's ELIXIR Warehouse, *Fleet-market,* LONDON.
Mr. *Jackson,* Sir, by the Desire of Mr. *James Daw,* of St. *Stephens,* near *Saltash,* in *Cornwall,* a Man above Sixty Years of Age, maketh Oath and faith, that I, the said *James Daw,* has been for near Twenty Years past afflicted with a Consumption, and had Advice from all the eminent Physicians of that Place, but to no Purpose, at length grown so very weak and thin, that every one who saw me, concluded I could not live a Week, but being advised to try your True DAFFY's ELIXIR, sold by Mr. *John Taylor,* and by taking Three Bottles only of your Original Elixir, was perfectly cured, and am now, considering. my Age, as well as ever I was in my Life, and desire this may be made publick for the Benefit of others in the same Disorder. As witness my Hand the 17th Day of *February,* 1763, . *James Daw.*
Attested by Mr. *John Taylor.*
N. B. Several Persons since the above Cure, by taking the above Elixir, have been cured in different Disorders, and others have found great Benefit.

THE following is a Copy of a Letter sent to Messrs. *Jackson* and Co. the only Preparers of the True Original DAFFY's ELIXIR, at their Royal Patent Wholesale Warehouse, *Fleet-market, London.*
Mr. *Jackson,* Sir, in Duty bound, and for the Benefit of others that may labour under the like Disorder, I have here sent you a short Account of a very extraordinary Cure your True Original DAFFY's ELIXIR has wrought upon my Daughter *Mary* about 20 Years of Age; she being afflicted with a terrible Disorder for a long Time, and at length grew so bad, that she could neither go nor stand, and always in excessive Pain, that she could get no Rest Day nor Night, and every one that saw her expected it would be her Death; and applying to Dr. *Read* of *Troubridge,* he told me it was the Dropsy, with a Complication of other Disorders, and that he hoped he could give her something to relieve her; accordingly she took several of his Medicines, but found no Relief, but still grew worse; upon this I applied to Dr. *Jarvis* of the same Place, and he told her that he could do her no Service, without a long and tedious Course of Physick, which I, being a poor Woman, could not possibly pay him for; but applying to Mr. *Martin,* Grocer in *Troubridge,* who sells the only True ORIGINAL DAFFY's ELIXIR, prepared by you and Company, and bought a Bottle of him, and before she had taken it all, she found great Relief, was able to sit up and free from Pain, and by taking the second Bottle was perfectly cured, and able to go to her Work as usual, and continued so for about two or three Months, when she was took ill again, but by taking another Bottle of the above DAFFY's ELIXIR was perfectly cured, and is now, blessed be GOD, as well as ever she was in her Life. As witness my Hand the 14th Day of *June* 1763. *Mary Hewish.*
Witness *Miller Hewish.*   Daughter of *Miller Hewish,* of *Troubridge,* in the County of *Wilts.*

MRS. *Ann Haw*, of the Parish of *George-Ham*, in the County of *Devonshire* : Who was many Months Violently afflicted with the *Gout, Rheumatism*, and *Dropsy*: With a Complication of other Distempers, that none of her Friends or Relations expected her Life :——She had tried abundance of *Medicines*, but found no Benefit by them : — In her taking but two Bottles of this Original *Daffy's Elixir*, made a perfect Cure of her.—Which she desires for the Benefit of Others, may be made Publick. *October* 26.

I *Sarah*, Daughter of *Gabriel Chilcot*, of *Dyley*, in the Parish of *Lidigard St. Lawrence*, near *Taunton*, *Somersetshire* : Was in *February* last, grievously afflicted with a violent Swelling all over my Body, so that I could get no Rest, Day nor Night; concluding it to be the *Dropsy*: My Friends had the Advice of a Doctor, having taken many *Medicines*, with great Expence, to no Purpose: —Was at last advised to make Trial of the Original *Daffy's Elixir*, [*Which has Performed many Hundreds of Suprizing great Cures, when all other Medicines have failed :*]—By my taking less than two Bottles, it made me Discharge a Gallon of Water at a Time: And I bless *God*, am now perfectly restored to Health, to the Astonishment of all my Friends and Neighbours. As Witness my Hand. *Sarah Chilcot.*

I *Moses Hancock* of *Milverton*, near *Taunton*, being a long Time afflicted with great Swellings in my Body and Limbs ; together with the Stone and Gravel, which occasion'd great painful Obstructions in my Urine ; which made me so weak, that I could scarce walk or stand :—I took a great many *Medicines*, but found no Benefit at all by any of them, continuing still in tormenting racking Pains : All my Friends perswading me to make Trial of the Original *Daffy's Elixir :* In taking at Times, less than three Bottles, by the Blessing of *God*, has made a perfect Cure :—I desire this may be Published to the World, for the Benefit of Mankind. As Witness my Hand. *March* 31. *Moses Hancock.*

April 4, *Parish of* Taunton, *St. James's Somersetshire.*

These are to Certify, that I *Mary*, the Wife of *James Slade*, was above a Month past, taken in a sudden violent Manner, with great pains in my Side, supposed to be the *Plurefy* ; which I thought would have been my Death : I was Blooded, but found no Ease : In taking but four Spoonfuls of the Original *Daffy's Elixir*, it perfectly carried off all my Pains : and I bless *God*, am now able to carry on my Business, as usual. Witness my Hand. *Mary Slade*, Wife of the above *James Slade.*

☞ *Pray be careful not to Buy a Spurious Sort, made by various Pretenders, who know nothing of the Preparation, and who, to make their rubbish Elixir go off, have counterfeited this Seal and Bill of Cures. For your Health's Sake, Take Notice, That the Genuine Bill of Cures has the same Seal as in the Margin.*

Pray be careful to Observe, that the Printed Bills have the Crown and Sceptres in the Top of the Arms.

Where this Original ELIXIR *is sold, may also be had by Virtue of the* King's Royal Patent.

Jackson's Tincture,
Dr. Bateman's Pectoral Drops,
True and Genuine British Oil,
Dr. Bateman's Golden and Plain Spirits of Scurvy-Grass
Dr. Stoughto's Great Stomachick Elixir,
Dr. Anderson's or the True Scots Pills,
Dr. Godfrey's General Cordial,
Hungary and Lavender Water, &c.
Turlington's Balsam of Life,
The Bathing Spirits,
Hadfield's Tincture,
Dr. Hooper's Female Pills,

The famous Patent Ointment which cures the Itch at once dressing, without the least danger, and never known to fail.
The famous Corn Salve that cures hard or soft Corns in two or three Weeks ; and always gives present Ease when applied,
Jackson's only true BRITISH POWDER for the TEETH and GUMS, in which it has gained the greatest Applause both in Town and Country,
The Court or Ladies Black Sticking Plaister,
Dr. Bostock's Cordial,
Superfine Durham Flower of Mustard,
Dr. Radcliffe's Famous Purging Elixir,

All under Sanction of the King's Royal Patent, under the Great Seal of Great Britain.

for a curious variety of things. These included three Delft punch bowls for 1s. 10d., two cruets for 8d., a carving knife and fork for 1s. 9d., a japanned waiter for 3s. 3d., a pair of spurs for 6s., and fiddle strings at 2s. 3d. to 3s. 6d. They included also some lime, planks, laths, bricks, brass and a cart and wheels. Such sales suggest a surviving tradition of the general store which sold anything and everything, but they may simply mean that the Dents, as good tradesmen, were ready to meet some of the more unusual demands of their customers. The Rev. Mr. Knowsley at Musgrave was a very good customer for other things besides a carving knife and fork and a cart and wheels.

The customers who bought their goods from William and Abraham Dent form an interesting study, though it is not possible to get a full picture of them. They did not all live in either the town or the parish of Kirkby Stephen, but most of them lived in the parish or in the neighbouring parishes of Warcop, Great Musgrave, Brough, Ravenstonedale and Crosby Garrett. It was natural for Kirkby Stephen to attract trade from the west and south west, for it was the nearest market town for places like Crosby Garrett and Ravenstonedale, or at least Ravenstonedale Town, for the upper reaches of the dale might be drawn towards Sedbergh. Certainly a number of the Dents' customers lived in Crosby Garrett, including Mr. Robinson, the schoolmaster, The Rev. Mr. Nicholson, who bought cloth, powder and shot and fiddle strings, and Miss Bird, who bought everything, sometimes 'by maid' and sometimes 'by man'. A number lived in Ravenstonedale, too, including Dr. Beck, who bought flour and treacle, and Richard Shaw, who bought large amounts of treacle.

North of Kirkby Stephen there must have been competition from Brough, which had at least two mercers, drapers and grocers in 1784,[1] and from Appleby, which had at least eight shops at that date. Only two customers from Appleby figure in the Dents' day book, but there were a good many from Brough, including John Thompson, esquire, who bought groceries and cloth, The Rev. Mr. Hodgson, who also bought cloth and groceries, and Joseph Wootton, who bought the Delft punch bowls and cruets among

[1] W. Bailey, *British Directory* (1784), iii, pp. 549-50.

other things. To the east of Brough there were customers at Stainmore, where, among others, James Rain, glover, got his alum from the Dents, and Jonathan Ewbanke got everything from hops to Horace. To the south-west of Brough, at Musgrave, the best customer, or at least the best credit customer, was The Rev. Mr. Knowsley, who seems to have got all his necessaries from the Dents. Further west, at Warcop, there were two good customers, The Rev. Dr. Ward and Thomas Rudd, whose wife did the Christmas shopping of sugar, currants, raisins and candy on 21 December 1764. Farther afield, at Sedbergh, books were sold to Thomas Highmoor and raisins to The Rev. Mr. Bateman, but this trade was dominated by John Cockbain's insatiable appetite for treacle.

The more distant customers are more difficult to explain; their custom must have arisen from some personal or trade relationship with the Dents or with Kirkby Stephen. It is not clear, for example, why The Rev. Mr. Richardson at Huddersfield should have bought his cloth from the Dents, or why Mary Taylor 'with' Christopher Teasdale, esquire, at Houghton-le-Spring should have shopped in Kirkby Stephen. On the other hand the Richard Harrison of London, who bought cloth from the Dents in 1764, may have been the bill broker of that name with whom Abraham Dent later had dealings. Similarly trade connections may explain the existence of customers east of the Pennines in Wensleydale and Swaledale. The Dents sent regular supplies of tea to John Harrison and William Stuart of Hawes, who were partners in a hosiery business. They sometimes supplied Abraham Dent with stockings, which were credited to them and partly paid for the tea. Later Abraham recommended Harrison and Stuart to one of his customers for stockings and he finally married into the Harrison family. Similarly the customers in upper Swaledale, Widow Alderson and John Metcalfe at Keld, and William Irwin and Daniel Addison at Muker, may have had contacts with Abraham Dent through the stocking trade. These more distant customers formed only a small proportion of those who bought their goods from the Dents, but they are a warning against taking too parochial a view of retail trade.

The customers came, not only from a fairly wide area, but also from a fairly wide social range. There cannot have been a great deal of the 'carriage trade' at Kirkby Stephen, but perhaps Sir George Dalston at Smardale Hall, who bought paper and tea from the Dents, came into that category. There was certainly a substantial middle-class trade, in which the clergy figured prominently as customers. At least eleven parsons bought goods from the Dents between 1762 and 1765, including The Rev. Henry Chaytor, the incumbent at Kirkby Stephen, and The Rev. William Fawcett, his curate. This clerical trade may have been influenced by the fact that Abraham Dent was a churchwarden in the 1760s, for these ties of mutual obligation can be important in country places. Within living memory a country doctor might choose his grocer, not for the quality or price of his wares, but because the grocer and his family were 'good patients' of the practice. The Dents had their doctor customers too: Dr. Beck of Ravenstonedale, Dr. Wilson of Redgill and Dr. Thomas Rudd of Hartley. Another Thomas Rudd was an apothecary in Kirkby Stephen, as was Richard Rudd, and both of them shopped at the Dents, as did two of the local attorneys, Mr. Fawcett and Mr. Jackson. Finally in the professional group were the schoolmasters, of whom Jonathan Ewbanke of Stainmore was the best customer. Others, who made occasional purchases, were Mr. Robinson, the schoolmaster at Crosby Garrett, Richard Yates of Appleby, whose widow was buried at Kirkby Stephen in 1794, and Mr. Wilson, the schoolmaster 'in town'. One of Wilson's pupils, Master Keymer, who was obviously a boarder, was supplied with cloth, hanks of worsted (was he being taught to knit?), paper, sealing wax, a Greek grammar and a 'Justin'. At the end of July 1765 the Dents arranged for Master Keymer's return home, paying 12*d.* for a box and cord, 6*d.* to Mr. Parkin, the writing master, £1 11*s.* 6*d.* for 'expences on the road', £3 2*s.* 0*d.* 'to the Machine', 1*s.* 6*d.* to Pearson 'for self and box to Kendale', a shilling tip to Mr. Wilson's maid and 4*d.* for a post letter. Young Keymer was no doubt going to London by the Flying Machine stage coach which began to run between Kendal and London in 1763 and which took two nights and three days to make the journey. At £3 2*s.* 0*d.* he would at least have an inside seat.

Parsons and schoolmasters suggest themselves as customers for books, but in fact the former do not seem to have bought their books from the Dents, though The Rev. Mr. Bird at Crosby Garrett did buy a copy of *Aesop's Fables* for 1*s.* and The Rev. Mr. Hodgson at Brough bought '1 Parish law bound'. It was otherwise with the schoolmasters. Jonathan Ewbanke bought editions of Virgil, Terence, Ovid and Horace, and Mr. Wilson bought Martin's *Dictionary* and Salmon's *Geography*. James Highmoor at Flitholme and Thomas Highmoor of Sedbergh bought Greek and Roman authors, as did Robert Islip of Soulby. They must surely have been schoolmasters. The pupils might be supplied by their parents or uncles. John Fothergill, an innkeeper in Kirkby Stephen, bought paper, quills and cloth as well as school books for his nephew, and Robert Bousfield, a waller, bought a grammar for his son. Thomas Bradley, clogger, paid 4*s.* for a lexicon and 1*s.* 10*d.* for a *Youth's Guide;* it is unlikely that they were for himself. The elementary primers and reading books had a wider circulation than had the classical texts, but the county historians were unduly patriotic in claiming that, because of the large number of schools in Westmorland, it was rare 'to find any person who cannot read and write tolerably well'.[1] The marriage registers show a number of bridegrooms, and more brides, who made their marks.

It would be wrong to think that the Dents dealt only with the middle class. They sold to the tinker and tailor, the mason and slater, the carpenter and glazier, the bleacher and dyer, the innkeeper and carrier. They sold sugar, treacle, flour and candles to James Petty, labourer, flour to James Fawcett of Soulby, tinker, and a paper book containing two quires to George Brown, Scotchman and pedlar. Servants, who sometimes did the shopping for their masters or mistresses, might also be clothed by them. Robert Rudd of Sowerby bought thick-set and buttons for his servant man. In October 1763 William Parkin of Lunds bought for his servant man 13 yds. thick-set at 1*s.* 8*d.* yd., 5 yds. shalloon at 1*s.* yd., 2½ yds. flannel at 1*s.* yd., harden, pocket fustian, buckram, twist, thread, tape, two dozen coat buttons and three dozen

---

[1] Nicolson and Burn, op. cit., i, p. 9.

waistcoat buttons. The bill was £1 15s. 7½d. Similarly Christopher Harker of Enterbar bought bleached linen in 1763 for his maid servant, and later in the year bought for her, or for another maid, 1¼ yds. of scarlet cloth at the high price of 12s. yd., 1⅛ yds. of snail,[1] ribbon, cord, buttons and silk, at a total cost of 16s. 6d.

The Dents both sold goods and lent money to their own servant, whose wages were £2 10s. a year. The following entries in the day book, which are unusually illiterate, show the nature of the transactions:

	£	s	d
6 December 1763 Isabell Dent our Servant			
Lent		1	
paper 2½d. 1 Hankerchiff 2s.		2	2½
Lent money 3s. 1 yd. black Ribin 4d.		3	4
paper 2½d. 1 yd. Ribin 4d. 1½ yd. Do. 10½		1	5
9 May [1764] Green Searge &c. 10d. pocketts 11		1	9
		9	8½
Pd in full for wadges Due at Whitsuntide 1764		10	4
and Rest Dr. for black Silk Cap Sheen		14	
Received		10	
October 4⅛ yd. black tamay 5½d.			5½
10 Nov. 1½ Doz. Bloa (?) Lint @ 8s. 6d. Half on't to John[2]		6	4½
blue Searge 3s. 4.		3	4
17 [Nov] Green binding 2½d.			2½
		10	4½
Check 4 yds.		4	6
1764 December 6th pd 10s. in full for Wadges Due at Martinmas Last		10	1½
	1	5	0
5 Dec. Rest Dr. at a Cap Sheen		4	
2 brat (?) Aprons [no price]			
May 22 1765 filliting & thred 3½ Scarlet Callamca 12d. Silke 3d.		1	6½
pd for Stamped Lin gown 26s.	1	6	0

___

[1] Chenille, a velvet cord.

[2] Perhaps John Dent, a clockmaker, who died in 1774, aged 33.

<table>
<tr><td>toWeaver and Spinain Lin Cloth 8s. 1½d.</td><td></td><td></td><td>8</td><td>1½</td></tr>
<tr><td></td><td></td><td>1</td><td>19</td><td>8</td></tr>
<tr><td>Recd atWhitsuntid 1765 by ½ yearWadge</td><td></td><td>1</td><td>5</td><td>0</td></tr>
<tr><td></td><td>Dr.</td><td></td><td>14</td><td>8</td></tr>
</table>

All this gives the impression of a fairly normal, rather than of a particularly generous, treatment.

The Dents sold and customers bought, but what was the scale of the operation ? It is very difficult to determine the total turnover from the surviving records. In 1763 the sales on credit amounted to £498 19s. 4¾d. This figure includes some sales into which an element of barter entered. Thus the Dents bought coals from Robert Nickolson of Winton, and the coals were credited to his account for cloth and groceries. Similarly John Thompson, junior, a plasterer, was credited for work done (at 1s. 6d. a day in 1765), and Anthony Cleasby, a carrier, was credited for the carriage of treacle, sugar and hops, as was John Brunskill for the carriage of flour. Alexander Simpson, having bought groceries and tobacco for 6s. 8¾d., was able to present Abraham Dent with the following beautifully written bill.

	£	s	d
April the 25 1763			
a Day work	0	1	0
3 Pints of Early pease	0	1	3
Carrot seed	0	0	1½
Spinage seed	0	0	1
Lettuce seed	0	0	1
Thyme and margorem	0	0	2
Radish seed	0	0	1
Parciley seed	0	0	1
1 Oz Onion seed	0	0	3
Cabige Plants	0	0	4
	0	3	5½
To Leveling a walk in the Churchyard	0	3	0
	0	6	5½

Which left Alexander owing $3\frac{1}{4}d$. Finally Andrew Whitfield, who did the cobbling for the Dent family, was able in part to pay for his cloth and groceries by his 'shows mending'. About November 1765 he presented the following bill.

	s	d
Mr. Dent Dater [debtor] for Shows Mending		
20 March 1765 Doughter Shows Sold and Spact	0	8
April 24 Mrs pumps Sold and Spact	1	3
May 3 Mrs Cloth Shows Spact	0	4
June 23 Mr. Wm. Dent Shows Sold Spact	0	7
July 11 Doughter Shows Sold and Spact	0	8
19 Mrs Cloth Shows Spact and Mended	0	6
Agust 13 Doughter Shows Spact	0	3
15 Mr Abraham Shows Spact Mended	0	8
Sept. 3 Doughter Shows Capt	0	2
10 Mrs Shows Spact	0	$3\frac{1}{2}$
Octbr Mr William Dent Shows Sold	0	4
	5	$8\frac{1}{2}$

This reduced his grocery bill from $7s$. $9\frac{1}{2}d$. to $2s$. $1d$. A later bill shows that Whitfield repaired Mrs. Dent's pattens and clogs and Mr. Dent's boots.

The credit sales of just under £500, while including these barter transactions, do not include the loans which the Dents made to their customers. Such loans were entered in the day book, and amounted to £87 18s. 4d. in 1763. There were 42 loans in all, ranging from 1s. to seven guineas. Twenty-seven of the loans were for a guinea or over. There was a wide range of borrowers, from Dr. Rudd of Hartley, who borrowed four guineas, to Isabel Dent, who, it will be remembered, borrowed 1s. and later 3s. No interest was charged on these loans even to persistent borrowers like Matthew Dixon, who borrowed two half guineas in March 1763 and two guineas in May. No doubt it was all done to oblige the customers, rather as to-day a country grocer will cash a customer's cheque during those lengthy periods when the banks are not open. Indeed on occasion Dent's shop seems to have acted as a source of ready cash for those who had come into town to do their shopping.

c

The credit sales were no doubt a convenience for the customers too, but it is not always possible to tell what length of credit the Dents granted to their customers. The length varied greatly. Thus John Barnett bought groceries to the value of £4 6s. between 24 October and 9 November 1762 and paid for them on the latter date; John Terry bought cloth, buttons and thread for 8s. on 23 January 1764 and paid for them a fortnight later. Ann Harrison bought groceries for £1 1s. 2½d. on 2 and 9 May 1763 and paid for them a week later; these were Mondays so she did her shopping on market day. At the other extreme Thomas Hutchinson of Hartley bought cloth to the value of 12s. 10d. in July and August 1762 and only paid for it on 16 June 1767. In some cases debts were brought forward from an 'old day book' which has not survived. In other cases customers were 'sent a note' to remind them of their debts. Some customers paid in instalments. Thus William Walton of Brough bought cloth and groceries for £1 18s. 8½d. between February 1762 and June 1764 and paid for them in two instalments; he paid 10s. 6d. on account on 17 February 1764 and the remainder on 27 February 1765. Similarly Mrs. Jane Brecan bought soap, pins and her Christmas groceries on 16 December 1762 at a cost of £2 18s. 7½d., which she paid in three instalments on 29 December 1762 (a market day) and 13 and 31 January 1763 (another market day).

These credit sales were clearly of two sorts. Many of them represented small purchases which the customer was unable or unwilling to pay for at the time of purchase. No doubt they were paid for in due course, but the date of payment is often not given. Some of these may simply represent purchases by children for their parents or by servants for their masters and mistresses; on 7 June 1762 John Nanson of Kaber sent his maid to buy a spelling book for 6d., which he paid at some later and unspecified date. Other credit sales represented accounts which substantial customers were allowed to run. Thus the companies which bought gunpowder seem to have had regular dates for settling their accounts, of which 27 February and 27 May were apparently the most common. Individuals such as Bartholomew Dixon of Winton and The Rev. Mr. Knowsley of Musgrave ran long accounts which involved giving them credit for six months or more. There was probably nothing unusual in these forms of credit that the Dents extended to their customers.

These credit sales did not equal total sales, and what proportion they bore to the total is not known. Another approach to this problem of the turnover is to look at the Dents as the customers of their suppliers. The Dents paid £677 for goods in 1763, £882 in 1764, £847 in 1765, £750 in 1766 and £947 in 1767. It is not certain that all these goods were bought to sell again through the shop, but most of them were. They were obviously bought at wholesale prices, whereas the credit sales were retail, but unfortunately there is not the detailed information necessary for working out the retail price margin or for estimating what stock was carried over from one year to another. The figures would suggest that annual sales in the shop ranged from about £900 to £1,250 in the years 1763–67 and that rather more than half of the sales were made on credit, but this is partly guess work. It is clearly time to look at the suppliers and to hope that their goods were more reliable than these crude statistics.

Chapter III

The Shopkeeper: The Suppliers

In the study of retail trade it is easy to forget that the shopkeeper is a middleman between the manufacturer or wholesaler and the consumer. Yet it is as important to discover where the shopkeeper obtained his goods as it is to show what he sold and to whom he sold it. It is just as important, but it is not easy even in the case of the Dents who kept a ledger of purchases. The ledger runs from 1756 to 1777 and gives the name and usually the place of the supplier and the cost of the goods he supplied, but unfortunately it rarely specifies what those goods were. Nevertheless, from comments in the ledger and from the chance survival of bills, it is possible to get a general idea which goods were obtained from which supplier. The outline is there even if the details are often lacking.

Kirkby Stephen was an interesting case from the point of view of supply. It was an inland town with no water communication at all; it was not near to a port, not even to Westmorland's only port, Milnthorpe; it was not very near to a large town, and was itself much too small to support wholesalers of its own, except in stockings. In such circumstances, where did a shopkeeper get his supplies? He certainly did not get them from two or three large wholesalers. Between 1756 and 1777 the Dents bought from about 190 suppliers. In the single year 1763 they bought from 47 suppliers. As they bought goods for £677 in that year, the average was £14 8s. per supplier, but the range was from 11s. 6d. to £98 4s. 8½d., and the eight largest suppliers provided 65 per cent of the total.

The goods sold in the shop were not produced locally. The chief local product, knitted stockings, rarely if ever figured in the retail trade, presumably because people bought their stockings direct from the knitters or knitted their own. Even the agricultural produce came largely from outside the county, though a little wheat was bought from John Ellison of Barras Hall, James Petty and John Sawkell of Brough, and James Bird of Hellbeck near Brough. Some flour was bought from Thomas Cannon of Brough in 1767, but this was exceptional. In 1756–58 the Dents had bought

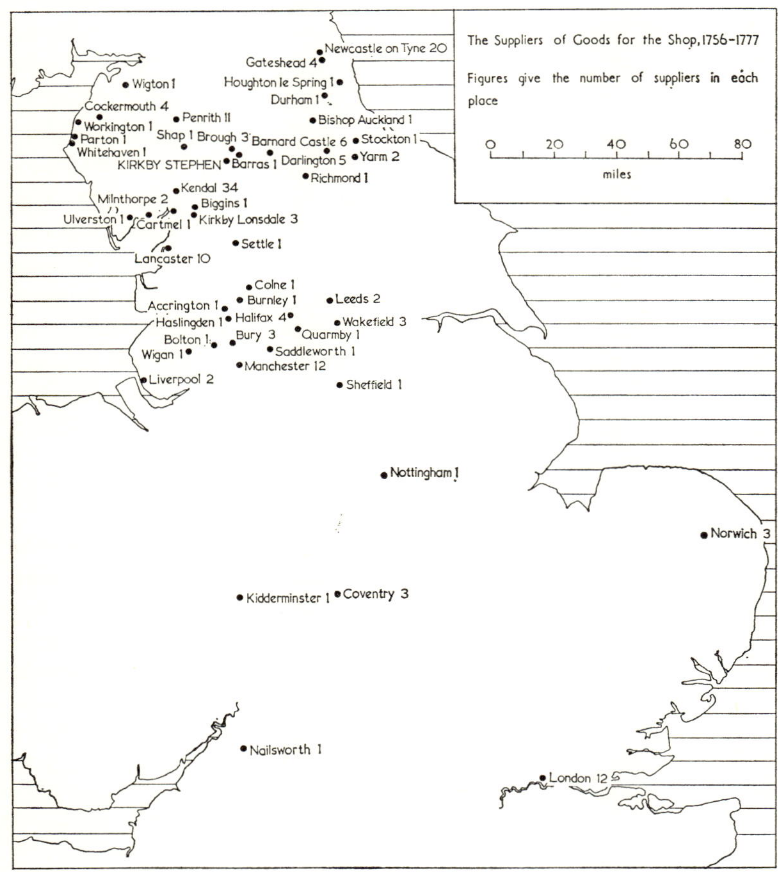

large amounts of flour and barley from William Hindrie of Darlington, but in the 1760s and early 1770s their main source of supply was Barnard Castle and their main supplier John Monkhouse. Monkhouse supplied them with goods worth £53 14s. 3½d. in 1764, of which £49 9s. 0½d. was for flour at prices ranging from 13d. to 22d. a stone. This wide range seems to have been due to different qualities, for the price varied considerably for flour supplied on the same day. The other goods were a little barley, 55 loaves at 5*d.* each, 32 'peper cakes' at 2*s.* 6*d.* a stone, and some split peas at 7*s.* 8*d.* a bushel. The peas drew the comment 'Memorandum James Rain bought A.D. [Abraham Dent] 1 bushel split pease 6*s.* at Newcastle. Carriage 15*d.*' Monkhouse supplied no more peas, but he continued to supply large amounts of flour and some barley: £70 worth in 1765, £51 in 1767, £50 in 1769 and £101 in 1770.

Monkhouse was not the only supplier of flour at Barnard Castle. Matthew Wiseman supplied small quantities of fine flour (at 23*d.* to 25*d.* a stone) in 1765 and Sampson Middleton a few sacks in 1771. Mathias Strickland at Abbey Mill was more important. He supplied the Dents with flour worth £11 9*s.* 4*d.* in 1762 when they noted that six sacks were underweight to the extent of three stones. The following year his bill came to £17 6*s.* and in 1764 to £51 16*s.* 10*d.* Despite this increase in his sales, he was uneasy about the future, and on 8 December 1764 wrote as follows, apparently to Abraham Dent.

Sir

I have Sent you 2 Load of fine flower But I am Surprice that you Didd Nott Send soner. I think you will forsack mee Sone [soon] and I Do Nott Now [know] your Reason for I allwase use you well and you Now I Denied Several peple In Kerby of flower when you and I Began trading, So I Desire you Will Lett me Have your Costom till I Live in this part the World. My friend monkhouse as Bee att my Lanlord to take my mill over my Head. So I Beleve I Can Nott Gett akill Bult[1] Without paying Intrust for the money, So pleas to send me a little money If It Sute you, for I was forst to Give my Lanlord Is year Rent and It Is Nott due till may day Next. So the flower Can Nott Be aford under 20 per St.[2] So 2 Sacks Is   3–0–0
      and 2 Before was   2 14 0

and pleas to Send your Sacks and I will Send you 2 Load of superfine against Crismas. So pleas to Excuse Hast from your friend and Well Wisher With my Complement to your famly

Mathias Strickland

[1] A kiln built? More probably a mistake for a mill built.   [2] Stone.

The Dents duly received the two sacks of flour for £3 on 10 December. On 15 February Strickland wrote again acknowledging the receipt of £9 9s. and added 'as for this 32 Stone I doo Nott Now How to aford It under 20 per St But I shall Send you a brown Lofe to make it Lower If you pleas to Exsept It as my Nabours Dose With my Complements to Mrs Dent'. Strickland supplied a little more flour in May 1765, but that seems to have been the end. Perhaps Monkhouse had taken the mill over his head.

Though agricultural produce came in largely from outside the county, the Dents did buy a good many things from suppliers in Westmorland. The obvious centre for this wholesale trade was Kendal, 24 miles from Kirkby Stephen and the largest town in the county, though not its capital. Between 1756 and 1777 the Dents dealt with about 34 suppliers in Kendal, but only seven of them ever supplied goods worth more than £20 in a single year. The bigger suppliers dealt mainly in groceries and stationery. Thus John Whitwell supplied such groceries as treacle, Spanish juice, rice, soap, sugar, figs, carraway seeds and hops. His trade with the Dents was modest until 1759 when his bill came to £38 13s. 3d., which included, according to the Dents, some hops and treacle overcharged. He supplied the same amount of goods in 1762, when the rice was described as 'ordinary' and the powder loaves as 'dear'. In 1763 the bill fell to just under £25 and a consignment of soap was 3 lb. short weight. In 1764 the bill rose to £52, only to fall to just over £40 in 1765 and to a mere £11 10s. in 1766, when 'sugar at 46s.' was 'worth 42s.' and 'figgs charged 30 same time had as good at 28'. Despite these complaints, Whitwell sold the Dents goods worth £77 12s. 11¾d. in 1767, but his sales fell to half that figure the following year. After 1769 John Whitwell disappears and seems to be replaced by Thomas and Anthony Whitwell. They sold the same sort of goods and inspired the same sort of complaints: in 1770 the rice was 3 stones short weight and the 'isinglass charged 6s. 6d. as good from Darlington at 5s. 6d.' Their sales were smaller than John Whitwell's had been, for they never exceeded about £40 in a year. Two other Kendal grocers sold goods to the Dents which exceeded

£20 in occasional years. Matthew Bell, whose sugar loaf was 'too dear by $1\frac{1}{2}d$. a pound' in 1757, whose hops were dear and short weight in 1758 and whose rice was overcharged by 3*d*. in 1762, nevertheless sold the Dents goods worth £23 3*s*. 9*d*. in 1766. George Benson, who sold goods for £9 7*s*. 3*d*. in 1767 and received a bill on Coales of London for £19, wrote to Abraham Dent on 15 January 1768 as follows.

Respected Friend

I have thy favour covering a Bill vallue Ninteen Pounds, which overpays thy account £9 12*s*. 9*d*., in consequence of which I send thee herewith Cash per Pearson Nine Pounds thirteen shillings, and I thank thee for the remittance, and when further is wanted they order will oblige.

Thy Friend
Geo Benson.

Further was wanted, and Benson continued to supply groceries to the tune of £28 in 1770 and nearly £40 in 1771.

The other big suppliers were the Ashburners and John Moore. The Ashburners were printers, paper makers and booksellers. Thomas Ashburner supplied the Dents with paper, magazines, books and no doubt Daffy's Elixir between 1759 and 1764; James Ashburner supplied the same things between 1764 and 1772. Occasionally there was some variation: cockles for 1*s*. 8*d*. in 1769, fish for 1*s*. 6*d*. in 1770, and 'a wigg' for 14*s*. in 1771. The Ashburners, and especially James, were substantial suppliers; the bill came to nearly £50 in 1765 and to £53 11*s*. 9*d*. in 1769, when Abraham Dent noted 'inquire price of printing ball bills on cards'. John Moore, esquire, supplied the paper for legal instruments which bore a stamp duty. The duty was high. In the early 1770s it was 2*s*. 6*d*. on every sheet used in an 'indenture, lease, bond, or deed not otherwise specially charged'.[1] Thus on 17 September 1774 Moore 'sent to Mr Dent by Mr Ashburner's boy Paper demy 1 Quire duty 2*s*. 6.—£3 2*s*.' In other words the paper cost 2*s*. and bore a 2*s*. 6*d*. stamp on each of the 24 sheets. Two months later Abraham Dent received six pairs of parish indentures from

---

[1] S. Dowell, *A History of Taxation and Taxes in England*, iii, p. 290.

Moore, but on these the duty was only 1*s*. a pair. Between February 1774 and June 1778 Dent paid Moore £192 for paper and stamps. Part of this sum represented increases in the duty which had been made in 1776 and 1777 and which raised the duty to 5*s*. a sheet. Thus in January 1778 a quire of demy paper still cost 2*s*., but the duty was now £6 or 5*s*. a sheet. Dent settled his accounts with Moore by remitting bills, usually drawn on the London firms which Dent supplied with stockings. Thus on 26 January 1778 he 'sent by Robert Rudd's servant 1 Bill on Nicholas Pearse, esq.' for £60. Pearse was a London clothier who bought stockings from Dent.

There was a host of minor suppliers in Kendal from whom the Dents got some goods: tobacco from John Thompson, which drew the comment in 1765 '7 lb. 8 oz. twist tobacco charged and there was only 6 lb. 12 oz.', hops from Wilson Robinson, sugar, starch and Spanish juice from Mrs. Isabella Dickinson, lace from Thomas Collier and Richard Peddler, bombazine and callamanco from Joseph Symson, silk handkerchiefs at 5*s*. each from John Moseley, some of which were returned as 'tore in carriage', sail twine, pack thread and mitts (at 4*s*. a dozen when coloured and 3*s*. 4*d*. when white) from Ephraim Hodgson, thread from William Thompson, pearl buttons, described as 'dear' in 1756, knives, tongs and rum puncheons from William Bordley, bone from William and Robert Newby, two dishes and two plates costing 8*s*. 'for Comunion Service' from William Strickland, brazier, and bundles of cards from William Fothergill, who reported to Abraham Dent on 19 January 1776 that he had sent half the order for cards and that the other half would follow next week, as 'this idle Xmas has run us behind hand'. The cards, at 12*s*. to 14*s*. a bundle, were presumably wool cards.

No town in Westmorland, apart from Kendal, was important as a centre of supply. The Dents bought a few goods, apparently groceries, from James Wilson of Milnthorpe, and a little paper from Potter Fletcher of the same place, though it was described as dear in 1760 and 'very bad' in 1765. They got harden from Joseph Laycock of Biggins and coal sacking and twine from James Jopson of Kirkby Lonsdale, though the twine was said to be '2½*d*. per pound over dear' in 1760. James Woods, again of Kirkby Lonsdale, supplied lint, and seems also to have dressed hemp for the Dents. Finally John Batty of Kirkby Lonsdale supplied soap, which the Dents paid for partly by meeting the carriage costs of his tallow; in 1756 they recorded opposite his account 'paid Richard Fothergill 20*s*. for carriage of 12 firkins of tallow from N. Castle to K. Stephen and forwarded them by Henry Sawkeld to Sedbergh'.

In Cumberland the main centre of supply was Penrith, where eleven people sent goods to the Dents between 1756 and 1777, though usually in fairly small quantities. This trade seems to have been largely confined to different sorts of cloth. Thus Henry Blacklock sent small amounts of linen, harden and sacking, William Bliss linen and checks, William Lancaster also checks and Thomas Mounsey 'doub. gumed mens gloves' at 9*s*. 6*d*. a dozen, women's gloves at 10*s*. 6*d*. a dozen and women's mitts at 8*s*. 6*d*. a dozen. The following bill seems fairly typical of this trade.

Penrith Apral 17 1764 Mr Abram Dent Bout of Jonathan Thompson

	£	s	d
39 yd. of Lin and tow cloth at 11*d*. p. yd over cast 12*d*.	1	16	9
36 yd. ½ of Do Do Do	1	13	5
22 yd. of check at 12½*d*. p. yd.	1	2	11
16 yd. of check at 1*s*. p. yd		16	
	5	9	1

the above I hope will Pleas the and the Remainder of thy order I shall send at the weeks end but for the 1 Peace of white Cloth

Thy Friend
Jonathan Thompson

Abraham Dent carefully subtracted the 'over cast'. Apart from Penrith, there was a single supplier at Workington and one at Whitehaven, a surprisingly small number for the Cumberland ports. At Parton, near Whitehaven, Adam Dixon supplied 'Mr Dantt' with 2½ doz. 'shame' [chamois] and a 'raper' in 1768. Cockermouth was more important. There George Fearson supplied shalloon in a variety of colours, black, blue, olive, copper and claret, and in amounts costing from £1 5s. to £9 12s. a year. Thomas Smith also sent shalloons and on a bigger scale; his bill was £20 16s. 3d. in 1766. James Wilson sent handkerchiefs among other things and Annah Pearson sent 'seages', whatever she meant by that.[1]

Further south, in Lancashire, two centres of supply were important, Lancaster and Manchester. Ten individuals or firms in Lancaster supplied the Dents with goods, but it is not always possible to tell what those goods were. William Barnes sent coffee, and Eskrigge and Jackson large amounts of soap; in 1769, when the firm seems to have become Eskrigge Gardner & Co., their bill came to £30 4s. 1d., but this may not all have been for soap. The most important item however was sugar. This was supplied by William Watson, whose sugar was sometimes short weight, and Lennard Herd, but the biggest supplier was Lawson Rawlinson & Co., whose bill came to £83 4s. 10½d. in 1764 and to £86 15s. 3d. in 1765. Not all of this was for sugar, they supplied gunpowder among other things, but £65 8s. 2d. was for sugar in 1765. On 10 October 1765 Henry Hargreaves, acting for Rawlinson, wrote to Abraham Dent that some sugars had been despatched 'by Labrow and I wish em safe to hand. You'll, no doubt, think the prices high, but are the lowest we are selling at and I do think they'll go a deal higher, that if you can at Newcastle do better you'd do well to lay in a stock'. The prices included lump at 78s. cwt., and some other type of sugar at 74s. cwt. In an undated fragment of a letter Hargreaves wrote, presumably to Abraham Dent, 'I asked Mr Rawlinson after your Cousin Wm Dent and he told me he hoped he would not come home this year. He'll be much wanted, he says, in the West Indies and he thinks will be prevail'd on to stay over year.'[2] It is a tantalizing reference for nothing seems to be known about cousin William or what he was doing in the West Indies. If he were employed there by the Rawlinsons, this might explain the Dents' connection with that firm.

In Manchester a dozen suppliers sent goods to the Dents, but

---

[1] Perhaps they were serges.   [2] Meaning 'over the year'?

again it is not always clear what they sent. As might be expected, most of the goods seem to have been various sorts of cloth. Thus Richard Mather sent striped linen and black worsted shag, which was 1½ yds. short measure in 1763, but his bills, which came to over £30 in 1766 and 1774, must have included other sorts of cloth. Richard Barton & Co., also supplied shag as well as baize and flannel, which drew the comment 'flannil dear' in 1760. The flannel may have been dear, but the Bartons, described as fustian manufacturers in 1781,[1] continued to supply considerable amounts of cloth. So too did George Webster, described as a cotton merchant in 1781,[2] whose bill came to £51 9s. in 1774. Finally Nathaniel and Falkner Phillips, fustian and small ware manufacturers and silk merchants, supplied a wide variety of laces, superior striped, all cotton, London, boys, which it would need a mercer to interpret. Outside Manchester, frieze was obtained from George Pickup of Accrington, flannel from George Grimsby and Richard Aspinwall, both of Bury, calamanco from Henry Smith & Co., 'nigh Colne', and baize and shag from Hugh Duckworth of Haslingden. Duckworth's bill of 7 February 1764 was fairly typical of this trade.

	£	s	d
1 piece of stout Baize 48 yards at 10½	2	2	0
1 piece of fine Red list at	2	7	0
18 yds of Drab shag at 22d.	1	13	0
19 yds of Do at 22d.	1	14	10
3 yds of ell wide wrapper	0	2	0
	7	18	10

It is also typical that against the first entry, someone, probably William Dent, has written 'only 46 yd.' and against the third entry '17½'.

The Dents seem to have got little except cloth from Lancashire south of the Ribble, though in 1764 they got a parcel of whale bone for £8 13s. from Mouncey & Co. of Liverpool, and in the early 1770s they were getting some gin from Samuel Hodgson

[1] W. Bailey, *Northern Directory* (1781), p. 245.
[2] Ibid., p. 262.

& Co., also of Liverpool. More interesting was an order which Abraham Dent gave and which received the following reply.

Mr Abraham Dent   Wigan January 21 1756
Bought of John Latham

	£	s	d
To Clockwork wt. 60 lb. at 14*d*. per	3	10	0
To Bells wt. 6 lb. at 18 per	0	9	0
To 3 Setts 30 hours Pinnions at 1*s*. 1*d*. per	0	3	3
To One Sett Eight Days Pinnions at	0	1	10
Wraper and Cord to be Returned	4	4	1

The above I hope will come safe to hand and prove to content and as I am a Stranger to you I have charged to pay on Delivery, which I hope you cannot take amiss. But before you'l want any more I shall enquire your Charrecter which, if good, as I hope it is, I will alow you Comon Credit with the next and all other parcells you may want, and am Sir your most Obedient Humble Servant

John Latham

These Pinnions I send you on Tryal as are made by a Toolmaker of the Best of Steel and cut down in an engine and every one who has of em likes them.

The letter was addressed

To Mr Abraham Dent Clockmaker Kirby Stephen with a Parcel to Receive four pounds four shillings upon Delivery.

It is unlikely that Abraham Dent was a clockmaker; the goods were obviously bought for a customer. This can hardly have been John Dent, who may have been a relative and was certainly a clockmaker, for he was only 15 in 1756. Whoever Abraham was buying for,[1] he gave Latham another order in April 1756; this time he was allowed credit, for he did not pay until September. When Latham acknowledged payment on 6 October 1756 he added 'I have Rop or gut for Clocks or Drill bows if any is wanted, have likewise Lacker', but no further orders seem to have followed.

[1] A note in the ledger, apparently in William Dent's hand, suggests that the goods were for 'Bro. Geo' (?Brother George). The cost of carriage from Wigan was 3*s*. 9*d*.

Across the Pennines in Yorkshire it was much the same story of getting cloth, though Joseph Wilson & Co. of Sheffield supplied some tobacco in 1768. Thus Thomas Holme of Halifax supplied blue cloth at 3s. 6d. yd., and John Hinchcliffe, also of Halifax, supplied flannel and doubtless other cloths, for his bill came to £42 10s. in 1771 and to £77 1s. 8d. in 1774. Other substantial suppliers were Michael Haigh of Quarmby, Thomas Clawson of Yarm and Giles Rickaby of Wakefield, but it is not clear what exactly they supplied. There is no doubt, however, that Wormald and Fountain of Leeds, whose bill came to over £40 in 1759, supplied cloth; it was in this firm that Benjamin Gott began his career as a cloth manufacturer.

The north-eastern counties, Durham and Northumberland, were more important than Yorkshire as suppliers. From Barnard Castle the Dents got, not only large supplies of flour, but also some cloth. The cloth came from Matthew Birkbeck, who in return got regular supplies of tea from the Dents. On 9 August 1769 Birkbeck wrote to Abraham Dent, 'two weeks since I writt to you by Jackson carryer for thre pound of Common Tea such as we used to have from you, but none is come to hand. I desire you'l send one pound of Congoe with them, if anything be wanting in my way, your favours will greatly oblige'. The following day 3 lb. of Bohea and 1 lb. of Congou were sent, and in 1770 Birkbeck supplied just over £10 worth of goods. On 4 December 1771 he wrote again to Abraham Dent: 'To your order I have sent you one Stripe, which I hope will please you. I am in a most melencoly sitywation at this time, its too tedious for me to relate. I make no doubt but you'l hear of our suferings. I desire you'l send me two pound of Common Tea and two pound of Coffee. If anything is wanting in my way, your further orders will greatly oblige.' The 'one stripe web' cost £1, but there were no further orders or further evidence of the nature of Birkbeck's 'suferings'.

County Durham was more important as a supplier of groceries than as a supplier of cloth. The Dents got large supplies, which included hops and treacle, from Thomas Rudd of Stockton, whose bill came to £75 1s. 0½d. in 1761; at the same time they seem to have supplied Rudd with tallow and candlewick. Similarly they got goods, including tea, from John Pease of Darlington, again largely in return for tallow. By September 1763 this firm was described as Pease and Dent, though whether the William Dent who signed a receipt 'for Mr. John Pease and self' was related to the Kirkby Stephen Dents is not known. Another Darlington supplier was John Pratt, who sent small amounts of groceries between 1767 and 1774; they included pepper, capers, isinglass and salt of tartar. More important was Edward Clark of Gateshead who supplied soap, starch, Spanish juice and gun-powder among other things, and whose goods produced a run-ning commentary from the Dents: 'sope a pound short' in 1756, starch dear and 'powder charged more than aggred for' in 1757, 'sope overcharged 6d. a firkin' in 1760 and 'sand not worth car-riage' in 1762. Despite these delinquencies, Clark continued to supply fairly large amounts of goods, as did John Atkinson of Gateshead, though in his case there is no clue as to the nature of the goods.

The suppliers in County Durham were outnumbered by those in Newcastle-upon-Tyne. Between 1756 and 1777 at least twenty individuals or firms in Newcastle supplied the Dents with a wide variety of goods. Newcastle, which was some sixty miles from Kirkby Stephen via Barnard Castle, was clearly an important centre of supply, though it is not always possible to tell what goods came from there. Thus John Soulsby's bill came to just over £40 in 1768 and Joseph Ramsey's to over £20 in 1765, but in neither case is there any indication of the nature of the goods supplied. It seems fairly clear, however, that Newcastle was important as a centre for the supply of groceries. Thus the Dents got prunes among other things from Gilbert Wilkinson, pints of British blue from Thomas Simpson, and a wide range of goods, including tea, treacle, almonds, gunpowder, quicksilver, starch, raisins, prunes, currants, hops and lint from Atkinson and Hall. Although they 'overcharged at treakle 1½d.' and their gunpowder was dear and their raisins and prunes were short weight in 1761, and their lint was 'charged 9s. a dozen not worth 8s. dozen' in 1765, Atkinson and Hall's bill came to nearly £100 in 1763, to about £270 in 1766, and to £217 in 1770. Another big supplier was Monkhouse and Hopper whose bill, apparently for hops and spirits, came to £171 in 1772 and to £115 the following year. Hops were also bought from Coates and Ismay. Most of these goods must have come into Newcastle by sea, but whether they were imported direct from foreign countries or came coastwise from London is not certain. The latter seems more probable for things like sugar and dried fruits and, of course, hops, especially as freight rates may well have been low in the colliers which returned from London to Newcastle in ballast. Thus in 1769 four Newcastle importers, Rawlinson & Co., Benson & Co., William Backhouse and Nicholas Dunn, were getting large amounts of groceries, haberdashery, ironware, hardware and apothecary ware from London by ship. None of these importers supplied the Dents with goods directly, but they may well have supplied the Dents' Newcastle suppliers. Benson & Co. and William Backhouse seem to have dominated this trade, and the variety of their cargoes suggests that they were general merchants trading on a big scale. At Stockton, a smaller port, Dent's supplier, Thomas Rudd, was probably the Rudd & Co., which was getting groceries and other goods from London by sea in 1769.[1]

Not all the goods from Newcastle were groceries or gunpowder. Some cloth was obtained from Pattison and Bowker, whose thick-set was 'quite dear' in 1757. More interesting was William Charnley, a bookseller and publisher who supplied the Dents with some of their paper, magazines and books, though the paper and books were sometimes described as 'dear'. Charnley's account with the Dents, which gives weekly totals of the goods, rather suggests that he supplied them with newspapers, but there is no direct evidence of this. There was certainly no Westmorland newspaper available at this time.

Though the Dents got most of their supplies from the northern counties, there was a scatter of suppliers elsewhere, with some concentration in London. Three Norwich firms sent goods, probably cloth, though this was rarely specified even in the case of Crowe and Patterson, whose bill came to £43 15s. 3½d. in 1759. Lillington and Penfold, however, certainly supplied crape in

---

[1] Exch. K. R. Port Books, 268/4.

1767 when their bill for 168 yards came to £12 14s. Three Coventry suppliers also sent goods, probably ribbons, for two of them, Messrs. Bird and Smith and Anthony Harrison were ribbon manufacturers in 1874.[1] Thomas Rawson of Nottingham sent stockings and 'fine worsted for knitting' in 1773, but these probably belonged to the stocking rather than the shop trade. From Kidderminster John Watson sent unspecified goods which drew the comment '1 piece marble not to order', whatever that implied.

Finally about a dozen London suppliers sent goods to the Dents between 1756 and 1777. Samuel Yeats sent 44 yards of scarlet and black cloth for £20 15s. 10½d. in 1768, John Longden, drysalter, sent 'petre, allom and pearl ashes' in 1766, and Henry Wallis sent watches in 1770. Hops were obtained from Hardcastle and Cattley, Hop Merchants, Old Swan Stairs, and from Messrs. Sterry and Coates. All these suppliers were not very important, but two others were. Thomas Elton and Co. sent considerable quantities of goods, which certainly included cloth and lute strings; they seem to have been haberdashers. Mr. John Law near St. Paul's Wharf supplied rum, gin, brandy and some sugar, but it is not clear how much of the spirits was bought to sell through the shop. London seems rather less important as a centre of supply than might have been expected, but it was a long haul from the capital to Kirkby Stephen, and some London goods may have been shipped by the coast to Newcastle.

The presence of so many suppliers in different parts of the country suggests a developed transport system. The main man in that system was the carrier, a strangely neglected figure. It is clear that there were regular carriers between Kirkby Stephen and some of the northern centres of supply. James Rain and John Robinson operated between Kirkby Stephen and Newcastle, Anthony Cleasby and Christopher Stubbs between Kirkby Stephen and Stockton, Thomas Pearson and Ephraim Jackson brought goods from Kendal, and the former also from Lancaster, Henry Sawkeld served Sedbergh and Kirkby Lonsdale, and John Brunskill Barnard Castle. Stubbs, Pearson and Jackson were local men; Cleasby seems to have lived at Stainmore. The carrier

---

[1] W. Bailey, *British Directory* (1784), iv, pp. 826–7.

D

brought goods for the Dents and carried back empty soap boxes and treacle casks and sometimes goods that were returned, for example almanacs and books to William Charnley at Newcastle. Unfortunately there is very little evidence of the cost of this carriage, which is rarely recorded. In 1756 James Rain was paid 10s. for the carriage of 8 firkins of tallow from Newcastle, and in 1764 he charged 1s. 3d. for the carriage of a bushel of split peas from the same place. In 1771 it cost 5s. 6d. to carry 30 stones of lambs wool from Houghton-le-Spring to Barnard Castle, or 1·8 per cent of the cost of the wool. In 1774 when Abraham Dent sent hams to his customers for stockings in London, the carriage on 24 hams weighing 278 lb. was £1 9s., which was very roughly 11d. a ton-mile; carriage at such rates was expensive, but it was common enough at that period.

Carriers did not only carry goods, important as that was, they also carried money and other instruments for the settlement of accounts. Thus many forms of payment were carried to Newcastle by James Rain. In July 1757 he took 'a London Bill value £10' to William Charnley; two years later it was 'a Bill value £20 on Newcastle Bank'; in February 1760 £4 5s. was sent to James Wilkinson 'per James Rain', and in May Rain took a bill on Michael Morley to Charnley. In 1763 Rain was taking bank-notes and bills to settle the Dents' account with Edward Clark at New-castle. Similarly John Robinson took bank-notes and bills to Gateshead and Newcastle. Thomas Pearson and Ephraim Jackson took cash and bills to Kendal, where William Barnes occasionally drew on Abraham Dent through Jackson. On 25 February 1774, when Barnes was owed £2 0s. 7½d., he wrote to Abraham Dent, 'I have made bould to draw on you for Two Pound per favour of Ephm Jackson, which will be obliged to you to pay at the time, being drawn fourteen days from the above date. Am in great want of cash at this time. When you have occation shall be glad of an order from you.' The bill of the same date runs:

Fourteen days after date Please to Pay to Ephm Jackson or order Two Pounds as advis'd By Sir Your Humble Servant William Barnes. To Mr. Abraham Dent in Kirkby Stephen.

It is endorsed by Jackson. Barnes seems to have got no further orders.

Trade with so many scattered suppliers demanded not only a complicated system of transport but also a complicated system of payments. For some of the goods they obtained the Dents paid partly in kind. They sent tea to Matthew Birkbeck of Barnard Castle in exchange for cloth, and tea and cloth to John Monk-house, also of Barnard Castle, in return for flour. The Dents in turn sent some flour to William Fothergill of Kendal from whom they bought cards. The most interesting of these exchanges were with the paper makers. Potter Fletcher, the paper maker at Milnthorpe, was paid partly in rags, white at 1s. 11d. a stone and brown at 8d. a stone in 1766. James Ashburner of Kendal received some flour from the Dents, but he too got rags, and in much greater quantities than did Fletcher. Thus in 1773 Ashburner received about 770 stones of rags, the white at 2s. a stone and the coarse at 9d. The Dents seem to have got the rags through Joseph Norman, described as 'rag gatherer' in the parish register in 1784 when his son was baptized. These barter transactions. though they have some interest, were not really very important. They were not the usual way of settling with suppliers.

The Dents paid for their goods in a variety of ways, which would not be necessary with the banking system of to-day when it could all be done by cheque. Their ledger of purchases does not always record the actual method of payment, though it does record the supplier's receipt for the payment made to him. The left-hand page of the ledger gives the amount owed to the supplier and the right-hand page gives his receipt for that amount. Thus Hugh Duckworth of Haslingden supplied goods for £4 0s. 6d. on 4 September 1760. Opposite this entry is the receipt: 'Received 4 February 1761 of Mr. Wm Dent four pounds and sixpence in full p. me Hugh Duckworth.' The signature of the supplier, or some-times of his son or employee, is original, which means that the supplier or his agent had access to the ledger. But how was this done? It is possible that one of the Dents did a tour of their suppliers, taking the ledger with him, settling the accounts and getting the ledger receipted. A careful study of these receipts, comparing the date of the receipts and the places where the suppliers lived, shows that this was not always possible. Thus on 8 February 1763 John Walker signed a receipt in the ledger on behalf of Samuel Dales, Cheapside, London; on the following day, 9 February, Potter Fletcher of Milnthorpe signed a receipt. The ledger could not have been in London on one day and in Milnthorpe the next, not in the eighteenth century. It is just possible that Fletcher was in London on the 9th, but this seems to be straining coincidence a little.

An alternative explanation, apart from any theory that the Dents forged the signatures of their suppliers, is that the suppliers or their agents or travellers came to Kirkby Stephen, perhaps for orders, and there got their accounts settled and there signed the ledger. There is some evidence for this. On 8 June 1756 William Dent recorded that Thomas Holme of Halifax was debtor to him for 'a post letter with advice of his coming this jorney'. In three or four cases, too, the suppliers seem to have received payment from Mrs. Dent, though it is not possible to be certain about this. Perhaps the most serious objection to this explanation is that the amounts are occasionally so small that they would hardly seem worth collecting in this way. Indeed it seems probable that both methods were used; that some suppliers or their agents received payment in Kirkby Stephen, and that others were visited by one of the Dents. It is known that Abraham Dent made business journeys to London. In 1768 when he owed Hardcastle and Cattley of London £8 19s. 3d. for hops, he sent them 'a bill on Mr. Brook' for £9 14s. 9d., and then collected the balance of 15s. 6d. 'when I was in London'. He may have made similar journeys to the north east, for occasionally two Newcastle suppliers signed the ledger on the same day, which suggests that this was done in Newcastle, not in Kirkby Stephen. In whatever way the receipts were obtained, it is clear that there was a good deal of movement of men as well as of goods.

It is equally clear that such a system of receipts implied the giving of credit. The Dents' suppliers were paid for their goods at irregular intervals. There was a gap in time between the Dents' receipt of goods and their payment for them; that gap simply represented the length of credit that the suppliers allowed the Dents. It might be possible to work out from the ledger of purchases the length of the credit in a great many of these transactions, but that would be a tedious and a rather fruitless operation. It is obvious from the ledger that there was no uniform or standard period between purchase and payment. Nor does any very definite pattern emerge which might relate the period of credit to the size of the purchase or the provenance of the supplier. Small suppliers like John Udall of Wigton, Jacob Collier of Kendal, and Thomas Cocker of Bolton might wait any period from a month to a year before being paid for their goods. The bigger suppliers gave the same sort of credit: four to six months in the case of Atkinson and Hall of Newcastle, seven months to a year in the case of John Whitwell of Kendal, and four to seven months in the case of Lawson Rawlinson and Co., of Lancaster. The London suppliers, small and great, gave a similar credit. John Longden, a drysalter of London, supplied 'petre, allom and pearl ashes' on 29 March 1766 and was paid on 4 October of that year. Sterry and Coates supplied hops on 23 June 1762 and were paid on 29 January following. Samuel Dales of Cheapside gave five to six months' credit in 1762–3. Hardcastle and Cattley, the hop merchants of Old Swan Stairs, supplied hops to the value of £17 0s. 1d. on 4 October 1766 and were paid by a bill on Elton on 3 July 1767.

The ledger of purchases rather gives the impression that the smaller suppliers had often to wait longer for their money than had the bigger suppliers. This would be natural enough given a large number of small suppliers who were scattered over a wide area and who had to make some personal contact with the Dents before they could be paid. One thing at least is certain. Though the credit granted to the Dents by their suppliers varied greatly in duration, such credit was granted in almost every purchase of goods for the shop. Given the methods of supply and the methods of payment, it is difficult to see how it could have been otherwise.

Credit may be allowed, but goods have to be paid for in the end. What form did that payment take? Basically there were two methods of payment in transactions which were not settled by barter; they were cash and bills.

Many of the suppliers seem to have been paid in cash, especially perhaps those whose accounts were small. It is not known how much of the cash was coin and how much bank-notes, but the former almost certainly predominated. When the Dents sent by carrier what they described simply as cash, this was coin, for they recorded the despatch of notes, sometimes keeping a record of the number. Some notes were sent in payment to suppliers. In 1773 John Jackson of Bishop Auckland was sent £10 'in 10 Newcastle notes of 20s. per John Thompson', and Monkhouse and Hopper of Newcastle were sent two Newcastle bank-notes of £5 each (in 1771 they were sent a York bank-note of £10 10s.). In June 1774 John Atkinson of Gateshead received 5 Newcastle notes of 20s. each, one Newcastle note of £5 and a Leeds note of £5 5s. There were other examples, but altogether they do not suggest that bank-notes played a large part in the payment for goods supplied to the shop.

It was otherwise with inland bills, which were much more important. Their mechanism has been admirably described by Professor Ashton in his account of Peter Stubs of Warrington, where the evidence is much fuller than it is in the case of the Dents.[1] Bills of exchange were used in two ways to pay for the goods that the Dents bought for their shop. In some cases the supplier drew a bill on the Dents. The following is an example.

Sr £21 13s.   Stockton May 14 1763
    Ten days after date pay Mr. William Calvert or order twenty one pounds thirteen shillings (Value in Account) with or without advice from Thomas Rudd & Co.
To Mr. Abraham Dent, Merchant, Kirkby Stephen

On the back of the bill appear the signatures of Calvert, Isaac Wilson and John Fawell. Thus the bill had been endorsed by Calvert, who had used it to pay a debt to Wilson, who in turn had used it to pay a debt to Fawell.

There are a number of such bills loose in the ledger. They bear no stamp, for they were not taxed before 1782, and no acceptance on the face of the bill. They could be very crude. For example

---

[1] T. S. Ashton, *An Eighteenth-Century Industrialist*, pp. 99–123.

Agust the 22 1767

ten dayes after the date hear of pay to James Madecolf or his order
fife poundes and plase to a Count of youre humble Servant

Wm Westwood

To Mr. Abrham Dent in Kerbestefan, Wastmourland, for £5.

This is endorsed James Metcalfe and Matthew Smith.

Only one of the surviving bills is printed, with blanks for the
date, names and amount. It is as follows:

£4   Kendal *December 6 1763*

Tow Weeks after date pay to *Mr. Thos Crudwson* or Order *fourr pounds*
for Value *Received* by Advice from *Js Thompson*.
To *Mr. Wiliam Dent Merchant in Kerby Stavin.*

The bill, which is endorsed Thomas Crewdson and Thomas Pearson, is a very elegant piece of printing. Surely it must be an
example of Ashburner's work?

The second way of using bills was for the Dents to remit to
their suppliers bills which they, the Dents, had received. Not a
great deal can be discovered about these bills, which seem mainly
to have been remitted to the bigger suppliers. Thus Atkinson and
Hall of Newcastle, who were big suppliers, received the following
bills in 1767.

April 28 Sent per John Robinson a Bill Kellam and Palmer, Fenchurch
St., London   £40
May 19 Sent per Robinson 1 Bill Hyde on Wimpey, London   £30
July 7 Sent per Joseph Rain 1 Bill on Coales of London drawn by
Mr Brathwaite   £30

Similarly Coates and Ismay of Newcastle, who supplied hops,
were paid £80 by bills in 1769–70, but two of these bills, Wilkinson, London, drawn by Anthony Cleasby for £20, and Michael
Fawcett drawn by J. Ernest for £20, were returned, and Coates
and Ismay charged 2s. $7\frac{1}{2}d$. 'by postage of Letter of Bills returned'.
It is not surprising that the Dents sent their bills by carrier where
possible.

Bills were also remitted to smaller suppliers, but it was not
always possible to send a bill of the exact amount owed. Thus

when James Woods of Kirkby Lonsdale was owed £26 5s. 6d. in 1771, the Dents sent him a bill for £20 (Bradberry on Bradberry) and £5 18s. 6d. in cash; the remaining 7s. was covered by wine the Dents had supplied. Sometimes it worked the other way as when George Benson of Kendal received a bill of exchange for £19 when he was owed only £9 7s. 3d.

These methods of payment were not mutually exclusive. It was common to use different methods of paying the same supplier. Thus on 16 January 1770 John Soulsby of Newcastle was sent

A Bill per post on Vandewall and Barton	£40	0	0
1 Newcastle note on Aubone Surtees & c.	5	0	0
3 Do on Bell Cookson & c.	3	0	0

Similarly when Edward Clark of Newcastle was owed £39 1s. in 1763–4, it was paid as follows.

Sent per James Rain 7 Bills on the Newcastle Bank	£7	0	0
Sent per Rudd 1 Bill on Newcastle Bank No. 645	£5	0	0
1 Bill on Whitfield London	£7	1	0
Cash	£20	0	0
	39	1	0

The Dents do not seem to have kept a separate bill ledger, though in the ledger of purchases there are four folios of 'Bills received since March 24 1765', which runs to the early part of 1769. This list at least shows how important the inland bill of exchange was at this time, though this has long been recognized. More unfortunate, there is no trace of any profit and loss account for the shop, and indeed no evidence that such an account was kept. This means that it is quite impossible to tell how profitable the shopkeeping was, especially as it was only one of a number of activities in which Abraham Dent engaged. Indeed it is not certain how long he continued as a shopkeeper. It is clear that he kept the shop after his father's death in 1774, and that he was buying goods for the shop until 1778. In 1778 there is a reference to a Shop Book, which has not survived. It is probable that Abraham Dent gave up the shop about 1780. In an account for that year with John Moore of Kendal, who supplied stamped paper, there is the statement, 'by stock on hand transferred to Mr. W. Wilkin £21 16s. 6d.', but it is not clear whether Wilkin was Moore's successor or Dent's. Certainly there is no reference to shopkeeping after 1780, and the shop does not appear among the shops in the Directory for 1784. Dent could hardly have handed the shop over to one of his sons, for Thomas was only 15 and Abraham junior 13 years of age in 1780. Neither was subsequently described as a grocer or shop-keeper. Dent himself was 51 in 1780, but if he gave up the shop then, it was no retirement from business; he was still a wine mer-chant and brewer and a dealer in stockings.

Chapter IV

The Wine Merchant and Brewer

ANY account of Abraham Dent as a wine merchant and brewer must be short and unsatisfactory, for these are the most undocumented of his business activities. His father was described as a wine merchant at his death in 1774, and Abraham himself was so described seven years later. It is possible that father and son were in partnership in the wine business down to 1774, but, as in the case of the shop, this cannot be proved. Thus down to 1774 it is impossible to tell how much of the wine business was conducted by Abraham and how much by his father; after 1774 Abraham was in charge. He had no monopoly, for Robert Yates of Kirkby Stephen was described as a wine merchant in 1775 when his wife Bridget was buried.

Wine and spirit merchants would be a more apt description for the Dents than wine merchants, for there is little evidence that they dealt extensively in wines. On 25 July 1760 Mark Maugham, writing on behalf of James Wilkinson of Newcastle, told William Dent that he had good red port and mountain wine and good cider should he want any, but in fact Wilkinson's bill came to only £1 17s. 8d. in 1760, and 6s. 8d. of it was for hoops. William Monkhouse and Company of Newcastle supplied some port and, apparently, mountain wine in 1769-70, as well as quantities of gin, brandy and cognac brandy, but it is not clear how much of their bill of £118 in 1770 was for wines and spirits. In 1769 and 1770 they paid for the Dents' wine licence, which cost £2 4s. 1d. in 1769 and £2 4s. 8d. in 1770. As Monkhouse and Hopper they continued to pay for the wine licence in 1772, 1773, 1774 and 1775 as well as to supply large quantities of goods, some of which were hops.

On the west coast two ports, Liverpool and Lancaster, supplied some spirits. At Liverpool Samuel Hodgson and Company sent gin in 1771 when a cask was '1 quart short of 40 gallons' and when

their bill came to £28 11s. 8d. At Lancaster Messrs Rawlinson and
Sons supplied unspecified gallons, almost certainly rum, between
1769 and 1772; in 1769 they sent about 67 gallons costing just
under £30. By 1776 when their bill, apparently for rum, came to
just over £115, they were trading as A. Rawlinson Sons and
Lindow. The following year, 1777, they sent 101 gallons of rum
at 8s. 10d. a gallon, with a discount of 4d. a gallon for ready money.
The rum was sent in December 1777 and paid for on 11 March
1778, largely by a bill at 60 days; the discount was 16s. 8d. or about
2d. a gallon. In 1778 they supplied about 300 gallons of rum, some
at 8s. 9d. a gallon, and in 1779 310 gallons, of which 103 gallons
were at 9s. and 100 were at 8s. 9d. a gallon. The remaining 107
gallons involved a more elaborate calculation:

	£	s	d
12 June 1779			
104 gallons rum at 3s. 8d.	19	1	4
Excise 4s. 8d. Custom 5d. per gallon on do.	26	8	8
Additional Duty of 5 per cent	1	6	5
For a short charge in the above puncheon 107 gallons			
called 104 difference 3 gallons @ 3s. 8d.	0	11	0
Excise 4s. 8d. and Customs 5 per gallon		15	3
Adittional Duty 5 per cent thereon			9
	48	3	5

Much of the rum was paid for by bills on Law and Holme of
London, usually at 60 days. After 1779 the account was 'carried to
new book', which has not survived.

Another Lancaster firm that supplied rum on one occasion was
Messrs. Simpson and Newby. On 8 November 1774 Abraham
Dent recorded, 'Bought Simpson and Newby 1 puncheon rum
delivered at the Bond Cellar Lancaster @ 8s. 7d. and to have sent
3 samples to chose out of, to pay first cost in April and to have 6
month credit on the Excise when ever I chuse to take it out.' The
puncheon contained 108 gallons and cost £46 16s., of which £21
3s. was the first cost, £25 4s. was the excise and 9s. was the
carriage to Kendal. The rum seems to have been delivered in
March 1775 and paid for two months later.

A more varied supply of drink was obtained from 'Mr. John

Law near St Paul's Wharf', who was a partner in the firm of Law and Holme, Distillers, of 28 Upper Thomas St., London. Law had some connection with Kirkby Stephen; he seems to have had relatives in the district. In July 1780 Abraham Dent wrote to Law and Holme, 'I am just taking a ride to Musgrave to go to Church and dine with Mr. and Mrs. Law.' A year later Law was in Kirkby Stephen. On 7 July 1781 Dent 'accounted with Mr. Law at K.S.'. Law returned to London in company with Dent's son Thomas and with a horse that Dent had provided, though whether they travelled on horseback or by carriage is not clear. Dent wrote to Law and Holme on 12 July 1781, 'I hope by the time you receive this Mr. Law and his fellow traveller will be arrived safe in London. I wrote to my son Dobson mentioning that the horse was to be disposed of in London, also to Mr. Law, that if he could get twelve guineas for him, the price he cost me, he or Mr. Holme would do the best in their power.' By the 20th Dent had received 'a line from my son Dobson', announcing the safe arrival of 'Mr. Law and my son Tom', and was anxious to hear 'how the horse performed his jorney' and whether he had been disposed of. Two years later, in July 1782, Dent was expecting 'Mr. Law hear about the 12th August to have some diversion on the Moors'. The other partner in Law and Holme was William Holme, who also had local connections. On 20 February 1787 Dent wrote to Holme from Kirkby Stephen, 'I called on your Father and Mother who I found in as good a state of health as I could suppose. They tell me they have some hopes of seeing you this summer. I should be very happy to see you at Sedbusk if you possibly can give me a call.' Holme did come north in the summer of 1787, but Dent missed him. On 23 July 1787 he wrote to Holme, 'I was sorry that I was disappointed in meeting you the morning you left Hawes as I purposed a good deal of pleasure in taking a ride with you as far as Mr. Andersons. . . . I shall be happy to hear that you arrived safe in London and that you found Mrs. Holme &c. all well.' It is evident from an earlier letter that Dent had never met Holme, despite his dealings with the firm and his visits to London. His contacts had been with John Law, and it looks very much as if Law had retired or died sometime about 1786.

The Dents did considerable business with Law and Holme. In 1772 they bought from them 106 gallons of rum, 73 gallons of gin and 48 gallons of strong molasses brandy at a total cost of £87. The prices of these spirits were recorded in the shopkeeper's simple code of capital letters standing for figures: thus

s. d.

106 gallons rum @ L/G   £41 10s. 4d.,

which meant that L/G stood for 7s. 10d. Opposite these entries in the ledger were the following recipes.

Proof in gin—for 100 gallons take full a pound of best salt of tartar, put it in a can with about three quarts of proof gin and three quarts or a gallon water, let them stand full ½ an hour, often stirring it, then add 1 pint of oyl of almonds, be sure its bright.
For 50 gallons gin 6 oz. of alom dissolved over the fire in 1 pint water, then put it in your cask stirring it well about and leave out the bung 2 or 3 days.

In 1773 the Dents bought 74 gallons of strong molasses brandy at 9s. 6d. a gallon, 101 gallons of gin at 6s. 10d., 110 gallons of Jamaica rum at 7s. 10d., and a hogshead of vinegar for £2 10s. The following year the brandy was down to 43 gallons, but the gin had risen to 117 gallons (at 7s. 6d.) and the rum, described as Jamaica old rum, to 120 gallons (at 8s.); there were also 12½ gallons of aniseed at 4s. 4d. a gallon and 12½ gallons of 'cinn', presumably cinnamon, at 6s. 6d. In addition there was £2 4s. 0½d. for 'Yeatts wine licence'. In 1775 the amounts were greater: rum 224 gallons (at 8s. 3d.), gin 236 gallons (119 gallons at 6s. 5d. and 117 at 7s. 6d.) and brandy, described as British, 74 gallons (at 11s.). There was also £2 10s. 8½d. for an unspecified 'wine licence and fine', the fine being presumably 6s. 8d. In 1776 there was no gin and the rum had fallen to 116 gallons (at 8s.); the brandy was up in quantity and down in price, 70 gallons at 9s. 10d. Aniseed reappeared, 12½ gallons at 4s. 6d., and there were 142 gallons 'sweets' at 2s. 3d. which was presumably sweet wine, and a butt of 'old Mounta', presumably Mountain, a variety of Malaga wine, which cost £30. No rum was bought in 1777, perhaps because

Abraham Dent was getting larger supplies from Lancaster, but there were 73 gallons molasses brandy at 10*s.* 6*d.*, 221 gallons of gin (110 gallons at 8*s.* and 111 at 6*s.* 8*d.*), and 16¼ gallons aniseeds at 4*s.* 6*d.* The accounts for 1778 are incomplete, but they include one interesting item:

March 31	Yeatts wine licence	77	£2	4*s.*	0½*d.*
	E. Dent do	77	£2	4*s.*	0½*d.*

This seems to suggest that Abraham Dent's first wife Elizabeth was alive in 1777 and that the wine licence was in her name, but it is possible that E. Dent was William Dent's widow.

There is evidence that Abraham Dent continued to get supplies from Law and Holme in the 1780s. On 28 March 1780 he wrote to them: 'It may be 4 or 5 months before I shall want more gin. If there should be any advantage to you or me you may send a puncheon more same as last. I am intirely at a loss how the duty on malt and spirits will be.' Unfortunately there is no record of the quantity he was buying then. In the 1770s the quantity had been considerable, and it had been paid for by inland bills. Abraham Dent had a large bill account with Law and Holme, who seem to have dealt in bills as well as in wine and spirits.

As wine merchants the Dents got supplies of wine and spirits from Newcastle, Liverpool, Lancaster and London, but little can be said about how they disposed of this drink. Some was sold through the shop in the 1760s, but this does not seem to have been the most important outlet. Some was sold to the suppliers of goods for the shop, to George Benson of Kendal, John Monkhouse of Barnard Castle and James Woods of Kirkby Lonsdale, but the amounts were small. Similarly those who supplied malt for the brewery got some wine and spirits from Abraham Dent. Thus Thomas Bass of Barnard Castle, who was supplying malt, got 12 gallons 2 quarts of wine at 3*s.* a gallon in 1774, and 22 gallons 3 quarts of rum at 9*s.* a gallon in 1775. The following year Mrs. Bass got 45 gallons of rum at 9*s.* a gallon, and a further 12 gallons in 1777 at the same price. This may have been for re-sale. Dent was paying 8*s.* 10*d.* a gallon for his rum in 1777, which suggests that 9*s.* a gallon was more a wholesale than a retail price. William

Chisman of West Auckland, who also supplied malt, was getting some rum from Dent in 1774–79. The quantity was not large, some 15 gallons in 1775 and 28 in 1776 for example, but it was large enough for Chisman to be getting it for other people. In 1775 two gallons were for William Harford at West Auckland, nearly 4 gallons for a Mr. Dixon, and 2 gallons for George Smuffitt. The next year at least five people were getting the rum as well as Chisman himself. Again the price was 9s. a gallon (though it rose to 10s. and 10s 6d. in 1777). Whether Chisman was re-selling the rum or getting it to oblige his friends or customers is uncertain. It is equally uncertain who bought the rest of the Dents' rum and their gin and brandy.

Although the Dents were described as wine merchants, and were indeed wine merchants, the surviving evidence does not suggest that they were very big wine merchants, though it should be emphasized that the evidence is incomplete. For the two years 1776 and 1777, when it seems to be reasonably complete, Abraham Dent bought wines and spirits for £245 and £171 respectively. Obviously too much reliance should not be placed on isolated figures of purchases, especially when nothing is known of the stock in hand. Even so, the impression is one of a not very large wine and spirit business, but this too should be considered in its setting. Abraham Dent was not the only wine merchant in Kirkby Stephen, and Kirkby Stephen was a very small town.

There is evidence that Abraham Dent continued as a wine merchant until 1783, but he was not included as such in Bailey's Directory of 1784, when only Christopher Alderson was described as a wine and brandy merchant. It is probable that he retired from this business about 1784. On 5 June 1784 he wrote to Law and Holme, 'In my last I forget to mention to settle on Goods Account, which you will now please to do and let me know what ballance I shall have to draw for.' There is no further reference to a goods' account with Law and Holme, and in 1789 Dent wrote to William Holme asking him to give 'my son Thomas' the present prices of brandy and rum as Thomas and a partner intended doing some business in the spirit trade and wished to buy from Holme. They also intended, Dent added, 'paying ready money'. It is not known how Holme responded to this letter, which clearly shows Dent himself was no longer in the business, but in 1790, when Thomas Dent's first son was baptized, the father was described as 'brandy merchant'. It was a short-lived description; on the baptism of a second son in 1791 Thomas Dent was described as a 'common brewer'.

Abraham Dent had been a common brewer too. On 15 May 1774 John Waller wrote to Dent from Plymouth, 'My Aunt tells me you are building a brewery in the Market Place, which I think you wou'd not do if the business did not answer. I heartily wish it may and everything that is good to you.' In June 1774 William Strickland, brazier, of Kendal supplied 'a copper' weighing 3 cwt. 2 qr. 16 lb. 8 oz.; it cost £28 18s. 8½d., and must have been part of the equipment for the brewery. That was the beginning of the elusive brewery about which so little can be discovered. According to the Directory of 1784 the brewery was run by a partnership of Dent, Portees and Mason.[1] Portees was apparently a James Portees who, in the early 1770s, was employed by Pease and Dent of Darlington, a firm which supplied the Dents with hops. Whether he was a partner in the brewery from the beginning, is not known. He bought a house in Kirkby Stephen in 1784 from William Barnett, innkeeper,[2] but two years later Abraham Dent, junior, referred to him as 'Mr. J. Portees of Liverpool, my father's late partner in the brewery'. He seems to have died intestate in 1803, when he was described as brewer, late of Liverpool.[3] The third partner, Mason, has not been identified; he was probably the John Mason who was described as a common brewer at his death in 1802 when he was aged 69. He may have belonged to the local family of Mason who were tanners, skinners and fell-mongers.

In 1786, when Dent mortgaged much of his property, it included 'all that common brewery with the counting house, shop and appurtenancies and the malthouse with the appurtenancies

---

[1] W. Bailey, *British Directory* (1784), iii, p. 605.
[2] Hallam MSS. (Westmorland Record Office).
[3] Administration dated 10 September 1803 in the Lancashire Record Office; the estate, unspecified, was under £300.

now in the possession of the said Abraham Dent and Company'. The property also included the Golden Fleece Inn, which Dent had bought from Joshua Ewbank in 1782 and the Sun Inn, which was in the occupation of John Dickinson.[1] Perhaps the inns acted as convenient tied houses, though in fact Dickinson seems himself to have been a brewer.

References to the Brewery Ledger and the Brewery Book show that separate accounts were kept for the brewery, but these have not survived. There is however some evidence of purchases which must have been made for the brewery. This relates to the purchase of malt between 1774 and 1778. At that time the purchases of barley seem to have been insignificant, which implies that the brewery was not then doing its own malting. Some malt was obtained locally; Robert Islip of Kirkby Stephen supplied 28 loads[2] for £42 in 1774, and Thomas Cleasby, another Kirkby Stephen maltster, supplied 44 loads in 1776 and 14 in 1777. Other local suppliers were Thomas Hutton of Soulby, who sent 34 loads in 1774, 26 in 1775, 50 in 1776 and 66 in 1777; Joshua Hutchinson of Hartley, who supplied 20 loads in 1774, 10 in 1775, 18 in 1776 and 9 in 1777; Thomas Bowness of Winton who supplied 155 loads in 1776, 181 in 1777 and 185 in 1778. Small amounts were also obtained from William Shaw of Stainmore and James Harker of Hartley.

Further afield, some malt was obtained from John Nicholson of Boulton in Derbyshire, but the more distant supplies came largely from County Durham. Thomas Bass, and later Mrs. Bass, of Barnard Castle supplied malt in amounts ranging from 196 to 504 bushels in a year. At Gainford Christopher Wright sent 112 bushels in 1775, and Robert Monkhouse 264 bushels in 1778. From Staindrop William Pearson sent 727 bushels in 1775. Finally at West Auckland William Chisman supplied flour and a little barley as well as malt. The malt ranged from 50 bushels to 317 bushels a year. Chisman's account is more interesting than the others, for it gives some break down of costs. Thus under 22 November 1775 there appears this entry:

[1] Hallam MSS. (Westmorland Record Office).
[2] The load was apparently 8 bushels.

E

54 bushels of malt Ditto 53 bushels makes 107
Charge of the above 107 made from 90 bushels of barley

90 bushels of barley @ 3s. 9d.	16	17	6
Duty for the whole	3	10	10
Making of the malt	0	19	0
To the Maltman 12d. per steep	0	2	0
Carriage to B. Castle from West Auckland	0	14	0
for buying and attendance at 1½d. a bushel		11	3
	22	14	7

Of the other constituents of beer, some hops were obtained from Monkhouse and Hopper of Newcastle and from Thomas and Anthony Whitwell of Kendal, but there is no mention of yeast. The recorded purchases of malt came to about 115 qrs. in 1774, 230 in 1775, 340 in 1776, 389 in 1777 and 290 in 1778. The average price was 33s. a qr. in 1774, 32s. 8d. in 1775, 29s. 11d. in 1776, 24s. 4d. in 1777 and 27s. 2d. in 1778. It is uncertain whether this malt represented all that was bought for the brewery in these years. If it did, it would give some indication of output. Assuming that four barrels of strong beer or eight barrels of small beer could be brewed from a quarter of malt,[1] then the output in 1777 would be 1,556 barrels of strong or 3,112 barrels of small beer. This was a modest output, but it should be remembered that beer was bulky in relation to its value and would not stand the cost of long distance land carriage. In an inland town like Kirkby Stephen, with no water communication, the sale of beer was limited to a local market. This cannot have been very large, and in any case Dent and Company had no monopoly of it.

After about 1778 there is even less information about the brewery. The partnership of Dent, Portees and Mason seems to have broken up about 1786. Shortly afterwards Abraham Dent went to live at Sedbusk in Wensleydale, and the brewery seems to have been taken over by his two sons, Thomas and Abraham junior. It was in their tenure in 1793. Four years later Thomas had become an army officer, but Abraham junior was still described as a common brewer when his daughter Isabella was baptized on

---

[1] P. Mathias, *The Brewing Industry in England 1700–1830*, p. 371.

25 September 1797. Abraham may have remained a brewer until his death, which occurred sometime between 1797 and 1804, or until the brewery was sold, along with other property in 1801.

It has been necessary to give this disjointed and unsatisfactory account of Abraham Dent as a wine merchant and brewer because otherwise the picture of his business activities would have been even less complete. He may not have been either a wine merchant or a brewer in a very big way, but he was both, and it is essential to see the whole range of his activities. That range was considerable, for it included a substantial business as a hosier.

Chapter V

The Hosier: The sixties and seventies

KIRKBY STEPHEN lay in the great Pennine knitting belt which stretched through Wensleydale, Swaledale, Dentdale and Ravenstonedale, and then went north to Stainmore and beyond. In this area hand knitting was probably, after agriculture, the main occupation. It included the knitting of gloves and mitts, caps and jerseys, as well as stockings, but there is no doubt that stockings were the main product of the industry. The origin and development of the industry remain obscure.[1] It may have arisen and developed to take the place of a declining rural cloth industry. There is evidence that the cloth industry in Westmorland was declining by the end of the sixteenth century,[2] though it did not, of course, die out. There was some cloth making in and around Kirkby Stephen in the eighteenth century, as the presence of weavers testifies, but it does not seem to have been important. Knitting was important.

In 1671 Sir Daniel Fleming described Kirkby Stephen as 'a market Towne well knowne . . . Here is a fine church, and the market in this Towne is much improved by the Trade of stockings, lately taken up and made in this Towne and parts adjacent.'[3] If Fleming were right, then the stocking industry arose in the seventeenth century, though when exactly would depend on the interpretation of 'lately'. It was certainly well established in the eighteenth century; Defoe wrote that Kirkby Stephen had nothing to offer 'considerable to our observation, except a great manu-

---

[1] The best study is M. Hartley and J. Ingilby, *The old hand-knitters of the Dales* (1951), but it is not, and is not meant to be, exhaustive.

[2] G. Elliott, 'The decline of the woollen trade in Cumberland, Westmorland and Northumberland in the late sixteenth century', *Trans. Cumberland and Westmorland Antiquarian and Archaeological Society*, N.S. lxi (1961), pp. 112–19.

[3] E. Hughes, ed. *Fleming-Senhouse Papers*, Cumberland Record Series, ii, pp. 16–17.

facture of yarn stockings'.[1] Later in the century Arthur Young had nothing to say about Kirkby Stephen, but concentrated on Kendal where the chief manufactory was knit stockings, 'employing near 5,000 hands by computation' and producing 550 dozen pairs a week, all of which were sent to London 'by land carriage, which is said to be the longest, for broad wheel waggons, of any stage in England'.[2] Whether Young's statistics were accurate or mere guesses cannot be determined. A later estimate, which claimed that Ravenstonedale, with a population of 1,138, produced 1,000 pairs of stockings a week in 1801, seems less credible.[3]

All this is common knowledge, but beyond this very little is known about the organization of the knitting industry, which is even more obscure than the organization of the domestic cloth industry. It seems clear that two types of people were engaged in it, the hosiers and the knitters, but both remain elusive. Abraham Dent was never described as a hosier, though he was one. If some of his business records had not survived, there would have been no evidence in other sources that he was engaged in the stocking trade. In the parish registers of Kirkby Stephen between 1770 and 1800 only one man, John Barnett, who died in 1782, was described as a hosier. Yet the position and importance of these men can be guessed from the estate of John Thompson, hosier, of Kirkby Stephen, who died in 1721. Thompson left £100 to be laid out in land, of which half the rent was to go to helping poor children in Kirkby Stephen to learning and the other half to helping poor boys to a trade. He left £20 to be added to the £100 which Philip, late Lord Wharton, had provided for the stipend of a dissenting minister in Ravenstonedale, and £400, a house, furniture and his two best cows to his wife Eleanor. The specific bequests totalled £747 10s. and this was no optimistic estimate of his resources. Thompson's personal estate came to £2,423 13s., and included £12 7s. 6d. for silver plate, £41 2s. for 'purce and

---

[1] D. Defoe, *A Tour through the whole Island of Great Britain* (Everyman edition), ii, p. 270.

[2] A. Young, *A Six Months Tour through the North of England* (1770), iii, pp. 170–1.

[3] W. Nicholls, *The History and Traditions of Ravenstonedale, Westmorland*, p. 242.

apperell, Bible and other books', and £2,299 11s. 6d. for debts owing to him (not including £104 considered desperate).[1]

If the hosiers are obscure, so too are the knitters. No one was described in the parish registers as a knitter, presumably for the same reason that no one was described as a spinner. Knitting and spinning were considered part-time occupations and as such were concealed under some other occupational or marital description. But even if the parish registers are silent, the concealment is not quite complete. In 1787, for reasons which are not apparent, the Justices of the Peace in Quarter Sessions ordered a household and occupational census to be taken in Westmorland. The surviving returns of this census are woefully incomplete;[2] there is none for Kirkby Stephen township and none for the parish, except for Kaber. The return for Kaber shows 34 households with a total of 156 inhabitants, 83 male and 73 female. Of the 'masters of the family', 17, described as engaged in husbandry, were in fact farmers. To these should probably be added William Bousfield, who was engaged in husbandry and who lived with his widowed mother. None of the farmers or their wives was described as 'knitter', but some of their children were. Thus John Pearson's household consisted of himself, his wife, three sons engaged in husbandry, two sons described as 'scholars', and three daughters whose occupation was given as 'knitting'. John Waistell, another farmer, lived with his wife, his son John, described as 'scholar', two sons-in-law, Anthony and Thomas Moss, both rather curiously described as 'scholars', and his daughter Sarah, who was a knitter. Similarly Lancelot Hutchinson lived with his wife, a son who was a scholar, a daughter who was an infant and a daughter Sarah who was a knitter; he had also a servant, Elizabeth Winter, who was described as a spinster, which seems to have been an occupational description.[3] Thomas Wilkinson, who had one son in husbandry and one at school, also had a daughter who was a knitter, as had William Thwaits and William Metcalf. George Binks, who lived

---

[1] Hallam MSS. (Westmorland Record Office).
[2] They are in the Westmorland Record Office.
[3] Sarah Buchamp, mistress of a family of two sons and two daughters was described as a spinster, as was one of her daughters.

with his wife and one son engaged in husbandry and one at school, had two daughters described as knitters. Finally among the farmers were Thomas Moss and William Hastwell, each of whom had a maid servant who was described as a knitter. Thus among farmers' families, according to the census, only daughters and women servants were classed as knitters. The daughters may well have been filling in time between leaving school and getting married.

Lower down the social scale the importance of knitting becomes clearer. Of the eight households where the master was a labourer, five included knitters; of the other three, in one there were no children and in the other two the children were still at school. In these labouring households the pattern could be similar to that among the farmers. Thus John Taylor, labourer, lived with his wife, one son who was also a labourer, and a daughter who was a knitter. But there were differences, for in the labouring households the wives and the sons might be knitters. Robert Wappup lived with his wife and five children, of whom two sons were infants, one was at school, and one son and a daughter were knitters. Similarly Thomas Brunskill had, among his five children, a son and a daughter who were knitters. The other three children were infants, which suggests that in this case infancy was followed, not by school, but by knitting. Thomas Collinwood, another labourer, lived with his wife Ann and a servant, Hannah Hornsby, both of whom were described as knitters. Francis Kipling's wife was also described as a knitter, but in this case the only son at home was a labourer like his father.

Finally there were the real knitting families, where the mistress was a widowed mother. Thus Isabella Wharton, widow and knitter, had six children at home, of whom two sons and a daughter were 'scholars', one daughter was a seamstress, and two daughters were knitters. Similarly Isabella Swail, knitter, had an infant son, and two sons and a daughter who were knitters. Another Isabella, Isabella Sayer, was the only person in Kaber who lived alone; she too was a knitter.

Among those whom the census described as knitters, females clearly predominated; there were 25 female knitters to 4 male. The same is true of Stainmore where the census records very few male knitters. But this may be misleading. Many of those described as knitters in the census were obviously full-time knitters. This may not have been true of the wives and servants; in the Stainmore returns the wife's occupation is sometimes more accurately given as 'housekeeping and knitting'. But it must have been true of the daughters and sons, for otherwise their occupations would have been differently described. No doubt knitting was a full-time occupation for some people, especially women and children in the lowest ranks of society, but this does not mean that it was not also a part-time occupation for farmers and labourers and their wives. This seems clear from an illuminating passage in a letter of 4 June 1784 which Abraham Dent wrote to Nicholas Pearse and Son, one of his London customers for stockings. Pearse had complained of the quality of the stockings supplied to him, and Dent replied that it was not possible to replace them in two or three months 'at this time of the year' because 'work of this sort is chiefly done from September to February when the people have no other employ, or else they could not be done for that price'. In other words the work was done between haytime and lambing time, which was the slackest period for farmers who had little or no arable land.

It may not follow, of course, that even in a slack period people will sit knitting stockings unless they want the money. It is easy to see that the wives and children of labourers, or the widows and their children, might need to knit in order to live, and that for them any talk of part-time work and slack periods would be inappropriate, but what of the farmers and their wives and families? Did they need to knit stockings in the sense that their farms could not otherwise support them? It has been suggested that domestic industry was necessary in areas where partible inheritance obtained, that is where land descended to all the sons and not just to the eldest. In such cases the family holdings became too small to support a family by farming alone, and incomes had to be supplemented by industrial work.[1] It does not seem that partible inheritance obtained in the Kirkby Stephen area. There much land was held by customary tenure, and transfers were made in the

---

[1] J. Thirsk, 'Industries in the countryside', in *Essays in the Economic and Social History of Tudor and Stuart England*, ed. F. J. Fisher.

manorial courts, but there is no evidence of any system of partible inheritance.

Even without partible inheritance, farms might be too small to support a family from the produce of the farm alone. Pringle pointed out that Westmorland farms were often small and that the farmer lived poorly and laboured hard. Some farmers, particularly near Kendal, 'in the intervals of labour from agricultural avocations, busy themselves in weaving stuffs for the manufacturers of that town'.[1] In Ravenstonedale the farms were small; they produced good butter and cheese but there was very little arable.[2] In Mallerstang, at the time of the tithe award of 1836–37, there were 3,000 acres of common and 3 acres of arable out of a total of 4,944 acres. There was plenty of land, but much of it was moorland which provided very rough grazing for the sheep. Common pasture was essential and was sometimes stinted, as apparently at Kirkby Stephen. Without it, the farms could not have supported their sheep and cattle. These farms were essentially family farms. At Kaber in 1787 only three of the farmers had farm servants living in. The Land Tax returns,[3] which are very imperfect, also suggest a large number of family farms. Only the most detailed work could establish, if it could establish at all, that the occupiers of such farms were compelled to supplement their agriculture with the earnings of industry. All that can be said with safety is this: the size of the farms and the type of farming suggest an environment suitable for the development of a domestic industry such as knitting. Even this simple analysis may be too sophisticated; in a region of small hamlets and isolated fellside farms the short winter days and especially the long winter nights had to be occupied by something in a century when there were no whist drives and television.

The knitting industry was widespread and important, but how was it organized? Were the knitters independent in the sense of owning their raw materials and selling the finished product? Or were they supplied with raw materials by the hosier who paid

[1] A. Pringle, *General View of the Agriculture of the County of Westmorland*, p. 302.
[2] F. W. Garnett, *Westmorland Agriculture 1800–1900*, pp. 22–3.
[3] In the Westmorland Record Office.

them for knitting the stockings? As with much domestic industry, it is easier to ask these questions than to answer them. The finer details of organization persistently elude the inquirer. It is largely a failure of sources; either records were not kept or, if kept, they have not survived. Even when some records have survived, as in the case of Abraham Dent, they are not very informative on this matter or very easy to interpret. Dent sold large quantities of stockings, but did he buy them in the first place or did he manufacture them in the sense of giving out the wool or yarn to the knitters and paying them for their work?

Dent's letters to his London customers certainly imply that he made the stockings which he sent them. On 8 February 1780 he wrote to Harley and Lloyd asking for an order and continued, 'I was in hopes that you would have had occation for much the same quantity this year, on which account I continued making as usual.' In a postscript he added, 'all the Guard Hose I made for some years you have had the whole so that I am at a loss how to dispose of them'. In a further letter to Harley and Lloyd of 20 March 1780, Dent wrote, 'if you should yet have occation for the quantity of hose you mention, I shall do the best in my power, but should wish to have had a month or two to have made them as they would have been much better than can be bought in the marketts'. It seems clear from this that Dent made as well as sold stockings, but this finds little reflection in the surviving accounts. On an unnumbered folio towards the end of the day book there is the heading '1764 Putt to knitt'. This is followed by '22 Feb.[1] John Thompson wife 2 hank worsted Rec^d', and similar entries to 5 April. In all 30 hanks were put to knit, including 2 to John Thompson, senior, and 7 to John Thompson, junior. In this case Dent was obviously giving out worsted yarn to the knitters.

Other entries, in a ledger of sales, are more difficult to interpret. On 1 February 1769 John Cleasby of Swaledale was supplied with 2 packs of wool and $78\frac{3}{4}$ lb. of soap. Opposite to this entry in the ledger is a long list of names, obviously of knitters, and of the stockings they had supplied from 16 February to 11 May. Thus

---

[1] The date was first written 'Jan', but 'Feb' seems to have been written over it.

13 March   1 dozen Guards[1]   Ed. Cherry   pd for
20 March   1 dozen common   Thos Fothergill pd him.

Many of the names are of men; thus George Alderson supplied a dozen pairs on 13 April, another dozen on 24 April and a third dozen on 11 May. These may of course have been knitted by his wife or family. This account ends '11 May paid for the above and £1 for 40 dozen. Paid at the same time 2s. 6d. till Lady Day last and 3s. for John coming 3 times with hose'. It is not clear what the half crown was paid for, but it looks very much as if Cleasby was acting as Dent's agent in Swaledale, distributing the wool and collecting the stockings, for which he was paid £1 for 40 dozen, or 6d. a dozen, and 1s. each time he brought the stockings to Kirkby Stephen.

Another entry in the same ledger is even more difficult to fathom. Between February and June 1769[2] Dent paid £131 5s. to Thomas Fawcett, who was the father of an attorney at Kirkby Stephen. In return Fawcett supplied 243 dozen pairs of stockings. On the face of it, this was a simple transaction; Dent was buying stockings from Fawcett and, from the dates of payment, was paying for some of them in advance. But the account shows clearly that Fawcett was being allowed '6d. for yourself per dozen', just as Cleasby had been. In this case, however, Dent could not have been supplying wool to the knitters, for he was paying Fawcett the full price for the stockings. It looks very much as if Fawcett was a small hosier who was buying stockings on Dent's behalf, for which he received a commission of 6d. a dozen. In the next, and last, account with Fawcett, which runs from July 1769 to January 1770, there is the following interesting entry in the list of stockings received: '2 August By knitting 1 dozen hose 5s. 6d.' Perhaps this was a special order, for there is no other evidence that Dent paid for the knitting of the stockings he received from Fawcett, but it is a very rare glimpse of what the knitters were paid. Their wages represent about 50 per cent of the cost of the stockings. According to Arthur Young Kendal knitters earned

[1] Guards hose.
[2] The entry is headed 1768, but this seems an error for 1769; the subsequent entries, beginning on 10 July, are headed 1769.

2*s*. 6*d*. a week, or 2*s*. if they were children of 10 or 12.[1] This suggests that those who were over 12 years of age knitted about half a dozen pairs of stockings a week, or a pair a day, excluding Sundays, when it may have been as wicked to knit as it was to sew.

Abraham Dent, it would seem, both manufactured and bought stockings. He certainly bought wool, though whether this was to give out to the knitters or to sell again is not clear. Arthur Young pointed out that the Kendal knitters mostly used wool from Leicestershire, Warwickshire and Durham; the local wool was used for Kendal cottons and linsey woolsey.[2] The records of Dent's wool purchases, which relate to the 1770s, also suggest that local wool was not much used in the stocking industry. Dent bought no local wool. Apart from one pack of wool bought from Mr. Butterwick of Yarm in 1771, all Dent's wool came from County Durham or Newcastle.

Some of the supplies from County Durham were small and casual. Ralph Child of Durham supplied 8 stones of lamb's wool at 9*s*. a stone and 7 stones of sheep's wool at 8*s*. in 1773; Charles Jackson of Barnard Castle sent a pack containing 16 stones of fine sheep wool at 10*s*. 6*d*. a stone in 1777; Thomas Laws of 'Wool-singham', presumably Wolsingham, sent a few stones in 1778 and 1781. George Bell of Houghton-le-Spring was a more regular supplier. He sent different grades of wool and charged carriage to Barnard Castle; the carriage was always 2*s*. 9*d*. a pack, though the pack varied from 15 to 17 stones. His account opened modestly in 1770 with '1 parcell 30 lb. of fine com.[3] £1' and 2 packs of '2^d [second] wooll', each of 15 stones at 10*s*. 6*d*. a stone. The following year he sent '2 packs 2^d lamb wool', again 30 stones in all at 10*s*. 6*d*. a stone. Bell sent no wool in 1772 and 1773 and only one 'pack head wool' at 11*s*. a stone in 1774. In 1775 the supplies were larger; '2 packs head sheep' at 12*s*. a stone, 1 pack 'head lamb wooll' at 12*s*. 6*d*. a stone and a pack second lamb wool at 11*s*. In 1776 they were larger still: 21 packs in all, most of them 15 stones each, but some of 16 and 17 stones, and the entries give the valuable information that there were 18 lb. to the stone.

---

[1] A. Young, op. cit., iii, p. 171. [2] Ibid., iii, pp. 171–2.
[3] Combing wool?

Prices were rising; the 6 packs of head sheep wool sent in January 1776 were at 12s. a stone, the other 7 packs of this grade, sent between May and November, were 12s. 6d. a stone. The head lamb wool was 14s. a stone and the second lamb wool 12s. 6d. In 1777 both supplies and prices had fallen; only 3 packs of head sheep wool at 11s. 6d. a stone were sent. Supplies, but not prices, picked up in 1778 when 6 packs were sent; in September 1778 head sheep wool was down to 10s. a stone and fine lamb wool to 11s. There is only one entry for 1779, '16 stone large combing' at 10s. a stone.

Thomas Pickering of Darlington was the only other supplier of wool in County Durham. He seems to have sold on the basis of a pack of 16 stones. Dent bought 6 packs (96 stones) from him in 1774,[1] when the bill came to £52, and 13¼ packs in 1775 when the bill was £115 14s.[2] The following year only 5 packs were bought, and no more was purchased until 1778, and then only 2 packs.

Abraham Dent got wool from five Newcastle suppliers, who sold by the pack of 14 stones. Some of them were not very important suppliers. Thomas Pattison sent 3 packs of second lamb wool in 1772, all at 10s. 6d. a stone, and John Burdon sent one pack of fine sheep wool at 11s. 6d. a stone in 1772 and one pack of second lamb wool at 10s. a stone in 1774. John Neal also sent 3 packs of second lamb wool in 1772, again at 10s. 6d. a stone; he supplied a further 8 stones at the same price in January 1773, but in October and November, when he sent 72 stones, the price was down to 10s. a stone. This was 6d. a stone cheaper than the fine sheep wool, of which one pack was sent in 1773 and two in 1774. The fall in prices in the later seventies, which occurs with George Bell's wool, is also found in John Wharton's brief account. He supplied 60 stones of fine sheep wool at 12s. in 1777, 62 stones at 11s. 6d. in 1778, and 60 stones at 10s. in 1779. On 28 April 1779, when the account closed, Abraham Dent added, 'Rests with me 1 pack combing wool at 11s. to be returned, brought by Rain.'[3]

The most important Newcastle supplier was Martin Fenwick,

[1] 3 packs fine sheep wool (1 at 10s. 6d., 2 at 11s. a stone); 1 pack lamb at 11s. 6d. stone and 2 packs second lamb at 10s. 6d. stone.

[2] Lock (i.e. fine sheep) wool at 11s. 6d. and 12s. stone; second lamb at 10s. 6d. and 11s. stone.

[3] James Rain, the carrier.

who sent 10 packs of wool between November 1770 and February 1771 which were 'charged to Mr. Barnett', presumably John Barnett, the hosier. Fenwick supplied Dent himself with 14 packs (of 14 stones each) 9 stones of wool in 1771, of which the 'fine sheep' cost 11s. a stone, the 'second sheep' 9s. 6d. and the second lamb 10s. 6d. The following year 10 packs were sent[1] as well as a single stone of 'fine combing wooll' which cost 13s. 6d. In 1773 Dent bought 7 packs of wool[2] and another stone of fine combing wool; in 1774 8 packs, all second lamb wool at 10s. a stone; in 1775 13 packs, and the second lamb wool was up to 11s. a stone and the fine sheep wool to 12s. 6d. The rise continued in 1776 when the 3 packs of second lamb cost 12s. a stone and the 2 packs of fine sheep 13s. a stone. By the autumn and winter of 1777 the price was lower; between October and December of that year Dent bought 5 packs of second lamb wool at 11s. 6d. a stone and one pack of fine sheep wool at 12s. And there the record ends.

Abraham Dent bought wool and sold stockings. That is clear. It is the transformation of the wool into the stockings that remains obscure. This was no simple process. The wool had to be carded or combed and then spun; the yarn had to be knitted; the wool or the stockings had to be dyed, and the stockings had to be washed, stretched and pressed. Over the first stage, there is some disagreement. Was the wool carded or combed? According to Arthur Young Kendal stockings were made from combed wool, and their manufacture gave employment to 120 woolcombers.[3] Thus they were worsted and not woollen stockings. According to Defoe Kirkby Stephen had a great manufacture of yarn stockings, and by this he meant woollen and not worsted stockings. In describing the dress of a 'middling tradesman', Defoe wrote that 'his stockings are, it may be, of Worsted, not of Yarn, and so they come from Nottingham, not Westmorland'.[4] No doubt worsted stockings were made in and around Kirkby Stephen. There were comb makers in the town, and in 1772 William Bonner was

---

[1] One pack of fine sheep at 11s. 6d., 3 packs second lamb at 10s. 6d. and 6 at 11s.

[2] Two packs of fine sheep at 12s. and one at 11s; 3 packs second lamb at 11s. and one at 10s.

[3] A. Young, op. cit., iii, p. 170.

[4] D. Defoe, *The Complete English Tradesman* (1726), pp. 401-2.

described in the parish register as a 'worstid carrier'. Dent himself had given out 'hanks worsted' to be knitted in 1764. Yet most of the stockings Dent dealt in seem to have been woollen. When he bought combing wool this was specified, and he bought very little of it. When he sold worsted stockings, these too seem to have been specified as such, and there were not many of them. To distribute 'hanks worsted' implies that the wool had been combed and spun before it was given out to the knitters, but it is doubtful whether this was the general practice. In Swaledale John Cleasby apparently distributed wool, not yarn, to the knitters. In the cloth industry it needed many hand spinners to supply one handloom weaver, but in knitting, according to Arthur Young, one spinner could supply the yarn for 4 or 5 knitters.[1]

Of the knitters something has already been said. Some of them were no doubt independent knitters, working on their own materials and selling their stockings in the Monday market at Kirkby Stephen, where the stocking sales were the first of the day's business. Others worked on materials supplied to them by the hosiers, and the evidence suggests that Dent got many of his stockings in this way. No doubt all stockings were knitted on curved needles and with the use of the knitting sheath or stick, a combination which greatly increased the speed of knitting.[2] At what stage the stockings were dyed or whether they were dyed locally is uncertain. In 1784 Dent wrote to a potential customer, William Burgess, and his letter throws light on this point. He wrote as follows:

I received your favour yesterday, not being at home till then, or should have wrote to you sooner. Colloured hose I never made any. Mr. John Harrison at Hawes in Wensleydale, Yorkshire, makes large quantities of them, his demands has been very great of late. A Mr. Stuart is in partnership with him. I don't suppose their [sic] is any person in this part can serve you better than they can. I have 40 dozen mens white hose such as I have served my friends with in London at 12s. per dozen. If you wish to have them give me a line by return of post, and I shall reserve them till I hear from you.

[1] A. Young, op. cit., iii, p. 170.
[2] On knitting sheaths see Hartley and Ingilby, op. cit., Appendix A.

Dent's friends in London were the army contractors who bought most of his stockings, apparently undyed; if necessary they no doubt had them dyed the appropriate colour for the rank and regiment of the wearer. If Dent did not dye his stockings, he certainly washed them. John Cleasby was supplied with soap as well as with wool, and Dent, at the end of one of his ledgers, calculated 'the drawback in sope', that is the part of the tax on soap which could be reclaimed when soap was used for industrial purposes. He worked on the basis of $\frac{3}{4}$ lb. soap to one dozen pairs of stockings. It was 'Brittish sope consumed in washing and scowering woolen men's[1] stockings'. Thus in February 1774 the drawback on the last year's production was 'for 1,141 dozen stockins at $\frac{3}{4}$ sope to a dozen is 856 lb. sope £2 19s. 4$\frac{1}{2}$d.' On 5 March 1779 Dent 'received drawback in sope 714 lb. at $\frac{3}{4}$ lb. to 1 dozen from 20 Feb. 1778 to 20 Feb. 1779 £2 9s. 7d.' The fact that Dent washed the stockings may be evidence that he also manufactured them ; if he had bought them in the market they would presumably have been washed already, but again it is not possible to be certain about this. After washing, the stockings were stretched on flat wooden 'legs' and then pressed in a stocking press. They were then ready for the market.

The sale of Dent's stockings is much better documented than is their manufacture. For the late 1760s and 1770s there is a ledger which records the sales, and for the eighties there is a letter book. The two sources do not, however, overlap. Most of Dent's stockings went to a market which is often forgotten; they went to the army. Most of them were military hose, and were described as marching regiments hose, guards hose and sergeants hose, though a few were marine or mariners hose and a very few were 'invalid hose'. As such they largely went to two great army contractors in London, Nicholas Pearse and the firm of Harley and Hillman, later Harley and Lloyd.

Nicholas Pearse, 'clothier in Lothbury', was a well-known supplier to the army. In 1785 when the Board of General Officers could not find any printed regulations relating to 'linnen linings for the Troops stationed in hot climates', it was suggested that

---

[1] Probably 'men's', but the word is almost indecipherable.

'the old established clothiers (Pearce for instance)' could 'produce some general order relative to this matter'.[1] Dent's first recorded dealing with Pearse was in 1767, when he supplied him with 420 dozen pairs of marching regiments hose at 12s. a dozen, 22 dozen pairs of sergeants hose at 31s. a dozen, and 132 dozen pairs of marine or mariners hose at 13s. 6d. a dozen. He also sent Pearse '1 dozen for yourself at £2 17s. and 1 at £1 1s.', and an unspecified quantity of hams. Westmorland hams were 'cured in the smoke of peat fewel' and were 'much preferable to those cured elsewhere in the coal fire chimnies'.[2] Dent also sent some hams to his other big London customer, the Honourable Thomas Harley[3] and John Hillman, merchants, but Harley and Hillman only took 100 dozen pairs marching regiments and 6 dozen pairs sergeants hose in 1767. This was less than the quantity sent to Messrs. Wilson and Chapman, 'clothiers at the Black Lyon in the Strand'. They took 100 dozen pairs marching regiments and 8 dozen pairs sergeants hose as well as 33 dozen and 4 pairs 'stout soldiers' at 13s. 6d. a dozen. Smaller consignments of 14 dozen pairs sergeants and 50 dozen pairs marching regiments hose went to J. Davenport, clothier in the Strand, and Edmund Burge, packer in Basinghall Street, respectively. Military hose dominated Dent's trade, but two London customers took a few civilian stockings in 1767. Robert Hare Killingley in Windsor Street took 26 dozen pairs 'men's yarn hose' at prices ranging from 12s. 6d. to 13s. 6d. a dozen, and 10 dozen pairs women's yarn hose at 10s. 6d. and 11s. 6d. a dozen. He was charged 1s. 6d. carriage to Kendal. Messrs. Frank and Bickerton in Rood Lane bought 6 dozen pairs men's grey hose at prices ranging from 10s. to 14s. a dozen and 6 dozen pairs women's hose at 9s. to 11s. a dozen and a dozen men's gloves at 6s. the dozen. They were charged 6d. for the wrapper. It is probable that these civilian hose had been made locally, though in 1767 Dent did

[1] War Office. Out-Letters Departmental, Board of General Officers, Vol. 28 (1781–90), f. 150.

[2] Nicolson and Burn, op. cit., i, p. 11.

[3] Thomas Harley (1730–1804), third son of Edward Harley, third Earl of Oxford; he was an M.P. for the city of London, and was lord mayor in 1768. The article on him in *The Dictionary of National Biography* says little about his business activities.

F

buy some stockings from Messrs. Bunyan, hosiers in Nottingham.[1] These were 51 dozen pairs 'Alt^d 2^d mens $\frac{1}{2}$ rolls' at 26s. 6d. a dozen, but they do not correspond to any of the stockings sent to London. Dent's total sales in 1767 were 928 dozen and 4 pairs of stockings, all to his London customers and all but 50 dozen pairs were military or naval hose. The total price was £613 16s. These were fairly substantial sales. They may help to confirm Arthur Young's opinion, expressed in 1768, that during the late war the stocking business 'was exceedingly brisk, very dull after the peace, but now as good as ever known'.[2]

Dent's stocking trade, whether brisk or not, was certainly fluctuating. In 1768 he sold 670 dozen and 11 pairs for £452 10s. 9d. Nearly all of them went to Pearse and to Harley and Hillman, and they were nearly all dispatched during the first six months of the year. Pearse took[3] 20 dozen pairs sergeants hose at the usual 31s. a dozen, 100 dozen pairs of marching regiments hose of which 83 dozen and 4 pairs were at 13s. 6d. and the remainder at 12s., and 188 dozen and 4 pairs of soldiers hose, a new category, though the price of 12s. a dozen suggests that they were similar to the marching regiments hose. Harley and Hillman also took some soldiers hose, 100 dozen pairs at 12s. a dozen, as well as 12 dozen pairs sergeants hose and 150 dozen pairs of marching regiments hose at 12s.[4] In October 1768 they were sent 3 dozen marching regiments, 2 dozen sergeants and 3 pairs guards hose as patterns. Supplies to the other London clothiers were much smaller; Messrs. Wilson and Chapman took 5 dozen pairs sergeants hose and 83 dozen and 4 pairs soldiers hose, and J. Davenport took 7 dozen pairs of sergeants hose. There was the usual purchase of some stockings from Nottingham, 36 dozen of the $\frac{1}{2}$ rolls from Bunyan and 16 dozen from Joshua Killer.

In 1769 sales were up; they apparently amounted to £742, divided between Pearse (£214) and Harley and Hillman (£528).

---

[1] He also bought from them a pair 'men's worsted stirrups'.
[2] A. Young, op. cit., iii, p. 171.
[3] He also bought 78 lb. ham at 6$\frac{1}{4}$d. a lb., on which the carriage was 13s. 4d.
[4] They also bought 30 hams of 535 lb. at 6$\frac{1}{4}$d. a lb.; the cost of carriage, in 2 packs, was £2 13s.

Details of Pearse's purchases are incomplete,[1] but Harley and Hillman took the usual sergeants and marching regiments hose as well as 5 packs containing 250 dozen pairs of 'invalid hose' at 12$s.$ a dozen and 75 dozen pairs of guards hose at 15$s.$ a dozen, which suggests that the patterns sent in October had been satisfactory. Both partners bought hams; Harley 12 hams of 201 lb. in all and Hillman 10 of 134 lb., all at $6\frac{1}{4}d.$ a lb. Sales fell considerably in 1770 when $749\frac{1}{2}$ dozen pairs were sold for a total of £519 4$s.$ Pearse, whose bill came to £224, bought sergeants and marching regiments hose, but he also bought a dozen 'men's fine ribbed worsted' for £2 17$s.$ and a dozen 'men's fine ribbed yarn' for a guinea. Harley and Hillman, whose bill was £286, also bought some men's ribbed worsted hose, 6 pairs at 5$s.$ a pair. A few civilian stockings went to Messrs. Frank and Bickerton, who had bought some in 1767. In 1770 they bought 2 dozen 'blue women's' at 11$s.$ a dozen and 12 dozen men's, some described as grey, at prices ranging from 10$s.$ to 14$s.$ a dozen. Again these do not seem to correspond to the 'rolls' or the 6 dozen 1 pair '2^{d} stout w^{t} long hose' at 26$s.$ 6$d.$ a dozen which Dent bought from Messrs. Bunyan in 1770.

In a letter to Dent of October 1771 John Waller expressed his sorrow 'at the dismal account you give of K. Stephen, its decline in point of business and the neighbours not being agreeable to each other'. Dent was apparently losing 'all relish of the place' and thinking of trying his fortune elsewhere, but Waller, writing from Plymouth, warned him that the times were very bad and that 'many trades people here have fail'd of late'. Waller thought 'a war might do something, but when that will happen God knows'. It was hardly an invitation to Dent to try his fortune in the south, and he remained at Kirkby Stephen. Despite his pessimism, Dent sold rather more stockings in 1771 than in the previous year: 792 dozen and 8 pairs for £559 13$s.$ By now the trade was entirely with the two big London army suppliers. Pearse bought £114 18$s.$ worth of marching regiments and sergeants hose, at the usual price of 12$s.$ a dozen for the former and 31$s.$ for the latter. Harley and Hillman, whose bills, including hams, came to £444 11$s.$, paid the

---

[1] The bottoms of some of the folios in the ledger have been torn away.

same price for the same sort of stockings, but they also bought 110 dozen pairs of guards hose at 15*s*. 6*d*. a dozen and 7 dozen pairs '3^{d} sergeants stoved' at the high price of 50*s*. a dozen. The latter seem to have been part of the stockings Dent bought from Joshua Killer of Nottingham. These comprised 25 dozen of the rather mysterious '½ rolls' and 7 dozen '3 men's white stoved' at 45*s*. a dozen. The white stoved had obviously been sold to Harley and Hillman at a profit of 5*s*. a dozen. At the same time Dent had bought from Messrs. Bunyan 28 dozen pairs 'men's stout long w^{t} [white?] worsted hose' at 26*s*. 6*d*. a dozen and 1 dozen '3^{d} alt^{d} white worsted pointed wetted stoved' at 34*s*. a dozen. It is not clear where the former were sold, but those at 34*s*. a dozen were sent by coach on 31 December 1771 and Dent charged 1*s*. for their 'carriage by the coach'. They reappear as one dozen guards sergeants hose at 36*s*. a dozen in Harley and Hillman's account on 4 January 1772. On 10 April 1772 Harley and Hillman bought 7 dozen and 4 pairs of guards sergeants hose at 36*s*. a dozen, 'from Nottingham', as Dent noted in their account. They had been supplied by Messrs. Bunyan on 30 March and appear in their account as '7 dozen and 4 pairs mens 3^{d} wetted and pointed white worsted stoved £12 1*s*.' The full record of Dent's sales in 1772 is not available, but they included at least 631 dozen pairs sold for £444.[1]

Dent's sales in 1773 were the highest so far recorded; 882 dozen and 4 pairs for £594 8*s*. Pearse bought 200 dozen pairs of marching regiments at 12*s*. a dozen and 18 dozen pairs sergeants hose at 31*s*. a dozen, and received '6 hogs cheecks and 4 dryd tongues' as 'a present'. Harley and Hillman bought the remainder, which included 23 dozen pairs sergeants hose which had come from Thomas Rawson of Nottingham. In 1774 sales fell slightly despite the worsening relations with the American colonies, which might have been expected to stimulate the demand for military stockings. On 25 February 1774, John Waller wrote to Dent from Plymouth, 'What think you of the *Somerset* and another ship having orders to prepare for sea with all expedition, which we are now very busy about? It is suppos'd we are intended for Boston in North America,

---

[1] In 1772 the hams sent to Harley and Hillman had gone up to 6¾*d*. a pound.

on account of the inhabitants there being very troublesome, but however some think we shall not get away, or if we do, there is no doubt we shall get back before winter.' They did not get away, and in May Waller was asking Dent, 'How does your hosiery go? I hope very well.' It was going to the tune of 747 dozen and one pair, selling for £515 13s., in 1774. Pearse, whose bill came to £184 13s., was buying the usual marching regiments and sergeants hose at the usual prices, but he was also taking a few civilian stockings: 3 pairs of fine worsted hose at 5s. a pair, 6 pairs of 'yarn loup and loup hose' at 2s. a pair, 2 dozen pairs of 'ribbed loop or loop yarn hose', again at 2s. a pair, and one dozen 'ribbed loop and loop worsted hose' at 2s. 6d. a pair. The remainder went to Harley, now described simply as the Right Honourable Thomas Harley, and no longer as Harley and Hillman. All the stockings he bought were military ones, including 5 dozen pairs of sergeants guards at 36s. a dozen, and all of them were bought between January and April. A dozen private guards hose were sent in November for a pattern.

Sales in 1775 reached new heights, though their full amount cannot be determined as some of the entries in Pearse's account have been torn away. The recorded sales totalled 1,315½ dozen pairs which sold for £888 6s. There was no change in the price of the stockings,[1] though Harley was now getting his ham at 6d. lb., and Pearse was paying the same price for his hogs' cheeks. Most of the stockings were still sent in the first six months of the year, but more than usual were dispatched between July and December. A few were sent by coach, for which Dent charged 'extra carriage', presumably the difference between the cost of sending by wagon and by coach. The extra carriage on 18 dozen pairs was 7s. 6d. At the end of the year Pearse wrote to Dent ordering his supplies for 1776. This is one of the few letters from Pearse that survive, and as such it is worth giving in full.

Mr. Ab. Dent   London 23 December 1775
  Sir

I received yours of the 28th September, 28th October and 30th November and the hose as advised. Your bills advised off shall be

---

[1] Marching regiments 12s. doz., sergeants 31s., guards 14s. and sergeants guards 36s.

duely paid, you must give me credit for the discount as you agreed when in Town.

You may provide for the ensuing year for me seven thousand pair of Marching Regiments hose and forty dozen Serjants. I rely on your providing the very best in your power, as I presume that I give my orders sooner than others and pay as well. If you can get a dozen pair of fine white ribbed hose of a large size, for my own use, shall be obliged; what you sent formerly were too small and shrunk much in washing. Send me also six dozen of the corser ribbed hose of two shillings per pair; let these hose be sent with the Marching Regiments to Mr. Lynds and you'll

Oblige Sir
Your humble servant
Nic. Pearse

P.S. I have not received the catchup you was so good as to say you sent—shall want no hams, its a trouble to you in providing &c. I can buy as cheap here.

The letter is endorsed

7000 pair at 12*d*.	£350
40 doz. at 31	62
	£412

Dent duly credited Pearse with discount at $2\frac{1}{2}$ per cent for the stockings Pearse had bought since August 1775 and for those that he had ordered in his letter. This must have been a special arrangement with Pearse, for there is no evidence that Harley claimed or was granted a discount.

The stockings ordered in December 1775 were sent in instalments, beginning with 100 dozen pairs of marching regiments hose on 26 January 1776. By the end of May all but 79 dozen and 8 pairs of the military hose had been dispatched, but it was not until July that Dent sent a dozen pair 'fine ribbed hose worsted' at 5*s.* a pair and not until November that he sent a dozen pair ribbed yarn hose at 2*s.* a pair. He was in London in April when he seems to have received the balance of the account due to him at that date. Harley, who still thought it worth while to get his ham from Dent at 6*d.* a pound, bought large amounts of stockings in 1776, but the grand total for that year was only 1,082 dozen and 8 pairs, costing £730 10s., which was a considerable decline on 1775.

Sales rose again in 1777, to 1,340 dozen and 3 pairs[1] costing £848 3s. and all going to Harley and Pearse. Harley's bill was £483 1s. 9d. and now he too was buying no ham. Pearse's bill was £365 2s. and he got a pot of char gratis, but was charged for 6 other pots (at 5s. 6d. each) and for 3 hogs' heads (at 3s. 10d. each). At the end of the year both customers gave their orders for 1778. On 23 December Harley, or rather Harley and Lloyd as the firm had now become, ordered 150 dozen pairs of private guards hose at 14s., 400 dozen pairs of marching regiments hose at 12s., 30 dozen pairs '3$^{\rm d}$ sergeants' at 30s., and 16 dozen pairs fine 3$^{\rm d}$ sergeants at 36s. These were sent between February and July 1778, but in some items the order must have been increased, for Dent sent 424 dozen pairs marching regiments and 188 dozen pairs guards hose. Pearse ordered 3,000 pairs of marching regiments hose at 12s. a dozen, 40 dozen pairs sergeants at 31s., and 6 dozen pairs coarse ribbed at 24s. These were sent between January and April, but again the order must have been increased, for Dent sent an additional 1,000 pairs of marching regiments hose in two batches in May and June. He also sent 6 pairs of fine ribbed hose to John Rogers of Newgate Street, who sometimes bought hams and hogs' cheeks and sometimes received them as presents. It is possible that Rogers was employed by Pearse, for when Dent was in London in April 1776 he was paid some cash 'by mistake of Mr. Rogers' and this is noted on Pearse's account. Total sales in 1778 amounted to 1,037½ dozen pairs, which were sold for £729 4s.

There is no information on the sale of stockings in 1779, for the ledger stops recording such sales in 1778. This does not mean that the sales themselves stopped, but simply that a new ledger was started which has not survived. When evidence becomes available again in 1780, it is of a different sort and merits separate treatment.

The existing ledger has its shortcomings as a source, but it does give the bare bones of Dent's trade as a hosier. It shows that his trade was considerable, though fluctuating, and that it was almost

---

[1] 1,191 doz. pairs marching regiments at 12s., 34 doz. and 3 pairs sergeants at 31s. and 115 doz. guards at 14s.

entirely in stockings for the army. Nearly all those stockings went to two London clothiers, Nicholas Pearse and the firm of Harley and Hillman (later Harley and Lloyd). With very rare exceptions, Dent sold his stockings at the same price to both customers.[1] In 1768 Pearse paid a higher price than Harley and Hillman for one batch of marching regiments hose, 13s 6d. a dozen instead of 12s., but this was most unusual. Prices were not only the same for the two buyers, but they were also remarkably constant. There was really no change in price between 1767 and 1778; in peace or war marching regiments hose were 12s. for a dozen pairs and sergeants hose were 31s. It must be assumed that such prices were determined by long-term contracts between the London clothiers and the army authorities. These prices were for stockings delivered in London; only on rare occasions, when stockings were sent by coach, did Dent make a separate charge for carriage, and then it was only for the extra cost involved. Stockings were often sent in packs of 50 dozen pairs, and a charge of 1s. or 1s. 6d. was sometimes made for the wrapper. They were directed, not to the actual buyers, but to their packers. Thus stockings for Harley and Hillman were sent to 'Mr. Wm. Worsfold, packer in Mark Lane'. Many of the stockings, perhaps nearly all of them, were taken by the carriers to Kendal and there transferred to the wagons for London. In the early 1770s William Todd of Hutton was taking some of them to London; they were noted as being sent 'by Pearson to Todd' or 'by Jackson to Todd', Pearson and Jackson being the carriers to Kendal. Between 16 February and 18 May 1771 Todd took 11 packs and a truss of hose to London; he charged £1 4s. for the carriage of a pack[2] and 3s. 9d. for the truss (which weighed 2 stones 11 lb.). Others were sent by Cave, 'waggoner to London', who also picked them up at Kendal. Most of this steady traffic went on during the opening months of the year; a fact which might give thought to those who believe eighteenth-century roads were impassable in winter.

[1] Though Pearse usually got a discount of $2\frac{1}{2}$ per cent, which was not granted to Harley and Hillman.

[2] One pack was charged £1 5s. 3d.; it apparently weighed 23 stones, which suggests that the other packs weighed 22 stones. If that were so, and assuming a stone of 14 lb., the cost of carriage was about 7·9d. per ton-mile.

The ledger recording the sale of stockings also shows how Dent was paid for them. He was not paid in cash, though on one occasion when he was in London he may have received the balance of his account in cash. He was paid by being allowed to draw on the buyers of his stockings. Thus in 1767 when Pearse bought stockings and a few hams for £392 13s. 9d., Dent drew eight bills on him to that amount; four were payable to William Monk-house, one was payable to James Fawcett, an attorney in Kirkby Stephen, one to Martin Fenwick, who supplied Dent with wool, one to George Bunyan, the Nottingham hosier who supplied stockings, and one to Lady Dalston, the wife of Sir George Dalston, of Smardale Hall near Kirkby Stephen. Dent drew on Harley and Hillman in the same way and sometimes to the same people. By this means he could pay his own creditors. The stocking trade gave him a useful reservoir on which to draw.

Chapter VI

The Hosier: The Eighties

No ledger recording Abraham Dent's stocking sales has survived for the years after 1778, but for the eighties there is a letter book, or part of a letter book, which contains copies of the letters that Dent wrote to his London customers. It contains other letters as well, though none of these relates to the shop or to shopkeeping, which again suggests that by then Dent had ceased to be a shop-keeper. Dent did not, of course, record or copy the incoming letters, and only two or three of these have survived. Despite the one-sided nature of the correspondence, the letter book gives a fuller and rather more personal picture of the trade than the ledger does. Dent did not always record the name of the addressees, but these can usually be deduced either from the contents of the letters or from the form of address; 'Honoured Sirs' was always Harley and Lloyd.

The letter book begins in February 1780[1] when Dent was getting anxious about his orders for that year. Early in February he wrote about this.

Dear Son Samuel

I wrote to you December the 18th in answer to yours of the 11th desiring to know as soon as you possibly could what stockins would be wanting for this year, and not having an answer makes me fear it has miscarried. At same time I desired your oppinion that if you should not have occation for such quantity as I could wish, I might apply to some others to dispose of them, but that is what I have a great dislike to do if my old friends could confer on me their favours as usual. I must wait with patience to have a line from you, which I hope will inform me that you are in good health, also your good family, which will give me great pleasure to hear.

I remain Yours Afectionately
A. Dent

[1] Some earlier folios are missing.

P.S. About the 25th Dec. you would receive 1 truss of Sergeants Hose 20 doz., which I forgot to mention to you that you would give them house room till I should order them elsewhere. If you chuce to have a look at them, they will be 26s. per dozen.

Samuel was Samuel Parker, who remains a mystery in two respects; it is not clear who he was and it is not clear what he did for a living. Dent addressed him as son and once referred to 'your Mother Dent', which suggests that Parker was his son-in-law. Yet there is no evidence that Dent had any daughters at this time except Elizabeth, who married William Dobson in 1778, and 'my son Dobson' was alive in 1780. It is possible that Parker was the son of Dent's second wife, Ann, by a former marriage. Whatever the exact relationship was, it is clear from Dent's letters that both Parker and his wife, whose Christian name is never given, were familiar with Kirkby Stephen and visited there. What Parker did in London is not clear. He obviously had some connection with the hosiery trade. Dent sent stockings to him, and in December 1781 wanted to know 'what quantity of hose I am to provide for you for 1782'. Yet there is no convincing evidence that Parker actually bought stockings from Dent. Those sent to him were usually destined for Harley and Lloyd. Parker may have been a packer who acted informally as Dent's agent, thus providing a link between Dent and his London customers, especially Harley and Lloyd. In 1768 there was a firm of London packers called Parker and Malleson,[1] but there is no proof that this Parker was either Samuel or related to him. In the seventies Dent was sending Samuel presents of gloves, fine plain worsted hose, hams and tongues 'for favours received', but the favours were unspecified. There is no evidence of any money payments, either in cash or by bills, between Dent and Parker, which suggests that their business dealings rested on kinship rather than profit.

Dent followed up his letter to Parker with one of 8 February 1780 to Harley and Lloyd.

Honoured Sirs

As you have favoured me for some years with a good order for Marching Regiments and Guard Hose, I was in hopes that you would

---

[1] J. Payne, *The London Directory for the year 1768*, p. 60.

have had occation for much the same quantity this year, on which account I continued making as usual, and not having a line from you as I requested in mine to you of the 20th November and 18 December last, makes me fear I shall have them laying on hand. If you could take 2 packs of M.R. and 2 packs of Guards, it would be gratefully accknowledged by

Honoured Sirs Your obedient and humble servant

A. Dent

P.S. All the Guard Hose I made for some years you have had the whole, so that I am at a loss how to dispose of them.

Meanwhile there was an order on hand from Nicholas Pearse, or Nicholas Pearse and Son as the firm had now become, which had probably been given in the previous December. This was for 5,000 pairs of marching regiments hose, which Dent dispatched in two instalments.

Nicholas Pearse, Esq., and Son   K. Stephen February 17 1780
Bought of Abm. Dent

900 pair of M.R. Hose in 1 sheet marked A.D.1[1]
900   do   do   A.D.2
200   do   do and 1 cagg catchup in 1 truss A.D.3

	£	s	d
in all 2000 pair @ 12*d*. to Mr. Lynds per R. R. to T. Baldwin	100	0	0
1 doz. pair Serg[t] Hose @ 26*s*. for sample by the coach from[2]	1	6	0
	101	6	0

Sirs

The M. Regt. Hose as above is forwarded this day to Mr. Lynds, which I hope will be safe their [*sic*] in about 14 or 16 days. As I did not think the catchup safe in bottles I racked it in to a cagg which I hope you will find good. It would be well to have it bottled again as soon as convenient. I have taken the liberty to send 1 doz. Sergt. Hose which I hope you will approve of, and if you [have] occation for such, shall be glad to serve you.

I am Sirs Your obliged humble servant

A. Dent

P.S. The 3000 Mar. Reg. shall be sent of [f] next week to Mr. Worsfolds.

[1] The A.D. is written in the form of a monogram.   [2] No place is stated.

The rest of the order was sent as Dent had promised.

Nichs. Pearse, Esq., and Son   Kirkby Stephen Feb. 24th 1780
Bought of Abm. Dent

		£	s	d
3000 pair M.R. Hose @ 12*d*.		150	o	o

In 4 sheets marked A.D.

4	5	6	7	to Mr. Worsfolds
62	62	62	64	Doz.

Brought from Feb. 17	101	6	o
	251	6	o

	£	s	d			
By discount	6	5	o			
By 1 doz. stockings damaged last year		12				
	6	17	o	6	17	o
				244	9	o

Sirs   K. S. March 1st.

As above you have account of your kind order which I doubt not will give satisfaction, and I have drawn on you this day to Law and Holme at 6 weeks, which I doubt not meeting with due honour. If you will be kind enough to accept a couple potts trout in about a months time they will be in good season or a few hogs' cheecks is much at your service if you will be kind enough to give me a line.

I am Sirs Your obliged humble servant
A. Dent

In the meantime the awaited order from Harley and Lloyd had come in, and this was dealt with.

Messrs Harley and Lloyd   March 1st 1780
Bought of A. Dent

100 Doz. M.R. Hose @ 12*s*.	60	o	o
in 2 sheets marked A.D. 8 & 9			
100 Doz. Guard Hose @ 14*s*.	70	o	o
in 2 sheets marked A.D. 10 & 11			
per Robt. Rudd to Kendale for Mr. Worsfold	130	o	o

Honoured Sirs

The above is your kind order which I doubt not pleasing. When anything more is wanted shall be happy in serving you.

I am Honoured Sirs Your humble servant
A. Dent

P.S. ½ doz. hams Mr. Lloyd desired me to send him; should be glad of a line at what time he would chuse to have them sent.

As the stockings were not sent direct to the buyers but to their packers, it was now necessary for Dent to inform the packers of their dispatch. This he did in detail so that the separate packs could be identified.

Mr. James Lynde   K.S. March 1st 1780
   Sir
I have forwarded to your care for Nich. Pearse, Esq., and Son two thousand pair of Yarn Hose and 1 cagg marked as under

     900 pair in 1 sheet marked AD1
     900 do   AD2
     200 do & cagg in a truss do AD3
     ‾‾‾‾
    2000

I shall take as a great favour you will be kind enough to have the sheets and cords taken care of and returned by the Kendal waggon, and what expence attends shall be thankfully repaid you.

                         I am Sir Your humble servant
                                   A. Dent

The rest of the stockings were sent to William Worsfold, who acted as a packer for both Dent's London customers.

Mr. Wm. Worsfold   K. Stephen March 1 1780
   Sir
I have forwarded to your care for Nich. Pearse, Esq. and Son, three thousand pair of Yarn Hose in 4 sheets marked as under

     62 doz. in 1 sheet marked AD4
     62 doz. in   do   AD5
     62 doz. in   do   AD6
     64 doz.   do   AD7
Also for Messrs Harley and Lloyd
     50 doz. in 1 sheet marked AD8
     50 doz.   do   do 9
     50 doz.   do   do 10
     50 doz.   do   11

I shall take it as a great favour you will be kind enough to have the

sheets and cords taken care of and returned by any of the Kendall
waggons and what expence attends shall thankfully be repaid by

Sir Your humble servant
A. Dent

[P.S.] I have made a larger quantity of hose this year than common if
any of your friends want.

Pearse and Son sent a further order on 16 March to which Dent
replied on 20 March:

I have received the favour of yours dated the 16th instant. I am sorry
to find the Sergeants Hose will not answer your purpose; whatever is
in my power I shall allways do the best I can. The 2000 pair you
ordered shall be ready for you whenever you please to give a line, and
if any more should be wanted shall be glad to hear from you. I am glad
to hear the catchup got safe to you. I have two or three ounces of
morrells[1] dryd, which I intended to have sent along with the catchup,
but I find was neglected. If you should think them worth your acceptance, I shall send them with the potts.

On the same day Dent wrote to Harley and Lloyd acknowledging two of their letters:

I was favoured with yours of the 2nd and 4th instant, but was then
abroad. If you should yet have occasion for the quantity of hose you
mention, I shall do the best in my power, but should wish to have had
a month or two to have made them as they would have been much
better than can be bought in the marketts. If you're in want of M.R.
Hose at 12s. can send you a few packs. I shall be happy to receive your
commands at any time, and you may be assured I will do the best in my
power for any article wanted that I have or can procure for you.

At the end of March Dent informed Harley and Lloyd that he
had 'taken the liberty' to draw on them for £50 to Law and
Holme at 30 days, and six days later, on 6 April 1780, notified
them that he had dispatched part of their order, 100 dozen pairs
marching regiments hose at 12s. a dozen. The remainder of the
order, 50 dozen guards hose at 14s., was sent on 20 April and Dent
hoped they would 'prove to your sattisfaction, which at all times
will give me pleasure to please you'. Both lots were sent to Samuel

---

[1] Perhaps morels, an edible fungus.

Parker at 3 Bow St., Covent Garden, to whom Dent wrote on 22 April.

Dear Samuel

You now have the 50 doz. Guard Hose which I hope will give content. The sheets and cords, when you can conveniently, can send them by any of the waggons to Kendal. And direct them for me at Kirkby Stephen, it will be well, for the carriers are come to that they will not find sheets so that I am at that expence. I shall thank you for a line as soon as you can to mention the sum my account I left with you amounted to. Also mention the last parcel of hose you had from me in 1779. I fear I have neglected puting down a pack which came when I was in London, for I have then made no memorandum of it. I hope this will meet with you and Mrs Parker and the rest of your family well. We are all well here and join in best wishes to you all.

I am, Dear Samuel, your affectionate Father A.D.

Harley and Lloyd's outstanding orders had now been completed, but Pearse and Son had still to receive the 2,000 pairs ordered apparently in March. On 28 April Dent wrote to Pearse himself, but largely on other matters.

I have this day forwarded for you by the Kendal waggon four pots of Eden trout, which you'll please to accept of, packed in 1 cask, which I hope will prove good as they are now in good season and is of the same as the small pot I sent you when I was in London. I am sorry I should make such a mistake, but char is in best season in December. Many familys prefer trout before char, but when the season returns, you shall have a few potts of char if better approved of.

P.S. The 2000 pair of hose is now ready whenever you chuse to have them sent.

The stockings were sent on 28 May: 2,000 pairs of marching regiments hose at 1s. a pair, which, with a discount of $2\frac{1}{2}$ per cent, came to £97 10s. On the same day Dent wrote to Pearse and Son saying that he was glad to hear that 'the cash of potts' had arrived safely and informing them that he had drawn on them to Law and Holme for £97 10s. at 30 days. Two days later William Worsfold was informed that the stockings had been sent to him and was asked as usual to return the sheets and cords by any of the Kendal wagons.

Dent had now completed all the orders in hand, but he still seems to have hoped that more might be forthcoming. He had written to Harley and Lloyd earlier in May informing them that he had drawn on them to Law and Holme for £28 13s. at 30 days and adding 'if any more M. R. Hose should be wanted soon or the latter end of the year, your favours will much oblige'. No order followed, and on 27 July Dent wrote again to Harley and Lloyd, 'As I have a payment to make in London at this time, I have taken the liberty to draw on you to Law and Holme for one hundred pounds 60 days after date of this, which I doubt not being duely honoured. If any Army Hose should be wanted more for this year, shall be happy to receive your orders.' Again no order followed; the trade was over for 1780. It had amounted to 934 dozen and 4 pairs of stockings selling for £576 6s. All of them were for the army, and they all went either to Pearse and Son or to Harley and Lloyd.

By November Abraham Dent was thinking about his orders for the coming year. On 24 November 1780 he wrote to Pearse and Son:

I take the liberty to ask the favour for the continuance of your kind orders as usual in the Army Hose for 1781 as I have a quantity by me, and shall at all times do the utmost in my power to serve you well.
P.S. A line as soon as convenient to know the number.

On 2 December a letter in almost the same words was sent to Harley and Lloyd. The same day Dent wrote to 'son Samuel'.

I have not been favoured with a line from you since my last of the 22nd of April last in which I requested you to examine the account of Messrs. Harley and Lloyd for 1779, which I left with you in June last. Now my dear Samuel, if you have got your great busstle over, which I doubt not but you have been much fatigued, shall be glad to have a line, for I fear I have made a mistake, but with your kind assistance all may be sett right. I hope this will meet with you, Mrs Parker and all your little ones in perfect health, which will give me great pleasure to hear of. Shall I have the pleasure of seeing you at K. Stephen this spring? If that should happen, I hope you will be able to find out my house and make a longer stay than you did last year. Your Mother Dent desires her best respects to you and all the family. My Old Virgin Ann

G

would be glad to see you again, and if their [*sic*] is a few dozen hose worse than the rest, she will throw them aside. I have ½ dozen bottles of catchup, if Mrs Parker should think them worth her acceptance for herself or friends shall send them when I hear from you.

Samuel Parker seems to have replied by return of post, for on 9 December Dent wrote again to him.

I am favoured with yours. Shall do everything in my power to get the 500 doz. of hose as good as I possibly can at 13s., to be delivered in the time you mention, and whatever Mr. H. [Harley] and you should wish to have me to do in this, nothing will be wanting, or any other plan you may think of. I should be happy to have seen you once more at K.S. I hope this will meet with you and family all well. All under my rooff desire their best respects.
P.S. I find that I had forgot in my last to you to mention that I had wrote to H. & L. [Harley and Lloyd] for the continuance of their favours.

It is clear from Dent's next letter to Parker, dated 1 January 1781, that the 500 dozen of hose was not yet a firm order. He wrote.

I was favoured with yours of the 5th ulto., and I wrote to you the 9th., which I fear has miscarryed as I have not been favoured with a line from you or Mr. Harley since. As you mentioned in yours that I should have an official order in a few days, in my last I mentioned to you that the 500 doz. hose at 13s. should be made as good as possible and that any plan that Mr. H. and you should think of, I should be happy to serve you. Your Mother &c. joyn in best respects, wishing you and family many happy returns of the season.

So far Dent had received no official orders for 1781, and he must have decided that it was time to remind his customers of this. On 6 January 1781 he wrote to Harley and Lloyd informing them that he had drawn on them to Law and Holme for £87 and adding 'when more hose is wanted shall be glad to hear from you'. It was not until 19 January that he wrote to Pearse and Son pointing out that he had received no reply to his letter of 24 November last, which made him fear that it had miscarried, and asking them to let him know what quantity of hose they would like to have and the time they would like them delivered in London. This seems to have produced results, for on 26 January Pearse and Son ordered 2,000 pairs of stockings, presumably marching regiments, at 1*s*. a pair. Dent dispatched them at once, informing Pearse and Son 'you did not fix any particular time of the hose being sent, so thought best to forward them in hopes more would be wanted, and shall be happy to serve you'. In a postscript he added 'I have taken the liberty to draw on you to Law and Holme for the above[1] at six weeks, which I doubt not meeting with due honour. When you chuse to have a few pots of trout, catchup or hogs' cheeks give me a line. Shall be glad you'l accept any of that kind we have in our parts.' The packer, William Worsfold, was notified of the dispatch and so too was Thomas Baldwin, who was responsible for getting the stockings from Kendal to London on the Kendal wagon. Baldwin was told that the stockings were in three packs marked AD 1, AD 2 and AD 3, 'the carriage of which you'l charge to me and debit me to yourself as I intend the whole to your care wheather by Rudd or Pearson'.

Meanwhile a firm order had come from Harley and Lloyd for 500 dozen pairs of hose at 13*s*. a dozen. Part of this order, 365 dozen pairs, was sent on 9 February 1781, when Dent notified Harley and Lloyd of their dispatch. They had, he said, been 'forwarded this day to Messrs. Burfoot & Bristows, Barge Yard, Bucklers Bury, London'; he hoped they would be approved of and encourage further favours, although 'they are not so equal as I could wish, but on the whole are worth more money'. Burfoot and Bristow were told that the stockings had been sent, and were asked, as usual, to return the sheets and cords. In a postscript Dent added 'I was in London July 79 when I had the pleasure of spending $\frac{1}{2}$ an hour with Mr. Bristow and Mr. John Dobson of Coxs Key. When you see Mr. Dobson please make my best respects to him.' Samuel Parker was also told, in a letter of 13 February 1781, that the stockings had been sent. To him Dent wrote a fuller account.

I was favoured with yours of the 3rd instant and to your wish forwarded 365 dozen of stockings to Messrs. Burfoot and Bristow's, same

---

[1] £97 10*s*. i.e. 2,000 pairs at 1*s*. less £2 10*s*. discount.

time advised Messrs. Harley and Lloyd, which I charge at 13s., but the pack No. 7 in which are 65 dozen are not so good as the rest, but you'l find many dozen better than the dozen I bought on the Hillside near Halfpenny House, which I think we gave 13s. 6d. for. If a few hundred dozen more should be wanted, let me know. You give me too little time to do so well as I could wish, though the whole of those sent are worth more money than charged. The rest will be forwarded this week and next. I hope this will meet with you and family all well.

A further instalment of 75 dozen pairs of stockings was sent to Harley and Lloyd on 16 February, when Dent wrote to Thomas Baldwin about their carriage:

By Thomas Pearson you have 75 dozen hose in one sheet marked AD 9, which forward by first waggon to Messrs. Burfoot & Bristow's and charge the carriage to my account. You did right to charge the last to me and what I sent before. As soon as conveniently you can, send account of what I have sent since we settled last and you will oblige

Your well wisher A. Dent

P.S. I thank you for the cockles you sent me.

The last instalment of the 500 dozen was sent on 22 February; it consisted of 70 dozen pairs, which was 10 dozen more than was needed to complete the order. Baldwin was urged 'by all means forward by first waggon as they should have been in London before March'.

In the middle of February Dent got one of his rare orders for civilian stockings. This was from John Smith at the Custom House, Whitehaven. Dent sent him 4 dozen pairs of stockings at prices ranging from 17s. to 21s. a dozen, and explained that this was 'more than your order. Well worth the money. I hope they will answer a good purpose for you or your friend.' Whether they answered or not, there was no further order from Smith. The more serious business of supplying military hose was continued in March when 75 dozen pairs at 13s. a dozen were sent to Harley and Lloyd, and Baldwin was asked to forward them 'by first opportunity to Messrs. Burfoot and Bristow's'. By then Dent was getting anxious about some of the sheets in which the stockings were packed and which he always asked to be returned. On 11 March 1781 he wrote to Thomas Baldwin about this.

I received a letter from Mr. Worsfold dated the 6th instant mentioning that he had sent the 3 sheets marked AD 1,2,3 by Hazard's waggon from the Castle, Wood Street, which [*sic*] the hose I sent to your care the 9th February. Forward them as soon as they come to hand as they are to have the same quantity sent as soon as possibly can.

The sheets did not come to hand, though Dent made 'all the inquirey' he could at Kendal about them, and told Worsfold that 'they should have come by one of the Kendal waggons from the Castle, Wood Street' and that Hazard's wagon came through Nottingham, implying that the sheets may have been mistakenly unloaded there for a Nottingham hosier. As late as June Dent was still asking Worsfold if he had the 3 sheets as 'the Bookkeeper at the Castle, Wood Street, say he never received any such bundle'. It is doubtful whether Dent ever got his sheets, but it all seems rather a minor hazard compared with those usually attributed to eighteenth-century transport.

Dent certainly needed sheets, for on 8 March 1781 Pearse and Son ordered 2,000 pairs of marching regiments hose at 1*s.* a pair and '2 dozen white worsted hose as a sample'; they also asked for some char and trout. The marching regiments hose and the fish could be supplied locally, but for the worsted stockings Dent wrote to Cox and Beardmore of Nottingham as follows.

By the first opportunity please to forward 2 dozen men's white worsted hose at 28*s.* per dozen. They are for to weigh something better than 6 oz. a pair. I should suppose that the 2^{d} would answer. They are for a sample. If they please, more will be wanted. Do the best you can. I shall not lay a great profit on them to bring matters about again.

P.S. Give me a line when they are forwarded that I may advise when they will be in London. Mark them AD 1 and fold $\frac{1}{4}$ sheet paper like a letter and direct it for Mr. Wm. Worsfold & Co., Mark Lane, London, with a parcel marked AD 1.

The fish, four pots of trout, was sent on 12 April, and later Dent wrote hoping it had arrived and proved good, for that was 'the season for them'. The marching regiments hose were sent in instalments during April and May. The worsted stockings consisted of one dozen 'men's white worsted narrow clocks' and one dozen 'men's worsted turned shapes', both at 30s. a dozen, so that Dent only made a profit of 2s. a dozen on them. He hoped that they would answer Pearse and Son's purpose and that he would hear by return of post what quantity was required, but no order for them was given. At the same time Dent was busy fulfilling new orders from Harley and Lloyd. He sent them 75 dozen pairs of guards hose and 60 dozen pairs of marching regiments hose at the end of March, which Baldwin was 'to forward by first opportunity this week or next'; the sheets and cords were to be returned, directed 'to the care of Thomas Baldwin, Kendal'. A further 120 dozen pairs of guards hose at 14s. a dozen followed in April.

At the end of April Dent received another order for civilian stockings. This was from John Wakefield, who may have been ordering from Liverpool, though this is not certain. At first Wakefield asked for '150 dozen men's white yarn hose at 18s. per dozen', but later he seems to have changed the order to 'an assortment'. Dent sent him an assortment early in May consisting of 153 dozen pairs of men's hose at prices ranging from 8s. 6d. to 17s. a dozen. Dent hoped that they would 'prove to content', but they did not. Wakefield was slow in paying, and Dent had to ask him on 1 January 1782 to 'be so kind as make me a remittance by bill or bills for the hose sent you in May last £103 14s. 6d.' Wakefield replied by asking 'to have discount for what is short of twelve months' credit'; Dent agreed to this, adding, 'I am sorry to find you did not think them so good as what you had from other Houses. Though they were not equal hose, on the whole I looked on them as the cheapest parcell of hose I have sold for some years. Any time when in my power I shall be happy to serve you on the best terms I possibly can.' Wakefield gave no further orders.

By June 1781 Dent had fulfilled all his orders, but he still hoped for more. On 13 June he wrote to Pearse and Son telling them that he had drawn on them to Law and Holme for £100 8s. 6d. at 30 days, and adding 'if any more hose should be wanted before the spring shall be happy to serve you. I fully intended giving you a call but had not opportunity before I left Town.' Five weeks later, on 21 July, he told Harley and Lloyd that he had drawn on them for £237 5s. to Law and Holme at 30 days and added 'if more

hose should be wanting the latter end of the year, I should be glad
to receive your commands'. On the same day Dent wrote to
Samuel Parker telling him that he had drawn on Harley and Lloyd
and that he had sent 'a pot of trout for a taste amongst you' and
that 'when the moor game is in full feather shall send you a couple
of brace of them'; he sent his best respects 'to the gentlemen of the
Accompting House'.

Dent received one further order for stockings in 1781. It was
a late one of 2 August from Pearse and Son, and was for 1,000
pairs of marching regiments hose at 1s. a pair and one dozen pairs
of guards hose at 14s. a dozen. These were sent on 9 August with
the request that if any more of either sort should be wanted 'shall
be glad to hear from you', and with the information that Dent
had drawn on Pearse and Son for £49 8s. 6d. to Law and Holme
at 30 days; this was the price of the stockings less the discount.
Dent drew on Harley and Lloyd for £94 5s. to Law and Holme
on 24 August and for £137 5s. on 16 October, when he added 'if
a pack or two of hose should be wanted at this time, shall be happy
to receive a line from you'. None was wanted. The stocking
season was over. In 1781 Dent had sold 1,406 dozen and 8 pairs of
stockings for a total of £913 19s. 6d. It was apparently the last year
in which he was to do business on anything like this scale.

In November 1781 it seemed as if Dent might be adding shoes
to the stockings. On 9 November he wrote from Kirkby Stephen
to Thomas Richardson in London.

I have never yet been favoured with a line from my friend in Scotland who I mentioned to you about shoes. I was talking with a person
of this place who says he can furnish you with 20 dozen. At his request
I sent as below and you have a copy of his charge. Shall be glad to have
a line to know if they will answer your purpose. I hope this will meet
with you, Mrs Richardson and family all well, which will give pleasure
to hear of.

$2\frac{1}{2}$ Dozen men's shoes at 48s.　　　　£6　0　0
　　　　　　　　　　　　Box　　　　　　　　10

Delivered at London for ready money.
P.S. They were forwarded and I suppose will be with you before this.

I have been from home since they was sent and quite slipt my memory to advise of them before.

Thomas Richardson was apparently related to the Richardson of Richardson and Mowbray, the Darlington bankers with whom Dent had dealings. Dent told Richardson and Mowbray on 11 December that he had had 'a line from Mr. Richardson at London', but nothing more was heard of the shoes. It would be interesting to know who was producing shoes on that scale at Kirkby Stephen.

By December Dent was thinking about the orders for stockings for 1782. On 2 December 1781 he wrote to Samuel Parker about this.

I take this opportunity to accquaint you that I and the rest of my family are all well. I sincerely wish this may meet with you and yours all in good health. I have this day drawn H and L [Harley and Lloyd] for £84. I should be glad to know what quantity of hose I am to provide for you for 1782. My best respects to Mrs Parker. Old Ann desires her best respects to you and hopes you'l pay us a visit in the spring. I shall be happy to see you if convenient.
[P.S.] I had a frank to L and H [Law and Holme]. Let me hear soon.

At the same time Dent informed Harley and Lloyd that he had drawn on them for the £84 to Law and Holme at 6 weeks and asked what quantity of hose they would require for 1782. He also asked Pearse and Son for a continuance of their kind orders as usual in the army hose as he had a quantity by him. This request was repeated in January 1782 and was followed by a personal call when Dent was in London early in February.

The first order for 1782 came in the middle of February when Pearse and Son asked for 2,000 pairs of marching regiments hose at 1s. a pair and 100 dozen pairs of guards hose at 14s. the dozen. The marching regiments hose were sent off on 14 February, when Dent assured Pearse and Son that the guards hose would be 'particularly good'; he was sorry he 'had not the pleasure of giving you a call again', presumably when he had been in London, and hoped that 1,000 or 2,000 more marching regiments hose would be wanted. The hams and fish, he added in a postscript, would be sent shortly. The guards hose were sent a month later, when Dent drew on Pearse and Son to Law and Holme for the full amount of the stockings. The hams were to follow 'as soon as properly dryed'.

So far no order at all had come from Harley and Lloyd, and on 9 March Dent wrote a rather anxious letter to Samuel Parker.

As I had not the pleasure of seeing you once more before I left London, I shall be glad to have a line to know you and all your good family are [?well], to whom my best respects. Mrs Parker mentioned to me that you wished to have seen me. Be kind enough to give me a line as soon as convenient, and what hose is wanting you'l let me know the time they are to be sent. I have on hand 3 or near 400 dozen M.R., which I was in hopes you would have wanted, but whatever quantity you have occasion for shall be glad to send you at the time you wish to have them.

This produced no response from Harley and Lloyd, but at the end of April Pearse and Son ordered a further 1,000 pairs of marching regiments hose at the usual 1s. a pair. These were sent, as well as '6 pots of Eden trout' as a present. The hams, which had been ordered in February, were sent in June. There were six of them, weighing 84 lb. in all at 5½d. a lb. Their carriage cost 9s. 6d. or 24 per cent of the price of the hams. In sending the hams, Dent had added his usual formula, 'if any more hose should be wanted shall be glad to have a line'. Apparently some stockings were sent to Pearse in December, but there is no record of their number. In 1782 Dent's recorded sales were only 350 dozen pairs of stockings; the price was £220, and they had all gone to Pearse and Son. The coming peace in North America was no doubt affecting the demand for a product so heavily dependent on a military market.

Dent does not seem to have written his usual requests for orders at the end of 1782, but that may have been because he was in London at the end of 1782 or the beginning of 1783. He was back in Kirkby Stephen by 10 January 1783. It was two months later before the first order arrived. This was from Pearse and Son for 1,000 pairs of marching regiments hose at 1s. a pair and 1,000 pairs of guards hose at 1s. 3d. a pair. Before the stockings were dispatched, Pearse and Son were enquiring about a consignment of stockings sent to them from Kendal on 8 May 1782 'by Shelly's waggon to Worsfolds'. Dent replied on 8 April 1783: 'Mr. Worrall is Bookkeeper for the Kendall waggoners No. 25 Wood Street. If you will be kind enough to inquire of him, I doubt not but he will know who they was delivered to. Their [*sic*] was a pack note as usuall to be delivered to Worsfolds marked AD 4 on the sheet. If they should not be made out, I shall write to Worrall and Shelly.' It is not clear what the trouble was, but it seems unlikely that the whole consignment had gone astray. In the middle of April Dent sent the stockings Pearse and Son had ordered in March; they were directed, not to Worsfold, but to Blackwell Hall, and were, according to Dent, 'very good'. Some ham and pots of trout were to follow. The stockings were sent by Thomas Baldwin, who was asked to forward them 'by first opportunity and let me know by return what weight and what wagon they are sent by'. Dent was taking precautions against future losses.

At the end of April Harley and Lloyd were sent 100 dozen pairs of guards hose at 14*s.* a dozen, which was 1*s.* a dozen cheaper than those supplied to Pearse and Son. These were dispatched in two packs to Samuel Parker, and again Baldwin was asked to 'let me know who they were sent by'. These stockings seem to have been sent in anticipation of an order, for in May 1783 Dent wrote as follows to 'son Parker'.

By this time you may think I have quite forgot you in not answering yours of the 23rd. April. I had the week before forwarded 100 dozen Guard Hose, such like as last year. If they are too many for you, be so good as give them a corner till I have the pleasure of being with you, which I hope will happen before the summer is over. I hope this will meet with your family and friends all well.
P.S. H and S[1] stockins may seem larger as they are streched and stoved and of coarse wooll. If you could have wished to have had such like, I could have fitted you with that sort. If anything more should be wanted in the autumn, a line I shall be glad to have. My best respects to Mrs Parker &c. I had almost forgot to tell you I have again taken a wife. Shall say more when I have the pleasure of seeing you.

[1] It is not clear what this means, unless it is a mistake for H and L, i.e. Harley and Lloyd.

It was a rather nonchalant way of announcing his marriage to a well-to-do widow.

Dent received only one further order for stockings in 1783. It was from Pearse and Son for 500 pairs of marching regiments hose at 1s. a pair. These were sent in a pack directed to Blackwell Hall on 21 August, when Dent wrote to Pearse and Son.

I was favoured with yours of the 14th. instant and you have as above agreable to your kind order. I hope many more will be wanted in the spring. The one pair shall be alowed for (when I have the pleasure of seeing you) that you mention was wanting in the bundle sent in April last. I am sorry I should neglect procuring you the hams, but if I can get ½ dozen to my sattisfaction, will forward them in a week or two. The 11th. of May last I sent by the Carlisle coach 4 potts of fish for your acceptance, I find I have neglected advising you of, I hope you received. At that time I had a matrimonial affair in hand, which I suppose has been the occation of my neglect, on which account I hope you'l excuse me.

The total sales for 1783 had amounted to only 308 dozen and 4 pairs, which were sold for £270, the lowest figure so far recorded.

Again Dent does not seem to have written round for orders at the end of the year, but in January 1784, in reply to a letter from Pearse and Son, he explained that 'the price of the Pattern Hose' was 2s. 3d. a pair for 'the better sort' and 2s. a pair for 'the other', and added 'the more time I have to make them the better'. These were guards hose and were much more expensive than those Dent had been supplying for the past four years, when the price had usually been 14s. a dozen pairs. They were presumably what had been described in the 1770s as sergeants guards hose. The patterns must have proved satisfactory for Pearse and Son ordered some of the guards hose as well as the usual marching regiments hose. Dent sent them 1,000 pairs of the marching regiments hose at 1s. a pair on 11 March 1784. They were 'in 1 sheet marked N.P. No. 12' and weighed 32 stone 2 lb., and were sent by R. Hewitson to Thomas Baldwin, who was asked to forward them by the first wagon to London and to let Dent know 'by return of Hewitson whose waggon they are forwarded with, as my friend desires to know who they are sent by'. My friend, that is Pearse, was told that they should be 'at the Castle Inn, Wood Street, Tuesday or Saturday the 23rd. or 27th instant', which implies that they took about a fortnight to get from Kirkby Stephen to London. Pearse was still worrying about the stockings sent in April 1783 when there was 'one pair short in the bundle', which probably explains why the pack sheet was marked N.P. instead of the usual A.D. and why a pack note was sent direct to Pearse in Lothbury.

Meanwhile Harley and Lloyd had given a meagre order for only 20 dozen pairs of guards hose at 14*s.* a dozen. They were, as Dent explained, 'such like as you have had for some years'. They were sent off on 17 April 1784, directed to 'Mr. Bean, No. 142 Drury Lane, London'. On the same day Dent wrote to Parker, through whom the order seems to have been received.

Your favor of 30th. ulto. I received, for which I am much obliged. I hope something more will be wanted in the course of a little time, and shall be glad to hear of you and family's wellfare at all times . . .
[P.S.] Mr. Pearse mentions to me he has 360 pair Guards Hose on hand since last year. If Mr. H. should have occation for any more, shall be obliged if you will give them a look. The Guard Hose to Mr. P. last year was charged 15*s.* a dozen and I have sent hose this year 27*s.* per dozen.

The hose at 27*s.* a dozen were the special guards hose that Pearse and Son had ordered earlier in the year, though they seem in fact to have been sent two days after Dent had written to Parker. They were the 938 pairs of guards hose at 2*s.* 3*d.* a pair which Dent sent on 19 April 'in 1 bale marked N.P. No. 1'. As this was a special order, the accompanying letter was especially commendatory.

Your kind favour I received. I have used my best endeavours to have the above hose particularly good, which I have not a doubt of giving sattisfaction both in quality and size. If any more should be wanted should [be] glad to have as much time as you possibly can give me to make them in. I am in hopes that these will please so well that your next order will be a considerable quantity, as every thing shall be done in the best thats possible. Mr. Harley has only had 20 dozen of Guards this year. I mentioned concerning what you have in hand to Mr. Parker and desired him to call on you if any more should be wanted.
I have taken the liberty to draw on you to Messrs. Law and Holme

for the above[1] at 6 weeks £102 18s. 3d. The hams and cheecks will be with you soon after.

Dent was in Liverpool in May, and on his return to Kirkby Stephen he wrote to Pearse and Son saying that he hoped that the guards hose had arrived. They had been sent by the York wagon, but he was not sure 'what inn they will be at'; he was sure they would be approved of, and added in a postscript, 'I fancy alteration should be wanted to be made next year. I shall do as near to your order as I possibly can.' All these hopes were dashed by a letter from Pearse and Son at the end of May, to which Dent replied on 4 June.

I am sorry to find by yours of the 27th ulto. that the hose which I had so great hopes of answering the purpose intended should not please. To replace in two or three months it is not possible at this time of the year, neither could I procure five hundred pair such like as you had last year in any reasonable time, even at 4d. or 5d. per pair more than charged to you at that time. As to the size, I had not a doubt that the least pair would have been large enough for the stoutest man. Work of this sort is chiefly done from September to February, when the people have no other employ, or else they could not be done for that price. As they are not approved of, I should willingly give my trouble which by taking of [f] 3d. per pair is much more than I ever had by any stockins, but if that will sattisfy I shall deduct that from the whole, though to my loss. If that will not do, must beg the favour of you to give them warehouse room until I can dispose of them otherwise. I am sure they are well worth the money they are charged, if the work is understood. Shall be much obliged to you to pay the £2 11s. for the carriage and charge it to me, and if you cannot get them disposed of, I shall remit you the ballance at any time you'l give me a line.
P.S. If I could have your order in September or October for any of the different sorts of hose you have had from me, it would be much better, and their [sic] is no person shall serve you on lower terms.

The unwanted stockings, which had originally raised Dent's hopes in a falling market, were difficult to dispose of. Dent wrote again about them to Pearse and Son on 6 July 1784.

I have yours of the 24th. ulto. before me. I am sorry I could not answer it before this as I have been from home. In mine of the 4 ulto

---

[1] The price of the stockings £105 10s. 6d., less £2 12s. 3d. discount.

to you, in some particulars you might judge I could not furnish with Guards such as last year. If no more is taken than you mention, what remains in hand I must beg the favour you will give them room in your house till I come to London or can dispose of them, but I hope the whole or part of what remained may be taken, as I am sure they cannot have better. Had they been hear [sic] three weeks ago, they would have been easily disposed of. Hear [sic] has been the greatest demands for variety of hose that has been some years.

6 hams cost me hear	1–18–6
the carriage I ordered to be charged to me I suppose about 7s. 6d.	7 6
	2–6–0

The unwanted stockings were not Dent's only worry. The guards hose sent to Harley and Lloyd in April had either gone astray or been damaged. They had been sent 'by the waggon that inns at the White Horse, Cripplegate' and had the usual pack note. Dent told Parker, who had enquired about the stockings, that 'the wagoner ought to make up the loss for the damage', but whether he did so does not appear. The only relief from these misfortunes was a late order of 28 October 1784 from Harley and Lloyd, and this was for only 30 dozen pairs of marching regiments hose at 12s. a dozen. These were sent by the York wagon on 4 December, and Harley and Lloyd were told that 'Mr. S. Parker will see that these are legged and stoved. In future if you chuse to have them undressed, mention and I shall make them stouter and better.' Dent noted that he 'wrote this from Sedbusk', where he seems to have spent Christmas and the New Year. The old year had been a bad one. Excluding the stockings that Pearse and Son had found unsatisfactory, Dent had sold only 133 dozen and 4 pairs for a total of £82.

The new year opened with a letter to Pearse and Son 'dated K.S. January 14th 1785 but sent from Hawes'. Dent wrote as follows.

I was favoured with yours of the 18th December last. I am sorry to find their [sic] is so many of the fine Guard Hose remains on hand. I have settled my book agreable to your letter and shall pay the greatest attention to serve you with any you are wanting on the very lowest

terms. Wooll is now as great a price as has been some years Viz. such as the stockins I make for you I will send a dozen or two at 15*s.*, but I fear the quality will fall short if they are to be of a large size. The five hundred pair of M.R. hose I hope to do as usual, and should be exceedingly happy to make the 938 pair to your sattisfaction. The demands for all sorts of hose that is made in our part has been very great. Hear [*sic*] is no stock in hand in any part of this country. As the Guard Hose that remains are stoved 1 hope the moth will not hurt them. As soon as I possibly can shall order them some other way, for they are well worth the money charged any where.
P.S. If you could have allowed 17*s.* a dozen for Guards might have them a full sized stout stocken to wear well, which if you should think of, give me a line as soon as convenient.

It was a curious letter, implying a heavy demand for stockings at a time when Dent's own sales were declining.

In February Dent drew on Harley and Lloyd for £14 to his son Thomas Dent at one month and asked them for 'a line for what hose may be wanting this Spring'. They seem to have ordered only 50 dozen pairs of guards hose at 14*s.* a dozen. At the same time a new customer, Messrs. Lowe and Lewis, apparently a London firm, put in an order, to which Dent replied on 13 February, writing from Sedbusk.

I was favoured with yours dated 5th inst. I am much obliged to you for your kind order, which shall be executed on the best terms I possibly can. At present hear [*sic*] is no stock in hand with any of our people that make M.[1] Hose, but shall send you a sample per coach on Tuesday or Fryday next. Would like to have them stoved. I doubt not getting made 2 or 3000 pair by the latter end of April for you, but shall be much obliged if you acquaint me by a line the longest time you can give to make what you may be wanting.

Lowe and Lewis ordered 1,500 pairs of stockings, which Dent told them, in March, he hoped would be with them by the latter end of April or the beginning of May. He added 'the severe winter has been very hard on the poor knitters of stockins. Coals scarce to be had owing to the great cover of snow which ground has not been clear of for 15 weeks.'

[1] Military?

By April Dent's sympathy for the poor knitters had evaporated. After sending Pearse and Son 500 pairs of marching regiments hose at the usual 1*s.* a pair and 480 pairs of guards at 1*s.* 3*d.*, he wrote to them on 9 April as follows.

I received yours of the 18th February which should have been answered before this, but has been in hopes to have had the whole of the Guards ready by this time. Never since I made hose have I experienced the difficulty in getting hose. Wool as high price as ever I knew it. Knitters saucy and not to be had to our wish. If size, quality and price could be properly ascertained and time given to make them, I can make them on as reasonable terms as any person. The potts of charr as soon as I possibly can shall be sent also a dozen of hams and the remainder of the Guards Hose, and if you are in want of more M.R. shall be glad to know.

Unfortunately at this point there is a gap in the letter book, owing to missing folios, and the entries are only resumed in October 1785. They begin again with the dispatch of 500 pairs of marching regiments hose at 1*s.* a pair and 6 hams at 6*d.* lb. to Pearse and Son; these Dent expected to arrive in London a fortnight after they had been sent off. Meanwhile Dent was still concerned about the special guards hose which he had sent to Pearse and Son in 1784 and which had been unsatisfactory. Originally there had been 938 pairs, of which Pearse had managed to dispose of 469. The remaining 469 pairs were still with Pearse. On 18 October Dent wrote about them to his son-in-law, William Dobson.

The 469 pair of yarn hose which is at Mr Pearses stands me to 2*s.* 1*d.* per pair in London. If their [*sic*] is not a chance of them for that money, I should wish to have 'em sent back again per Kendal wagon and a pack note with them directed for me at Sedbusk, Yorkshire, as many of them will have occasion to be dressed over again. They would have given more money here. They are of best lambs' wool.

As the stockings had been offered to Pearse and Son at 2*s.* 3*d.* a pair, the profit would have been 2*d.* a pair (less any discount) if the stockings had proved satisfactory. They were still in London in December when Dent wrote to Thomas Dobson[1] about them.

---

[1] The relationship of Thomas to William Dobson is not clear.

If the yarn stockin I mention toWm Dobson is not disposed of, you may send as much superfine black cloth as will make me a coat, also as much superfine as will make me a Kirk ganing[1] coat and pack it among the stockins. The colour I shall [leave?] for my daughter and your good wife to chuse for me. I would not have it a very dark one as it will not be made up till the spring.

Whether the unwanted stockings were returned to Sedbusk is uncertain; when last heard of they were still in William Dobson's possession. Though the record of sales in 1785 is incomplete, it does not suggest any marked improvement in Dent's trade. The new customers, Lowe and Lewis, might have been a hopeful sign, but there were no further orders from them.

The old customers remained, and they had to be canvassed for the coming year. In November 1785 Harley and Lloyd were sent a dozen pairs of guards hose at 14s. as a sample, and Dent asked to have their order 'as soon as possible for the time is now approaching to have them made'. The sample was sent at the request of James Mead, who seems to have been acting as an intermediary in the way that Samuel Parker had hitherto acted. The order followed in December; it was for 940 pairs of guards hose, which were to be provided 'against the usual time, viz. the latter end of April or beginning of May'. Pearse and Son had been approached as early as 2 October, but without result. Dent then applied what may have been his forcing tactics; he told Pearse and Son on 20 December that he had drawn on them for 15 guineas to Richard Stuart at two months, and if they wanted any guards hose 'a line shortly will very much oblige'. They replied on 28 December 1785 by a letter that has survived.

We received yours of the 20th inst. Your bill therein advised shall be paid. You may provide one thousand pair of Private Guard Hose at 1s. 3d. per pair to be delivered in May next, desire you will be particularly attentive to size and quality. They certainly ought to be better than others as we apprehend we pay more for them.

It was true that Pearse and Son often paid 1d. a pair more for the

---

[1] These words are difficult to decipher; 'ganing' is a dialect form of 'going', so it may mean a coat for going to church in.

private guards hose than Harley and Lloyd did, but even so their letter sounded a little curt.

Early in February 1786 Pearse and Son ordered 500 pairs of marching regiments hose, and a further 1,340 pairs in March. The latter were dispatched by Abraham Dent, junior, who added 11s. to the bill for 'pack sheets, cord &c.' Sixty pairs of marching regiments hose were sent in March to Thomas Harley (and not, as hitherto, to Harley and Lloyd); writing on behalf of his father, Abraham junior explained 'the rest of the M.R. and Guards shall be forwarded as soon as possible; fine wool is very dear and scarce or we should have had them forwarded before this time'. Dent drew on Pearse and Son on 18 April and his son did the same on 10 October, 'my Father being in Wensleydale'. These entries follow each other on the page of the letter book; there is nothing in between, which suggests that the letter book was ceasing to be a full record of transactions. If that is so, it is not possible to find what Dent's total sales were. In 1786 they amounted to at least 320 dozen pairs, which sold for £222 6s. 8d., but these figures do not include 'the rest of the M.R. and Guards' which were to be forwarded to Harley, or indeed any hose which might have been sent between April and October.

Early in December 1786 Pearse and Son ordered 'nine hundred pair of Guard Hose' for delivery the following March, and Dent promised that 'particular attention shall be paid to have them full as good as the pattern dozen'. He added that he had forwarded two hams of 25 lb., 'cost 12s. 6d.' The guards hose at 1s. 3d. a pair were sent in March together with 1,000 pairs of marching regiments hose at 1s. a pair and 6 hams weighing 102 lb. at $6\frac{1}{2}d$. lb.; the carriage of the hams to Kendal cost 1s. and from Kendal to London 8s. 9d. All arrived safely, but the stockings were not wholly satisfactory. On 27 May 1787 Dent wrote to Pearse and Son.

I am glad to hear the hose and hams arrived safe. The Guard Hose I am sure was much better than the pattern dozen sent you, so that theirs no doubt of their giving sattisfaction. I am sorry to find the Mar. Regts. has not answered, but shall replace thirty six dozen which shall be forwarded on Thursday first, which I hope will be with you in time. I have taken the liberty to draw on you today to Wm. Holme at one month for £75. In my next shall settle the discount if I have not the pleasure of being in London this summer.

Meanwhile orders had come in from Thomas Harley. Dent sent him 1,000 pairs of marching regiments hose at 1s. a pair in February, adding 'pack sheet and cord if not returned 5s.' In March 938 pairs of guards hose at 1s. 2d. a pair were sent by the Kendal wagon, and in April 300 pairs of marching regiments hose. This completed Harley's 'kind orders at present', but later in the year he ordered 500 pairs of marching regiments hose, which were sent on 6 October by the York wagon, presumably from Sedbusk. Later still, in November, he was sent 198 pairs of guards hose by Smith's wagon, apparently from Kirkby Stephen. Pearse and Son also put in a late order for marching regiments hose. They were sent 240 pairs on 27 October and a further 240 on 2 November, the former by Smith's wagon and the latter by 'Scar's wagon from Hawes to the York wagon'. On 2 November Dent wrote to Pearse and Son from Sedbusk.

I am sorry to find the Guard Hose was not so good as you expected. Wool is the highest price ever known and knitting higher than usual, but you may depend on it that I will serve you at all times on the most reasonable terms . . . Please to address your letters in future to me at Sedbusk, near Hawes, Bedal.

The late orders had brought Dent's sales for 1787 up to 443 dozen pairs, which he had sold for £286 10s. 4d.; all of them had gone to Harley and to Pearse and Son.

On 16 November 1787 Pearse and Son wrote to Dent at Sedbusk giving their orders for the following year.

We have yours of the 2nd inst., in consequence of the sudden reduction of the army again to its peace establishment we shall want less hose.

You need therefore only provide with great attention to the quality and size seven hundred and fifty pairs of Guard Hose more than we have already received from you—also seven hundred and sixty pairs of Marching Hose (with the same attention to size and quality) more than we have already received. These orders are instead of any former ones

you have received from us, and are all we shall want for the ensuing year. We must receive them on or before March next.
[P.S.] We sent your wrappers to the waggon which brought the last hose and they refused to take them; say in your next by what waggon we shall send them.

There is no evidence of any further order from Pearse and Son for 1788 and no evidence of any order at all from Harley for that year.

At the end of November 1788 Harley ordered 740 pairs of guards hose to be delivered in April; these were sent on 13 April 1789 and 'would have been sent last week but the great fall of snow kept all the carriers here'. They were sent from Sedbusk to the York wagon. Dent drew on Harley for the balance of his account in January, and asked whether any marching regiments hose would be required. Some were required, for 60 dozen pairs were sent in February and 20 dozen in April; in May Harley took 198 pairs of guards hose. Pearse and Son were also buying. Dent sent them 850 pairs of guards hose at 1s. 3d. a pair in March, pointing out that 'the price of wool is very high'. When Pearse and Son complained that 12 dozen pairs were 'inferior to the rest', Dent expressed regret and explained that 'the high price of wool and the deficient stocks of knitters' made it 'very bad to get them so equal as I could wish'. He sent 12 dozen as replacements, but hoped Pearse and Son would keep the inferior stockings, which they could have for 1s. a pair. Whether they did so, does not appear. On 3 July 1789 Dent wrote to Pearse and Son saying that he had drawn on them to William Holme for £45 at one month, and adding 'if any hose should be wanted shall be glad to hear from you'. And there the record ends. It is possible that Dent carried on his trade as a hosier for some time after 1789, but on this there is no evidence one way or another.

The change in the nature of the sources, from ledger to letter book, made it convenient to consider separately Dent's trade as a hosier in the 1780s, but this should not be allowed to obscure the continuity of his trade. The trade in the eighties was similar to that of the earlier period. It was based almost exclusively on the sale of military stockings, which were bought almost exclusively by the two London customers of the sixties and seventies, Harley and

Pearse. There was a similar continuity of price. For twenty years Dent sold his marching regiments hose at 1*s.* a pair; the private guards hose only varied from 1*s.* 2*d.* to 1*s.* 3*d.* a pair, and even this variation seems largely to represent different prices charged to Harley and to Pearse, for reasons which are not clear. Dent might complain about the high price of wool, but this was not passed on in the price he charged for his stockings. The increased price of the raw material combined with a constant price for the finished product suggests that it was the knitters who were squeezed. If the knitters were 'saucy', as Dent complained in 1785, it must surely have been because they were not dependent on knitting for their livelihood. If the price paid for knitting fell as the cost of wool rose, this might explain Dent's difficulties in getting stockings of uniform quality, and Pearse and Son's insistence on 'great attention to the quality and size'. Scamped work was an obvious weapon in the hands of workers in domestic industries, but too little is known of the knitting industry to be sure that this was what was happening to Dent's sources of supply.

There was continuity, too, in the actual mechanics of getting the stockings to the London market. They were sent by local carriers to Kendal or, on occasion when Dent was at Sedbusk, to York. The long haul from Kirkby Stephen to Kendal and thence to London seems to have taken about a fortnight. The slowness of the journey, during which men had to be paid and horses fed, partly accounted for the high cost of land carriage. Unfortunately there is little evidence on that cost. The 938 pairs of special guards hose, which were sent in 1784 and which proved unsatisfactory, seem to have cost £2 11*s*, in carriage or about 2·4 per cent of their price. Hams sent to London in 1787 cost 9*d.* a ton-mile in carriage, which seems roughly to have been the cost of sending stockings in 1771. This was a high cost, but not out of keeping with what is known of eighteenth-century land carriage. It is not the cost that is surprising, but the regularity of the transport. No doubt things went wrong; wrappers and cords were not always returned; the occasional pack of stockings got damaged or pilfered or went astray. Such things happen on most transport systems. There is nothing in Dent's letters to suggest that he felt that transport was a problem. He assumed that a pack of stockings sent by the Kendal wagon would arrive in London in what was then regarded as a reasonable time. This assumption seems to have been quite justified. Even the time of year seems to have made no difference. In the eighties most of the stockings were sent off during the four months of February to May; some late orders were dispatched in the months between August and December, but the main concentration was in February, March and April. These months, and especially February and March, can hardly have provided the best conditions for the wagons. But the wagons got through, whatever Arthur Young and others may have said about impassable roads. The real problem of eighteenth-century road transport was not so much the state of the roads as the cost of the carriage, which was prohibitive over long distances for goods of great bulk or weight and low value. It was a long haul from Kirkby Stephen to London, but a pack of stockings might be worth anything from £30 to £60, and as such it could stand the cost of the long haul. The same must have been true of goods supplied for the shop, some of which had a fairly long haul to Kirkby Stephen. Dent's activities as a hosier and a shopkeeper show that he operated in a national market, which was probably freer from impediments on the movement of goods than was the case elsewhere in western Europe. The importance of this in fostering the development of factory production has not, perhaps, been fully appreciated.

Dent's trade in the eighties was similar to that of earlier decades in organization, in the type of goods he sold and in the customers to whom he sold them, but it was very different in volume. Down to 1781 the trade had been large, sometimes exceeding a thousand dozen pairs of stockings in a year. After 1781 there was a dramatic fall to 350 dozen pairs in 1782, and the fall was permanent, for only in 1787 was this figure exceeded, and even then the total was a mere 443 dozen pairs. There are a number of possible explanations for this decline in sales. The most obvious is a fall in demand as the war with the American Colonies drew to a close. Almost all the stockings that Dent sold were military stockings, and, as Pearse and Son pointed out in 1787, a reduction of the army to its peace establishment meant that they required less hose. This would affect Harley's orders too. Dent himself sometimes seemed to imply that there was a heavy demand for stockings after 1781, but this may have been simply part of his sales' talk. There does seem to have been a fall in demand which it is not unreasonable to associate with the end of hostilities. It is possible, too, that hand knitting was meeting increased competition from the machine-made stockings of the Midlands, but there is little evidence that such competition was acute before the nineteenth-century. Finally there was the change in Dent's personal circumstances. After his remarriage in 1783 he gradually withdrew from Kirkby Stephen to his wife's native place, Sedbusk. By 1785 his letters were sometimes addressed from Kirkby Stephen and sometimes from Sedbusk. This continued until November 1787; after that Sedbusk was his home. He did some trade as a hosier from Sedbusk, but it was never large. Dent's sales had declined before his remarriage and certainly before his removal to Sedbusk, but these events may have influenced his business as a hosier just as they seem to have influenced his business as a wine merchant and common brewer.

Chapter VII

The Dealer in Bills

ABRAHAM DENT's business activities were many and varied; they involved a network of payments to him and by him, which cannot now be fully disentangled. In outline the system, if it can be called a system, seems obvious enough. The customers at the shop paid for their purchases either by barter, which was rare, or in cash or they were given short-term credit. The credit sales were recorded in a day book, or petty debt book as Defoe would have called it, and were presumably settled usually by a payment in cash. The suppliers of goods for the shop were paid by barter, which again was rare, or by cash or by drawing bills on Dent or by Dent supplying them with inland bills. Similarly the beer, wine and spirits in which Dent dealt seem to have been sold for cash, but the evidence for this is very slight. The suppliers of malt, wine and spirits were paid largely either by cash or by inland bills or both. That was also true of the suppliers of wool for the stockings. The knitters were presumably paid in cash, for there is no evidence of truck. Stockings bought locally from Thomas Fawcett were paid for in cash, but those bought in Nottingham were usually paid for by bill. Finally the army contractors, to whom the stockings were sold, paid by allowing Dent to draw on them.

All this meant that Dent was involved in a fairly complicated system of payments in which his various business activities were made to interlock. Thus his sale of stockings provided a fund of credit on which he could draw when he needed to pay for the goods supplied for the shop. The link in these transactions was the inland bill in which Dent had extensive dealings. Such dealings may have been endogenous in the sense that they simply provided a mechanism of payment in transactions which arose naturally from Dent's business as shopkeeper, brewer, hosier and wine and spirit merchant. On the other hand such dealings may have involved an exogenous element in the sense that they were greater than the nature and extent of Dent's business demanded. The incomplete survival of Dent's business records makes it difficult to reach a firm judgment on this point.

Dent had bill accounts with two types of people: those who supplied him with goods and those who did not. The suppliers of goods might draw on Dent or receive bills from him in settlement of their accounts, but in some cases they also supplied him with bills. Thus Thomas Elton & Co. of London supplied goods, including cloth, but they also supplied bills. Between 1756 and 1760 their account was largely for goods, but it included three bills; between 1761 and 1765, when their account averaged £112 p.a., about £40 p.a. was for bills or drafts supplied to Dent. Elton & Co's account came to £232 in 1766, £245 in 1767 and £171 in 1768, but it is not clear how far these sums represented goods and how far they represented bills. Very few of the items in the accounts are specified, and these are described as bills; it seems almost certain that the remainder were goods. Dent paid for these goods largely by bill, including in 1767 one for £34 18s. which was 'on Sir Charles Aisgill drawn by Roe of Maccklesfeild' and was 'sent Elton'. In the same year Dent sent Elton a bank post bill for £100 which he transcribed in full in his ledger of purchases.

The case of Law and Holme is clearer. The partners in this London firm of distillers had some local connection with Kirkby Stephen. They supplied Dent with quantities of spirits, but they also provided him with greater quantities of bills. For these transactions two separate accounts were kept: a goods account and a bill account. The goods account was usually settled by bill. Thus in August and September 1772 Dent bought spirits from Law and Holme for £79 18s. 0½d., and on 14 October this was paid by sending 'per post a bill at sight on Richard Harrison, Esq., Charing Cross, London £79 18s.' On occasion the spirits were partly paid for by transferring to the goods account any credit Dent had in the bill account. On 17 January 1774 £30 13s. 6d. was 'by ballance on bill account carried to goods account', where it duly appeared as 'by cash overpaid at bill account' and helped to pay for rum, gin and brandy supplied the previous year.

The bill account was much larger than the goods account. Between 31 August 1773 and 14 January 1774 Dent drew 27 bills on Law and Holme for a total of £564 13s. 6d. Of the bills 3 were at one month, 16 at six weeks, 5 at 30 days, one at 40 days, one at 50 days and one at 60 days. Some were payable to local people like Charles Kinsey, Robert Islip and Thomas Rudd of Sowerby. Others were payable to Dent's suppliers; a bill for £16 13s. was payable to Thomas and Anthony Whitwell of Kendal and it was entered opposite their account as 'sent a bill per Ep. Jackson on J. Law, London, at 60 days £16 13s.' Dent met these obligations partly by sending bills to Law and Holme and partly by 'my own draft', which was either on Pearse or on Harley and Hillman. More than half the account was covered by these drafts. Between 25 January and 10 December 1774 the bill account came to just over £1,000. Though details of the bills are not always given, it is clear that Dent was drawing bills on Harley and on Pearse to Law and Holme, who also received some cash paid by a Michael Dent, a Bank of England note for £30, and four Bank of England post bills for £80 in all. As before, Dent was drawing on Law and Holme to pay his suppliers, among them William Chisman of West Auckland from whom he got malt, and Martin Fenwick of Newcastle, who supplied wool.

After 1774 Dent's bill account with Law and Holme became larger, but less detailed. In 1775 it amounted to £1,347 5s. 2d. and in 1776 to £2,128 4s. 8½d. Again Dent was drawing on Law and Holme to pay his suppliers and others. He was paying into the account bills, some bank-notes and occasional oddments. Thus on 23 April 1776 John Law acknowledged receipt of £2 5s. from Mr. Swift 'on account of Mr. Dent', and this was duly credited to Dent's account. An earlier payment of £25 by Mr. Atkinson 'on Mr. Abraham Dent's account for the use of Ann Robinson of Crosby Garrat' seems to have been placed to the credit of Dent's goods account, not his bill account. On 11 July 1776 the latter account was credited with £4 16s. 1d. for 'light gold'. The light gold had presumably come into Dent's hands as a result of the recoinage of gold coin under an Act of 1773.[1] In Dent's day book there is a small printed handbill which runs:

THE

LIGHT GOLD,

CALLED IN,

By the KING's PROCLAMATION,

WILL BE EXCHANGED,

Without LOSS to the Holders,

From the 1st of May 'till the 19th of August, 1776.

By ABRAM DENT, in *Kirkby Stephen*.

Most of the light gold that Dent collected seems to have been sent to James Ashburner of Kendal, who received guineas and half guineas worth £825 between May and September 1776.

Dent's bill account with Law and Holme came to £1,414 12s. 8d. in 1777 and to £2,967 19s. 4d. in 1778, but the account gives no details of the bills themselves. From other evidence it is clear that Dent continued to draw bills on Law and Holme to pay his suppliers. Thus Martin Fenwick was paid for the wool he supplied by bills on Law and Holme, Thomas Hutton of Soulby was paid for his malt partly in the same way and Rawlinson Sons and Lindow of Lancaster received such bills for the rum they supplied. Similarly Dent continued to draw bills to Law and Holme on Harley and Pearse. Indeed by 1777 and 1778 all the proceeds from the stockings sold to Harley and Pearse were remitted in this way. Even so, the bill account seems large in relation to Dent's trade. In 1778 it was four times the value of the stockings that Dent sold and nearly three times the recorded value of goods that he bought.

These bill transactions with Law and Holme ceased to be recorded in the surviving ledgers after February 1779,[2] but they can be traced in Dent's letter book for the 1780s. In his letters to Law and Holme Dent reported what bills he had drawn and what had

---

[1] A. Feavearyear, *The Pound Sterling*, 2nd. ed. pp. 168–9.
[2] There are references to a bill account in the eighties, but it has not survived.

been remitted to cover such drawings. Thus on 4 March 1780 he
wrote to Law and Holme.

<pre>
I have drawn on you
Feb. 29th To Ralph Shaw at 30 days   12-0-0
Marc. 3rd. To James Fawcett at 30 days   30-0-0
                                                       ______
                                                       42-0-0

And you have inclosed 1 draft on Nicholas
Pearse Esqr. & Son for   244-9-0
6 Darlington notes £5 5s. each   31-10-0
                                                       ______
                                                      275-19-0
</pre>

Or again, in a letter of 24 June 1781, he wrote:

<pre>
I have drawn on you
June 13 To John Mason at 30 days   10- 0-0
   Do   To   do   at   do   5- 0-0
   Do   To William Barnett at do   10- 0-0
[June] 15 To Wm Harrison, Esq. I think 30 days   36-13-0
   Do   To Jos. Sympson at 6 weeks   10- 3-0
   Do   To John Harrison at do   14- 0-0
[June] 18 To Ed. Law at 6 do   15- 0-0
   Do   To do do   do   5-15-6
   Do   To Mrs Martha Bass   do   42- 0-0
   Do   To   do   do   at 30 days   50- 0-0
[June] 19 To David Nelson at 60 days   20
   Do   To Jas. Fawcett at 30 days   10
[June] 22 To   do   do   6
                                                     ______
                                                     234-11-6

and you have inclosed
1 Draft Nixon on Irwin   50   0   0
1 Do   Worswick on Albion Cox   8   0   6
1 Do   Bradberry on Bradberry   30
3 Notes Bank England   40
                                                     ______
                                                    128- 0 -6
</pre>

Yours I received of the 12th and 15th instant. Ainsley on Wilson £10,
Ainsley says it will now be paid, and Hanbidgge on Robertson I hope
will be paid. If not, return them both and charge interest and postage.

As these examples show, Dent was drawing on his London
stocking customers, as he had always done, and was also remitting

bank-notes. The latter included notes of Leeds, Leicester, York, Stamford and Darlington banks, but the most common were Bank of England notes, which were regularly remitted and which show some circulation of such notes in Westmorland.[1] On 2 April 1782 Dent sent Law and Holme 'one half of 4 Bank notes' value £100; ten days later he sent 'the counterpart' of the notes. This security device was also used in the nineteenth century and perhaps beyond.

In 1781 Dent drew on Law and Holme for a total of £5,682 18s. 9d.; the following year the recorded total was £4,167 14s. 10d., but there is a gap in the letter book from 5 November to the end of the year. In 1783 the figure was down to £279, but in 1784 it rose to £1,948 5s. 11d. The records are incomplete for 1785 and 1786; in 1787 only £289 2s. seems to have been drawn. There are traces of drawing on Holme in 1788 and 1789, but by then such transactions had become insignificant. They had not always been so, nor had they always been without difficulties. On 4 March 1782 Dent drew on Law and Holme to Richardson and Mowbray at 6 weeks; the amount was £262 10s. Three weeks later he wrote to Law and Holme: 'the draft on Richardson and Mowbray for £262 10s. I find is with you unaccepted. If I had not been disappointed by people which I have given drafts &c. to, you ought to have had good bills in your hand before this, but this will be a caution for the future and I hope save us trouble for the time to come . . . You shall have more drafts to make up the ballance shortly.' Dent duly remitted £69 on 29 March and a further £248 10s. on 2 April. Three months later he was still suffering disappointments. On 9 July 1782 he acknowledged the receipt of a bill account from Law and Holme and promised by the end of the week to 'make you remittance in Bank notes &c. for what I have drawn for'. Three days later he wrote explaining that 'disappointments will still happen; Mr. Kinsey is yet from home which I should have had a draft on last week as last year, and the rest shall be remitted shortly'. 'Kinsey, Esqr., on Saunders' for £100 was duly sent on 23 July.

---

[1] Sir John Clapham, *The Bank of England*, i. pp. 146–50, 167, for the geographical circulation of Bank of England notes.

The complications of this mechanism are well illustrated by a transaction of 1783–4. On 19 December 1783 Dent wrote to an Alexander Johnson saying that he was 'sorry the cask of gin should be sent to my friend at this time as she was provided with rather more than the same quantity by another hand, not expecting you would have sent it, as your servant promised it should be sent the week following that it was ordered. But it happened very lucky my being at home, as I can by some means have the matter adjusted.' In a postscript Dent added, 'As the affair has happened so unexpectedly, you may draw on me at four months or give me a line and I will send you a draft on London if more convenient to you.' Johnson did draw on Dent who, on 6 January 1784, wrote to Messrs. Bowser and Embleton, 'Yours I received inclosing Alexander Johnson's draft on me for £30 and to your request you have my draft for the same value at 40 days on Law and Holme, which will be duely paid at the time. I probabily may not advise of it for a few posts.' The following day Dent notified Law and Holme that he had drawn on them 'To Bowser and Embleton at 40 days 30-0-0'.

The sequel appears in a rather indignant letter from Dent to Law and Holme of 9 March 1784.

Inclosed you have as under which you'll be kind enough to place to bill account as I probabily may take the liberty in that way for a few months, which I hope you'll excuse. The £30 draft drawn on you came returned with charges as follows: bill £30, noting, commission, intrest and postages &c. 11s. 3d., which was paid to Stuart James Graham, attorney in Carlisle, who pretended to say his whole business was on account of the said bill, and charges me further as follows: 1784 February 25th Jorney to K.S. with a bill of yours payable Bowser and Embleton upon Law and Holme London, which was noted and returned. Out 3 days &c. for expenses £3 3s., paid for horse hire 11s. I was not at K.S. till some days after. The bill he left with Mr. Fawcett for £3 14s. I should be glad to have your oppinion whether I am to pay it or not. Had I refused payment of the draft, I should have paid the charge, though probabily their [sic] is no precedent of this kind.

2 Drafts   20   4   0
1 Bank England 20   0   0

There is no evidence that Dent got an opinion or that he paid the bill. In October 1784 he was writing to Law and Holme begging 'the favour you will take the trouble for a little time longer to do this buisness for me, as I have no other friends in London I can depend on'. If Dent were in difficulties and if Law and Holme had threatened to break their connection with him, they did not do so. They continued to do some business with him though only on a modest scale.

Law and Holme carried out a number of commissions for Dent or for his friends and acquaintances. In February 1780 they were instructed by Dent 'to get cash for the 2 prize ticketts you bought for Mr John Barnett, and what you receive please to give my account credit for them, as I have given him drafts for the full amount'. In November of the same year Dent himself was having a flutter. He wrote to Law and Holme: 'Hornsby & Co., No. 26 Cornhill, advertises shares of lottery ticketts, you'll be so kind as to purchase a share of two ticketts one guinea each and charge to me. I know nothing of the method, but you'll please to let me know when you write, which I hope will be soon.' Exactly twenty years before, Dent had held ticket no. 19 m 284 in the state lottery; he had kept both the ticket and the notification from Joseph Jones of Exchange Alley that it had drawn 'a blank'. Whether he was more successful in 1780 does not appear. On a rather higher plane, Law and Holme were told on 19 May 1780 that 'Mr. Cookson should have £11 paid at first fruits office at some opportune [time?]; you'll please to do it as soon as you conveniently can and charge to me'. Two years later they were asked to 'pay at the Tenth Office for Mr Cookson the tenths for K. Stephen', and to take out a beer and wine licence, apparently for Ann Railton. They collected the rent from 'Thompson's tennant in Piccadilly'; on 7 August 1781 Dent asked them to 'call on him in a few days' as 'Thompson told me yesterday he would write to him to pay you as usuall'.

Finally there was the case of Jeremiah Turner He boarded with Mrs. Ann Robinson of Crosby Garrett, who received £25 p.a. for his board and lodgings. This sum was paid, apparently by a William Atkinson, into Dent's goods account with Law and

Holme; Dent in turn paid the money to Ann Robinson and received a 'certificate' or receipt from her, which he forwarded to Law and Holme as proof of payment. On 24 March 1782 Dent wrote to Law and Holme, 'if you should see Mr. Richardson let him know that his relation Mr. Jeremiah Turner of Crosby is Dead . . . its the person Ann Robinson sent you a letter of attorney to receive [£]25 yearly for'. Five days later Dent sent Turner's death certificate to Law and Holme and told them 'when you have received for Mr. Turner's $\frac{1}{4}$ board and funeral expenses may credit my account and let me know the sum, which I shall pay her here. What James Taylor has mentioned below the certificate is very just, and I believe never a child took more care of a father than the family has allways done of him.' It was not until two years later that the business was settled. On 24 March 1784 Dent sent a bill for £14 3s. 7d. to Thomas Richardson, presumably Turner's relative. The bill was made up of:

Postage of your letter to me of March 11th. 84			9d.
Pd. Mr. Fawcett attorney for affidavit &c.		7	6
Postage of this to Brough			1
Ann Robinson's account of Mr. Turner's funeral &c.	13	15	3
	14	3	7

Richardson was told that if he paid the money to Law and Holme they would credit it to Dent's account and this would 'answer the same as if she had drawn on you'. Apparently this was done.

All these transactions had one thing in common; they involved the transmission of money between London and Kirkby Stephen. Thus Law and Holme were able to provide Dent with financial services as well as with goods. Others provided only services. This seems to have been true of the Harrisons of London. Between September 1772 and July 1773 Dent had a bill account with Richard Harrison, esq., of Charing Cross, London. This amounted to £1,087 in that period. Dent drew bills on Harrison, usually at a month or six weeks, partly to his suppliers such as Bunyan and Killer the hosiers of Nottingham, Monkhouse and Hopper of Newcastle, and the Whitwells of Kendal. He remitted to Harrison some bank-notes and promissory notes, but chiefly bills. The bills, as usual, were sometimes drawn on Pearse and Harley and Hillman. There is no trace of this account after 1773, but ten years later Dent had a bill account with John Harrison of London.

This Harrison family of London remains something of a mystery. It is not clear whether John Harrison was related to the earlier Richard. John had at least two brothers, William and Hugh. William had some connection with the north, which he visited in 1783. He and Dent met in January 1783, apparently at Kirkby Stephen, when Dent reported to John Harrison that his brother was 'in perfect health' and that they had agreed to meet again 'at Newcastle in ten or fourteen days'. Later William called on Mrs. Dent at Sedbusk only to find that she was away at Askrigg. Hugh Harrison seems to have lived in or near Kirkby Stephen, for Dent reported to John Harrison on 18 March 1783, 'your brother Hugh called on me yesterday; they are all well at home', and on 5 August 1783, 'your brother Hugh was not at markett yesterday'. The link between the Harrisons and Dent was closer than this, for they were related. On one occasion Dent addressed John Harrison as 'Dear Cousin'; cousin was a vague term, but at least it implied some connection by blood or marriage. It is tempting to see some connection between these Harrisons and the Harrison family of Sedbusk and Hawes, into which Dent married, but Dent called John Harrison cousin before he, Dent, married into the Harrisons. Moreover there were Harrisons at Kirkby Stephen, including John Harrison, an attorney, and Thomas Harrison, surgeon, apothecary and man midwife. It seems more likely that the London Harrisons and Dent himself were in some way related to the Kirkby Stephen Harrisons.

Dent's dealing with John Harrison started in 1782, but in that year he only drew on him twice, for a total of £79 12s. On 11 January 1783 Dent wrote to Harrison: 'From the conversation I had with your brother and you, I have taken the liberty to draw on you as annexed on the other side. In the course of ten or fourteen days, shall send you drafts to answer the purpose. Whatever expence you are charged with, I shall gratefully repay you at some opportunity.' The other side showed that Dent had drawn £32 to

James Mason at two months, £120 to James Portees at 6 weeks and £130 to Richardson and Mowbray, also at 6 weeks. In February Dent drew £200 to Surtees and Burdon, the Newcastle bankers, at 6 weeks, and asked them to send him their notes to that amount, but 'the above draft was returned, Surtees would not take more than a month'. Dent reported this to Harrison; he was 'at a loss what to do' and wanted Harrison's brother to advise him. Harrison's brother William must have had some connection with Surtees and Burdon for on 6 April Dent wrote to John Harrison: 'My draft to S & B on you I have by me yet and I find the Bank at Darlington[1] wants to do much the same way. I cannot think of giving them drafts on you at one month for their notes, but should be sorry to have any misunderstanding with Messrs. Surtees and Burdon on your brother's account.' Dent seems to have had no further dealings with Surtees and Burdon, but he continued to draw on John Harrison and to send him bank-notes and drafts. His account with Harrison for 1783 came to £3,099 11s. 2d.

The business ended as suddenly as it had begun. Dent drew on Harrison in February 1784, but in March their account was closed and Dent asked that any balance in his favour should be paid to Law and Holme 'as I have an account with them'. He was sorry, he told Harrison, 'that things have happened so awkwardly and that you have had so much trouble'. In a letter to Law and Holme, Dent hoped 'J. Harrison has given you the ballance due to me as you both of you know how the affair is'. They may have known how the affair was, but there is nothing in the records to explain the break. Obviously for a year John Harrison had largely taken the place of Law and Holme; in 1783 Dent's bill account with Law and Holme was only £279, with Harrison it was £3,099 11s. 2d.; in 1784 the account with Law and Holme was £1,948 5s. 11d., and with Harrison £32 15s. It is impossible to say what lay behind these changes.

In 1785 Dent opened another brief bill account with a relative in London. This was Thomas Dobson of 6 Leadenhall Street, but again it is not clear how Thomas was related to Dent's son-in-law, William Dobson. On 30 September 1785 Dent drew three bills on

<hr>

[1] Probably Richardson and Mowbray.

Dobson for a total of £115. Two days later he wrote to Dobson as follows.

I have taken the liberty

Sept. 30 To John Dawson at 21 days	80	0	0
30 do To Wm. Barnett at 1 month	22	17	0
30 To Thomas Baldwin at 6 weeks	12	3	0
	115	0	0

Dear Sir,

I have taken the liberty to draw on you as above, which I hope you will excuse as you shall have drafts in the course of eight or ten days to answer the purpose, and if its not too much trouble I probabily may continue to repeat such like for two or three months more. If you please to favour me with a line by return of post to K. Stephen to know if its inconvenient to you, which I should be extreemly sorry for. If otherwise, I shall be happy to return the favors now and allready received on my family's account. I hope yours are all well. I should have wrote to Billy and Bessy[1] before this, but has thought every week to have spared Abraham, who talked of writing to his sister when I left home. My best wishes attend you all.

Dent drew again on Thomas Dobson on 4 October and apologized to him that 'the value I have drawn on you should not have been sooner with you than this and of shorter date, but you I hope will be kind enough to get them discounted to answer the purpose and charge me with all expences, which will oblige me much for taking that trouble on you'. Dent had been drawing bills on Dobson at 21 days, a month and six weeks; the bills he sent in return were not sent until 14 October and they were at two months. This bill account, which totalled £180 3s. 6d., was closed on 9 December 1785 when Dent offered to pay 'what expence have attended the bill account, postage &c.'

Finally Dent had dealings with the Darlington bankers, Richardson and Mowbray. Richard Richardson and John Mowbray were surveyors and estate agents as well as bankers. Their London agents were Messrs. Dorriens, Mello, Martin and Harrison, which suggests that Harrison may have been John Harrison or his brother

---

[1] His son-in-law and daughter, William and Elizabeth Dobson.

William. In 1791 Richardson and Mowbray had an agency at Barnard Castle, which was held by Messrs. Harrison, Swainston and Son, grocers and drapers.[1] Dent seems to have acted as their agent in Kirkby Stephen in the early 1780s.

Dent had been remitting Darlington bank-notes to Law and Holme early in 1780, but his first surviving letter to Richardson and Mowbray is dated 16 October 1780 He wrote then:

I was favoured with yours of the 3rd. instant covering twenty notes each five guineas, on which account I have debited myself to you for £105. Shall as far as in my power make a circulation of them to your advantage. In the course of a week or ten days I purpose being in your neighbourhood and then shall give you a call.

A month later he remitted bills and a Newcastle bank-note to a total value of £106 10s., and asked Richardson and Mowbray to credit his account with them 'and send what notes you think proper either by post or as you think best'. 'I hope' he added 'this will meet with you and Mrs. Mowbray well; my best respects attend Mr. Richardson, though unknown.' The bills, note and letter were sent to Richard Steele of Barnard Castle for forwarding to Darlington. On 28 November 1780 Dent acknowledged the receipt of 40 notes of 5 guineas each and sent Richardson and Mowbray '1 draft Bradberry on Bradberry £50', adding 'I shall let you know how I quit notes'.

Presumably Dent 'quit' the notes satisfactorily, for on 1 January 1781 he told Richardson and Mowbray to send 'such quantity of notes as you think best and I shall do the best I can in disposing of them'. He himself sent five bills totalling £150 18s., which in a later letter he described more fully than was usual. They included a bill for £8 8s., Michael Warnhouse on Dale and Moser, London, payable to Thomas Titterington, Halifax, at two months, another of £15 10s., Samuel Bland on Thomas Bland payable at Sir Charles Raymond's, London, payable to George Simpson, Beverley at one month, and '1 draft my own on Law and Holme, London, payable to Richardson and Mowbray, Kirkby Stephen,

---

[1] M. Phillips, *A History of Banks, Bankers, and Banking in Northumberland, Durham, and North Yorkshire*, pp. 353–60.

January 1 81 at 6 weeks £105'. The last had been duly notified to Law and Holme on 6 January; it is interesting that the payee's address should have been given as Kirkby Stephen, unless it was simply a mistake for Darlington. Richardson and Mowbray evidently thought Dent had a ready market for their notes for they sent him 40 of 5 guineas each on 20 January and a further 100 on the 29th of that month. Perhaps they were too optimistic, for no more were sent until the autumn. On 21 September 1781 Dent wrote, 'I probably may have an opportunity of disposing of more notes than of late about Brough Hill.[1] May send what you think proper either by post or to B. Castle.' They thought proper to send 50 notes of 5 guineas each, for which Dent sent a bill on Law and Holme on 16 October, and added, 'by return of post may send such number as you think best'. They seem to have sent a further 50 notes. Dent wanted more and on 11 December wrote, 'you'll please to send 50 or 100 notes by first opportunity'. Again 50 were sent, which Dent acknowledged at the end of December.

Dent seems to have been too optimistic in his demand for notes at the end of 1781. On 14 April 1782 he wrote to Richardson and Mowbray that he hoped to be over at Darlington 'at or before May day' and that 'my accquaintance who had the chief part of the last notes has met with disappointments', but they could 'send a few notes' if they thought proper until he had the pleasure of seeing them. Dent may have received a few notes, for he sent '1 draft on Law and Holme for £133 4s. 6d.' at the end of April. Nothing more is heard of Richardson and Mowbray's notes during 1782, but on 11 January 1783 Dent wrote 'Inclosed you have my draft on Mr. John Harrison for £130 which [*sic* ?for] which you'll please to send me your notes in exchange'. The notes seem to have been sent by return. On 1 April 1783 Dent sent a further bill on Harrison for £115 11s. 6d., which was partly to cover a bill for £15 11s. 6d., Nelson on Bradley, which he had received from Richardson and Mowbray, who were asked 'to send your notes for the ballance'. It is doubtful whether they did. On 18 April Dent wrote to John Harrison, 'the draft for £115 11s. 6d. to Richardson and Mowbray I have only the £15 11s. 6d. in my

---

[1] Brough Hill Fair.

hand; I shall take a different method in a short time which I hope will be agreeable to the parties concerned'. Neither the method nor its agreeableness can be determined, but there were no further dealings with Richardson and Mowbray.

In his dealings with Richardson and Mowbray during the period from October 1780 to April 1783, Dent received about 400 bank-notes of 5 guineas each. He paid for them very largely by bills drawn on Law and Holme. On 26 August 1782 Dent wrote to Richardson and Mowbray, 'I purpose being at Croft next week, at which time I shall give you a call and if anything can be done to advantage in the bill way I shall with pleasure do for you'. But in fact Dent's bill transactions with Richardson and Mowbray were practically confined to sending bills in return for notes; he only received four or five small bills from Richardson and Mowbray. His benefit from these dealings with the Darlington bankers was a supply of notes which mainly seems to have been disposed of locally. These notes he obtained on credit, for the bills to cover them were usually sent some time after the notes had been received. Thus the 50 notes, value £262 10s. which were received on 12 December 1781, seem to have been paid for by the bill of 4 March 1782 on Law and Holme at 6 weeks, which was un-accepted.[1] There is no evidence that Dent derived any other benefits from his connection with Richardson and Mowbray.

Dent's bill accounts show the importance of the inland bill of exchange as a method of payment. Such bills were one of the means by which Dent paid his suppliers and received payment from his more distant customers. In that sense they provided a mechanism which was adjusted to his needs as a shopkeeper, wine and spirit merchant, brewer and hosier. Indeed these various activities were to some extent linked together by the mechanism of the bill, which brought the creditors in one branch of Dent's business into relationship with the debtors in another branch. Thus the suppliers of goods for the shop could be paid by bills drawn on the purchasers of stockings. In all this some credit was involved, but it was credit both given to and given by Dent, for it depended simply on the dates at which the bills matured. In

---

[1] Supra p. 117.

theory a creditor should have taken bills only at their present value; in other words he should have taken them at a discount, which would vary with the period the bill had still to run. There is hardly any evidence, however, in Dent's bill transactions that discount was calculated or demanded. This was true also of the bills in which Peter Stubs of Warrington dealt, for here again there was no evidence 'of any adjustment arising out of the usance of bills.'[1] It is easy enough to see that Dent used bills as a medium of exchange within the framework of his various business activities, but it is less easy to see what other uses he was making of them.

The difficulty is really one of interpreting sources which are themselves imperfect. The sources suggest that Dent's dealings in bills were at times much larger than the nature and extent of his business would seem to demand. This is especially true of the early 1780s, when the evidence implies that Dent had ceased to be a shopkeeper and when his trade as a hosier was declining rapidly. Thus in 1782, when he sold stockings to the value of only £220, his bill account with Law and Holme came to at least £4,167. This seems out of proportion to his need for bills in the conduct of his business as hosier, brewer and wine and spirit merchant. It suggests that Dent was dealing in bills for their own sake and not just as an adjunct to his other activities. Had his bill account survived for this period, the picture might have been clearer. From the letter book it is possible to calculate the extent of his dealings in bills, but the cryptic description of the bills themselves, especially those remitted to London, which do not give the name of the payee, makes it difficult to see exactly what he was about. As Dent's trade in commodities declined, his dealings in bills rose. Perhaps he was moving tentatively along that road which, in other cases, turned the shopkeeper and merchant into the banker. But he hardly achieved that metamorphosis.

[1] T. S. Ashton, *An eighteenth-century industrialist*, pp. 106–7.

Chapter VIII

The Gentleman

IN a deed of May 1793 Abraham Dent was described as 'late of Kirkby Stephen in the county of Westmorland, common brewer, but now of Sedbusk in the parish of Aysgarth and county of York, gentleman'.[1] This change of residence and of status was due in part to Dent's marriage ten years earlier. In May 1783 Dent wrote, in the postscript of a letter to son Samuel, 'I had almost forgot to tell you I have again taken a wife. Shall say more when I have the pleasure of seeing you.' John Waller at Plymouth received only 'an oblique report' of the event, and asked Dent, on 27 July 1783, 'Is it true that you are married to the lady you once hinted to me; if so, I most sincerely congratulate you on the occasion, wishing you both health and happiness.' The 'matrimonial affair', as Dent described it in a letter to Pearse and Son, took place on 9 March 1783 when Dent married Isabel Metcalfe of Sedbusk 'by licence'. The wedding was at Hardraw church, about a mile from the bride's home. The bride was a widow. She had married James Metcalfe, gentleman, on 24 June 1778 at Hardraw church. Three years later her husband died; he was buried at Hardraw on 29 May 1781. There seem to have been no children to this marriage, and it is not known to which of the numerous Metcalfe clans James belonged.

Isabel Metcalfe was the daughter of John Harrison of Sedbusk and his wife Jane. It is probable that Jane was a Stuart. The Stuarts were a family of substantial yeomen farmers with branches and property at Sedbusk and the nearby hamlet of Simonstone. John and Jane Harrison had a large family. Two sons and seven daughters are mentioned in John's will. Of the daughters at least three seem to have married into local yeoman families: Mary married a Whaley, Martha a Fawcett and Elizabeth a Tennant.

[1] Hallam MSS. (Westmorland Record Office).

John Harrison died in December 1777. His will[1] was witnessed by Thomas and Mary Stuart and Robert Pratt; it shows him as a man of substance. He left two houses, one of them thatched, two small fields with barn and cowhouse, and four cattlegates and a twinter gate[2] to his wife Jane for life with reversion to his son Thomas. Jane also received £100 and as much of the furniture as she cared to take. The remainder of the furniture went to Thomas and his sister Isabel. Thomas also got 'all my books', a silver tankard and the residue of the personal estate. Isabel got £100 and a silver gill and two table spoons. Of the married daughters, Mary Whaley got £70, Martha Fawcett £25, a guinea for a ring, and all Harrison's houses and garths in Simonstone, and Ann Lonsdale £15, which was a legacy left to her by her grandfather John Falder, and a guinea for a ring. Three more married daughters and a son, John, each got only a guinea for a ring. Thomas, clearly the elder son, was the sole executor; he was described as a yeoman. The other son, John, seems to have been the John Harrison who was a partner with William Stuart in a hosiery business at Hawes. It will be recalled that Dent had business dealings with Harrison and Stuart, supplying them with tea and occasionally buying their stockings. It may have been through such contacts that he first met Isabel.

Isabel had inherited £100 and some furniture and plate from her father, but when she married Abraham Dent she was much wealthier than that. She owned land and cattlegates and a lavishly furnished house in Sedbusk. All the real estate and the contents of the house had been the subject of a settlement or trust in Isabel's favour before her marriage to Dent. She had clearly inherited them from her first husband, James Metcalfe, who had been well-to-do. By his will[3] of 18 February 1780 Metcalfe had left £100 to each of his kinswomen, Hannah Harrison of Hawes and Jane Fawcett of Simonstone, the daughter of The Rev. Richard Fawcett. To John Harrison, the elder, of Hawes he had left £500 in 4 per cent Consols

[1] Wills of the Eastern Deaneries of the Archdeaconry of Richmond (Archives Department, Leeds City Library).
[2] The right to pasture a twinter i.e. a two-year-old sheep.
[3] Prerogative Court of Canterbury, Webster 311 (1781).

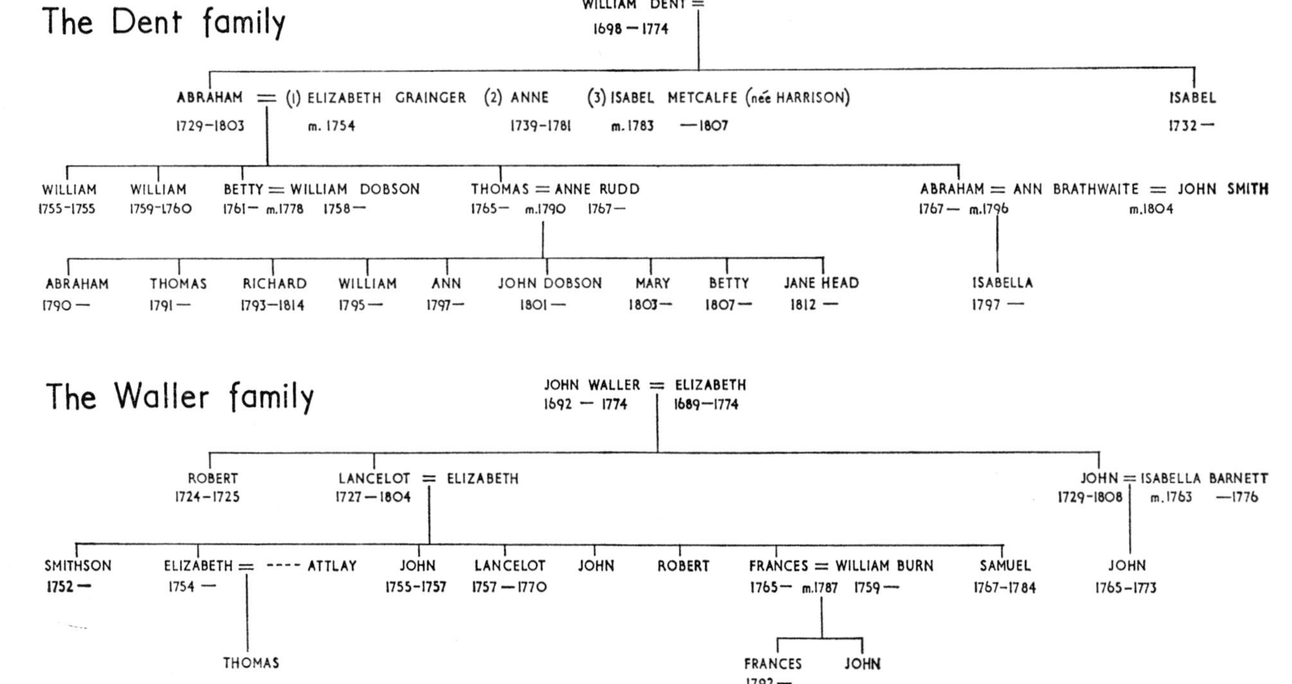

The Dent family
WILLIAM DENT =
1698 — 1774
ABRAHAM = (1) ELIZABETH GRAINGER (2) ANNE (3) ISABEL METCALFE (née HARRISON)
1729-1803   m. 1754   1739-1781   m. 1783   —1807
ISABEL
1732 —
WILLIAM   WILLIAM   BETTY = WILLIAM DOBSON   THOMAS = ANNE RUDD   ABRAHAM = ANN BRATHWAITE = JOHN SMITH
1755-1755   1759-1760   1761— m.1778   1758 —   1765— m.1790   1767—   1767— m.1796   m.1804
ABRAHAM   THOMAS   RICHARD   WILLIAM   ANN   JOHN DOBSON   MARY   BETTY   JANE HEAD   ISABELLA
1790 —   1791 —   1793—1814   1795 —   1797—   1801 —   1803—   1807—   1812 —   1797 —
The Waller family
JOHN WALLER = ELIZABETH
1692 — 1774   1689—1774
ROBERT   LANCELOT = ELIZABETH   JOHN = ISABELLA BARNETT
1724—1725   1727—1804   1729-1808   m.1763   —1776
SMITHSON   ELIZABETH = ---- ATTLAY   JOHN   LANCELOT   JOHN   ROBERT   FRANCES = WILLIAM BURN   SAMUEL   JOHN
1752 —   1754 —   1755-1757   1757 —1770   1765— m.1787   1759 —   1767-1784   1765-1773
THOMAS
FRANCES   JOHN
1792 —

in trust to pay the interest to his, Metcalfe's, sister, Ann Metcalfe of Hipperholme, £1,000 also in 4 per cent Consols in trust to pay the interest to another sister, Elizabeth Metcalfe of Hipperholme, and another £1,000 in 4 per cent Consols in trust to pay the interest to his beloved wife Isabel for life. After Isabel's death the interest on her £1,000 was to go to such kindred of Metcalfe's father as Isabel directed. The residue of the estate, both real and personal, was to go to Isabel absolutely; she and her brother, John Harrison of Hawes, were the executors. The witnesses were Michael Fawcett and Henry and Thomas Stuart. It is not known what the residue of the estate amounted to, but it must have been substantial. Nor is it clear how far Dent had access to his wife's fortune. On 4 March 1785 he wrote from Sedbusk to a Jeremy Marshall, 'I received yours of the 19th ulto. inclosing a Leeds bank note value £14 5s., when paid will be for one year intrest due the 18th of February last on a bond to the late Mr. Jas. Metcalfe.' There is no doubt that Dent had made a good match in the worldly sense.

For some years after his marriage Dent spent part of his time at Kirkby Stephen and part at Sedbusk. It is not clear how far Isabel divided her time between the two places. She was at Kirkby Stephen in the spring of 1783 when Dent was hoping she would accompany him on a trip to London and was even talking of a 'trip to Scotland'. Nothing came of the Scottish trip, but Dent went to London in September, apparently accompanied by his wife. Before leaving, Dent received an apologetic letter from Charles Kinsey of Smardale Hall.

I understand from Mr. Dillon that you intend to set off for London in the morning, which is a peice of unexpected news to me as I hoped to have seen you and Mrs. Dent here before your departure, seeing it is a long journey and very uncertain to whosoever undertakes it whether they may ever or never again see the friends they leave behind, as God knows who may or may not be before two months are over, and that I now learn is the time you mean to stay.

I find by what Mr. Dillon has said to Mrs. Kinsey that it is taken amiss that we have never paid a formal visit to Mrs. Dent since your marriage. I would beg leave to say that we are very far from having ever intended to shew you any slight or disrespect whatever, but we never understood that you had ever been as yet disposed to receive company in the formal or ceremonious way of visiting, as your stays as well as Mrs. Dent's have hitherto always been transitory and uncertain at K. Stephen . . . Please to present our best compliments to Mrs. Dent to whom and yourself we sincerely wish a safe and pleasant journey and a good sight of Mr. and Mrs. Dobson[1] to whom we beg to be kindly remember'd.

It was a rather alarmist view of a journey to London, where in fact the Dents seem to have stayed for only a fortnight.

Dent was back in Kirkby Stephen by the beginning of October 1783, and he seems to have spent much of the winter and the following spring there. In the spring he toyed with the idea of buying a chaise, which had been left at Kirkby Stephen by William Harrison, the brother of the John Harrison of London with whom Dent had business dealings. The chaise was stored in Charles Kinsey's coach house and was 'kept clean'. 'I should have been glad to have had it', Dent wrote to John Harrison, 'but it runs too wide for many of the roads and gates we have to go, and his cypher and arms on the harness makes it appear awkward.' Awkward indeed, for Dent may have been on the way to becoming a gentleman, but he could hardly sport arms, and someone else's arms at that. No doubt a chaise would have been useful for travelling between Kirkby Stephen and Sedbusk, and indeed Dent may have had some sort of vehicle for these journeys. However undertaken, these journeys must have been fairly frequent until 1787 when Dent went to live permanently at Sedbusk. There is little doubt that he simply went to live in his wife's house; he 'hung up his hat' as they say in those parts.

Nothing is known of Dent's family life after he went to live at Sedbusk. He was then a man of 58; his wife's age seems nowhere to have been recorded. There were apparently no children of this marriage, though Dent in his letters to William Holme, written from Sedbusk in 1788 and 1789, usually concluded 'my wife and daughter joyn in best wishes to you and family'. It is uncertain who this daughter was. So far as is known Dent had only one daughter,

[1] Dent's son-in-law and daughter.

Elizabeth or Betty, who married William Dobson and lived in London. It is possible that Elizabeth had been widowed or deserted and had returned to live with her father. In 1807 a Mrs. Dobson, who was living at Brough, was interested in Isabel Dent's estate; she must have been Dent's daughter, for Isabel had made bequests in her will to Betty, wife of William Dobson. This implies that William was still alive in 1804 when the will was made. Moreover in his will of 30 July 1808 John Waller left 20 guineas to Elizabeth Dobson of Brough, 'daughter of my late friend and old companion her father', which again shows that Dent's daughter was living in the north.[1]

Dent's sons did not follow their father to live at Sedbusk. They remained at Kirkby Stephen. The elder, Thomas, was 22 years of age in 1787. His early career is obscure. In 1780, when Thomas was 15, his father approached The Rev. Dr. Henry Chaytor by letter about a possible military career for his son. In his reply of 23 December 1780, Chaytor wrote, 'I received your letter and think you have done perfectly right to both apply to Mr. Jerry Robinson and write to his brother in London respecting your son. I know very little about the Army, but shall be extremely glad to do any thing in my power that may contribute in the least towards accomplishing what you wish for your son, and you may depend on my writing a line to Mr. Robinson on the occasion in a post or two.' In his reply of 5 February 1781 Dent reported that he had met Jerry Robinson at Appleby in January, and continued, 'I told him that I had not received a line from his brother and that I was afraid mine might miscarry. He said he did not doubt but it would arrive safe and that he did not like it the worse my not having a line from Mr. Robinson. As I desired if there was a probability of my son in the Marine service I should be sorry to be too troublesome so must wait with patience, as I have no doubt but you will do the needfull on your part.' Whether Chaytor did the needful or not, there is no evidence that Thomas went into the army at this time, though he did go up to London in the summer of 1781 and apparently stayed there until at least January 1782. He was certainly back in Kirkby Stephen by the following year.

[1] Prerogative Court of Canterbury, Ely 1002 (1808).

Thomas never seems to have played any part in his father's business as a hosier, but he did become a spirit merchant and a brewer, perhaps taking over the brewery, in company with his younger brother, when their father moved to Sedbusk. On 21 April 1790 Thomas married Ann Rudd, a local apothecary's daughter, and less than five months later, on 5 September 1790, their first child, a son Abraham, was baptized. At that time the father was described as a brandy merchant. Other sons followed: Thomas in 1791, Richard in 1793 and William in 1795. At their baptisms their father was described as a common brewer. By 1797, when a daughter Ann was baptized, Thomas Dent had become a Lieutenant in the Durham Fencibles. Four years later, when another son, John Dobson Dent, was baptized, the father had become a Captain, still in the Durham Fencibles. Later still, in 1803, when a daughter Mary was baptized, Thomas Dent had sunk to Lieutenant, this time in the Cumberland Militia. By then of course he was a gentleman, and had indeed been so described in 1801 when his wife Ann bought a cottage, house and garden in Kirkby Stephen from William Orton, for which she paid a fine of 7s. 6d. and a rent of 9d. p.a. to the Lowthers.[1] Thomas was still a gentleman in 1807 when his daughter Betty was baptized, but in 1812, on the baptism of yet another daughter, Jane Head, he was described as late Lieutenant in the Cumberland Militia.[2] By what means Thomas sustained his 'port' as a gentleman is not apparent.

Abraham Dent's younger son, Abraham junior, was 20 when his father moved to Sedbusk. He had in the past helped his father in the hosiery business, writing letters on his behalf and occasionally dispatching packs of hose. This activity seems to have stopped after 1787. In the 1790s Abraham junior was a common brewer, probably in partnership with his brother Thomas. He married Ann Brathwaite of the parish of Warcop on 9 February 1796, and they had one child, a daughter Isabella, who was baptized on

---

[1] Lowther MSS., Kirkby Stephen Manor Court Book, 1778–1810, f. 171 (Cumberland Record Office).

[2] The Monthly Returns of the Militia (War Office, 17/893) imply that Thomas Dent remained a Lieutenant in the Cumberland Militia until at least 1814, when there is a gap in the records. An Abraham Dent, who may have been Thomas's eldest son, was an Ensign in the Cumberland Militia in 1806.

25 September 1797. Abraham junior died young, though the exact date of his death is not known. It must have been before 27 February 1804 on which day his widow married John Smith, widower, of Liverpool.

When Abraham senior moved to Sedbusk in 1787 he had retired from shopkeeping and probably from the wine business and brewery. He was still doing a little trade as a hosier, and continued with this until at least 1789. This trade was not large enough to provide him with an adequate income. Was he therefore dependent on his wife, who had enough for both, or had he an 'unearned income' from property or other investments? It is a difficult question, which hardly admits of a definite answer, but it is worth looking into so far as the sources allow.

The Dents had certainly owned property at Kirkby Stephen, but it is not easy to discover its extent and value. Property there was held on a customary tenure with the payment of a fine on transfer and a small annual rent to the lord of the manor. Subject to these payments and subject also to the consent of the manorial court, land and houses were freely bought and sold, though the manorial court recorded only the fines and rents and not, of course, the purchase price. Moreover the manor seems to have belonged to more than one lord at one and the same time, and it is therefore difficult to be sure whether the land a man held from one lord constituted his total holding.[1]

Abraham Dent's father, William, had owned a little property at Kirkby Stephen, but at his death in 1774 this seems to have consisted of only three cattlegates in Kirkby Stephen Intack and a messuage and tenement. The messuage and tenement were charged with a 'fine certain rent' of 4s. p.a., which was a high figure for these customary rents and suggests that this property included the shop and perhaps also the site of the brewery. Abraham succeeded to this property as his father's heir at law and the transfer was ratified at a manorial court on 25 October 1774. Abraham himself had been buying and selling property for more

---

[1] Nicolson and Burn, op. cit., i, p. 544 where the manor is said to belong to the Earl of Thanet, the Musgraves and the Lowthers; certainly Thanet and the Lowthers seems to have been lords simultaneously.

than twenty years before this, and indeed seems to have made his first purchase, a close of land, in 1747 when he was only 18. The records of these transactions are usually too uninformative to be of much interest, but by 1778 Abraham had acquired, in addition to the property inherited from his father, three houses, a close, the three closes known as North Waitby Thorns, and a close of meadow of 6 roods called Low Waitby Thorns. The close of meadow was subject to a customary rent of only 9*d*. p.a., but it had been bought for £53 in 1764 by William Wharton, who sold it to Abraham in 1772. By 1778 Dent had built the brewery, and in 1782 he acquired 'all the customary messuage and dwelling house called and known by the name of the Golden Fleece Inn, with the barns, stables, outbuildings, yards and gardens with the appurtenancies within the said Manor', for which the customary rent was 2*s*. 9½*d*. p.a. Later, though it is not clear when, he also acquired the Sun Inn.[1]

These purchases do not seem to have been a sign of economic strength, for by 1786 Dent was plainly in some financial difficulty. On 12 April 1786 he mortgaged his property at Kirkby Stephen to James Fawcett of Kirkby Stephen, gentleman, in return for a loan of £500 from Fawcett.[2] Eight months later he was drawing on Christopher Lonsdale, presumably the husband of Isabel Dent's sister Ann. On 18 December 1786 Dent wrote to Lonsdale from Sedbusk as follows.

Having been disappointed of the payment of two hundred pounds, on consulting my wife the most convenient method we thought would be to draw on you, as by the time that my draft will be due, I shall have it in my power to remitt you the value. We shall be happy to have a line on the receipt of this to know how you and Mrs. Londsdale are. I hope you will excuse the liberty I have taken in this matter, and if you have occasion to have anything done in this part, you may freely command.

P.S. My draft is made payable to Thomas Dent, December 18th at 6 weeks for 200. We should be glad to have your oppinion in regard to stocks as money here may be lent on good security at 5 per cent.

---

[1] These transactions can be traced in Lowther MSS., Kirkby Stephen Manor, Verdicts, and Court Book, 1778–1810, ff. 3–7, 59 (Cumberland Record Office).
[2] Hallam MSS. (Westmorland Record Office).

To this Dent's wife added a line: 'I hope it will not be inconvenient to grant Mr Dent this faver as I shall deem it a great obligation from Dear Sir Your most obliged and ever well wisher Isable Dent. Excuse this scrawl I have been poorly.'

Dent met his obligation to Lonsdale by drawing on a Mr. Housen of London, to whom he promised, on 20 January 1787, to 'send . . . up bills to answer the amount'. He explained to Housen, 'I feared being disappointed of a large sum, which proves the case'. There was nothing very unusual in these transactions, though they have a certain note of urgency. On the day on which he wrote to Housen, Dent paid £20 in interest to James Fawcett, and a month later, on 19 February 1787, he borrowed a further £130 from John Burn, esq., at $4\frac{1}{2}$ per cent. For securing this, Fawcett joined Dent in a promissory note to Burn, and Dent's property at Kirkby Stephen was to be the security for indemnifying Fawcett for the £130 as well as for the £500 previously borrowed.[1]

These debts were presumably repaid, though this may well have been done by borrowing again. The position is obscure, for in 1791 Dent entered the property market again in a small way. He sold two houses, one of which paid a customary rent of only $2\frac{1}{2}d.$ p.a., and bought three cattlegates in Kirkby Stephen Intack.[2] Two years later, on 8 May 1793, he was mortgaging his property again, this time to Henry Day of Langton in the parish of Bongate. The sum borrowed was £550 at $4\frac{1}{2}$ per cent. Whatever was the purpose of this loan, the sum was not enough, and on 6 December 1793 Dent borrowed a further £300 at 4 per cent from his wife. This was done with the consent of John Harrison the elder of Hawes, hosier, and the Rev. Richard Fawcett of Hardraw, clerk, who were obviously the trustees in the settlement which had been made before Isabel's marriage to Dent. Again the security was Dent's property at Kirkby Stephen, subject, of course, to the existing mortgage to Henry Day and subject to 'all the estate, right, title, interest, property, benefit and equity of redemption, claim

---

[1] Hallam MSS. (Westmorland Record Office).
[2] Lowther MSS., Kirkby Stephen Manor Court Book, 1778–1810, ff. 110, 114, 121 (Cumberland Record Office).

and demand whatsoever at law and in equity of him the said Abraham Dent.'[1]

It is very unlikely that these debts were repaid except by borrowing again on mortgage, for on 19 June 1801 Dent sold his property at Kirkby Stephen to Thomas Monkhouse, Christopher Pickard and Joseph Thompson. It is almost certain that the purchasers were in fact mortgagees of the property, which they immediately resold in lots to five separate buyers.[2] This loss of property at Kirkby Stephen was not made good by any corresponding gains at Sedbusk. Dent paid 13s. 5d. in land tax for property at Sedbusk in 1801, but this was for property which belonged to his wife. She paid the tax between the death of her first husband and her marriage to Dent, and was assessed for the same sum after Dent's death, when the tax had been 'exonerated' or redeemed.[3]

Borrowing need not imply bankruptcy or involve moral turpitude; it need not even imply serious financial difficulty. Yet in Dent's case it does seem to have reflected a real financial embarrassment, which marked almost the last twenty years of his life. The reasons for this can only be a subject for speculation. It would be possible to take the cynical view that Dent was financially embarrassed by the early 1780s and that he married a well-to-do widow to rescue himself from that embarrassment. This may have been so, but there is no evidence that can prove it. Dent certainly borrowed from his wife, and there is a curious and obscure reference to his interest in her holding of Consols. On 9 April 1784 Dent wrote to Law and Holme asking them to

take the trouble to call on Mr. Thompkin at the Bank, who is one of the Clerks at the Bank at the 3 per cent Consols, and to know if a Mr. Calvert has called on him concerning 3000 Stock Mrs. Dent has their [*sic*], of which shall say more about shortly. Last April I received 50 guineas for the half year's intrest which includes intrest of £500 more

---

[1] Hallam MSS. (Westmorland Record Office).

[2] Lowther MSS., Kirkby Stephen Manor Court Book, 1778–1810, ff. 193–202, where the property is said to have been surrendered (in the manorial sense) to Thomas Monkhouse, esq., of Winton, who in turn granted it to five men; but the Court Book of 1774–1895 states clearly that Dent sold the property to Monkhouse, Pickard and Thompson.

[3] Land Tax Returns for High Abbotside (North Riding Record Office).

than the above, which is in her brother's name, but I suppose Mr. Calvert will settle it as Mr. John Harrison, my brother in law, has wrote to him.[1]

Unfortunately there is no record of what more Dent said. Indeed the whole reference to the Consols is puzzling. The interest of 50 guineas for a half year would imply that the entire stock of £3,500 was in 3 per cent Consols, but there is no record that Isabel Dent inherited or held any 3 per cent Consols.[2] Abraham may have been referring to the £3,500 of 4 per cent Consols that James Metcalfe left in his will, but Isabel had only a life interest in £1,000 of this stock. She certainly seems to have held no Consols at her death. It may, however, be fanciful to read anything very sinister into Abraham's interest in his wife's Consols.

It may not, however, be fanciful to believe that as Dent rose in the social scale to the status of a gentleman, his financial position declined. Men do not dispose of their property or borrow, even from their wives, without cause. In Dent's case the cause is not known. By the 1780s he had ceased to be a shopkeeper and his business as a hosier was small. Moreover about the middle of that decade the brewery partnership broke up. There seems to be some coincidence between this event and the beginning of Dent's borrowing. Is it possible that the brewery was a failure, despite the fact that Dent's sons later took it over? Certainly between 1782 and 1786 Dent made heavy payments by inland bills to James Portees, amounting to just over £900, and to a John Mason, who may have been the other partner in the brewery, amounting to £570. But the purpose of these payments is not known, and it would be idle to speculate. Even the final reckoning is not known, for Dent either did not make a will or, if he did, it has not survived.[3]

Abraham Dent died in 1803; he was buried at Hardraw on 3 March of that year. His widow survived him; she was buried, also at Hardraw, on 16 April 1807. She had made her will after

---

[1] Land Tax Returns for High Abbotside (North Riding Record Office).
[2] I am indebted for this information to Mr. E. M. Kelly of the Secretary's Office of the Bank of England.
[3] Or at least it is not at Somerset House, Carlisle, Leeds, York or Preston.

her husband's death, and disposed of her property 'in pursuance and exercise of the power and authority given to me in and by the settlement made previous to my marriage with my late husband Abraham Dent'. It was the long and detailed will of a widow who had a good deal to leave and had no children of her own.[1] Isabel, or Isabella as she is called in her will, left £40, some plate, a pair of small mahogany drawers and a large looking glass to her brother Thomas Harrison, and a brown silk gown and a petticoat to Anne Harrison. To her nephew Edward Fawcett she left her house in Sedbusk, including that part in the occupation of Cecily Fawcett, two fields called Rashdale and two cattlegates in Sedbusk High Pasture for life, with reversion to his daughter Isabella and her heirs. Edward also got 'my best green bed and bedding thereunto and also the press bed and bedding which stands over the dining room, with six mahogany chairs, one pair of mahogany drawers, one oack table which stand in the loby, the large cupboard which stands in the parlour, and also the sum of twenty pounds to buy two cows with'. Edward's wife, Bessy, shared 'my common clothes' with Elizabeth Wetheralt, Isabella Fawcett, and two of Isabel's married sisters, Jane Shaw and Mary Whaley. In addition Mary Whaley got a set of blue and white tea china, a damask table cloth, the best black cloak and a blue satin petticoat, and Isabella Fawcett got £20, a green silk gown, the green bed and bedding in the dining room, and six mahogany chairs and a pair of drawers.

Two other nephews benefited from Isabel's will. To her nephew Christopher Bushby she left her fields called Hill Dales for life, with reversion to his son John, subject to the payment of £2 p.a. to the wife of John Coultherd and £2 p.a. to Elizabeth, wife of John Wetheralt. Her nephew John Fawcett received £100, 'my silver pint', two silver table spoons, a large glass and a mahogany dining table in the parlour. Bequests of money included £10 each to Jane Nicholson and Henry Shaw, £20 each to George Smith (whose sister got a set of red and white tea china), John Allen and Mary Moss, £5 to the poor of Sedbusk, and £5 and a suit of

---

[1] Wills of the Eastern Deaneries of the Archdeaconry of Richmond (Archives Department, Leeds City Library).

mourning to the servant who waited upon Isabel at her death. All this, the mahogany, the plate, the china, suggests a comfortable and gentlemanly setting for Abraham Dent's old age. Nor were the Dents entirely forgotten in the will. Thomas Dent's son Abraham was left a writing desk, and Betty (or Elizabeth) the wife of William Dobson was left a silver gill, a lilac silk gown and part of the best lace. Finally Betty Dobson, Thomas Dent and Thomas's son Abraham were left 'all my share of the cotton mill at Aysgarth[1] share and share alike', subject to the payment of £50 to Isabella, daughter of the late Abraham Dent, who was presumably Isabella, the daughter of Abraham junior.

William Sadler of Bolton Hall and James Stuart of Simonstone were the executors and trustees, receiving £15 each for their trouble. Sadler was also left a clock and a silver coffee pot and stand, and James Stuart two pictures of Our Saviour's life and death. They were empowered to sell the land known as Brow close, High close and Low High close, and 7 cattlegates in Sedbusk High Pasture in order to pay off any debts and to discharge the legacies. Anything that remained was to be distributed among Isabel's nearest relatives; any plate, linen, china and furniture, not specifically bequeathed, was to be sold or distributed among relatives.

The land and cattlegates were sold at Hawes on 13 October 1807, which was a Tuesday and therefore market day. It is rather ironical that, when so much evidence has been lost, someone recorded every bid at the sale, and this has been preserved. The closes, which were meadow and contained about 10 acres, were sold as lot 1. The bidding started at 200 guineas from James Dixon, and the land was finally sold to Thomas Stuart for 416 guineas. The cattlegates were split into four lots: Thomas Stuart bought 2 gates for 64 guineas, John Bushby another two at the same price, but James Mason had to pay 67 guineas for the two gates in lot 4 and 38 guineas for the single gate in lot 5. Thus the sale realized £681 9s. Total receipts for 'Lands, debts &c.' came to £804 13s.,

---

[1] The 'great flaring mill' that, in John Byng's imagination, bred 'poaching, profligacy and plunder' as well as treason and rebellion (*The Torrington Diaries*, ed. C. B. Andrews, iii, pp. 81–2).

of which £407 12*s*. 10½*d*. was paid to 'sundry legatees', leaving £397 0*s*. 1½*d*. as 'ballance due to Mrs. Dent's heirs'.

The heirs had to wait some time for their money. Though Isabel's will had been 'carefully drawn' according to Mr. Breare, who seems to have been a legal adviser to the executors, it was disputed by Thomas Dent. In a letter to Breare of 23 January 1808 Thomas Dent claimed that he wanted 'nothing in the business but what is truly just and right', but he would only agree to 'a reciprocal release between the parties . . . under the following circumstances: that the present trustees to my Mother leave to me in the release an exclusive right of the equity of redemption of those premises bought by my father and sold by Mr. John Harrison, senior, to Richard Stuart of Sedbusk upon a mortgage title; and also everything left to me or any part of my family in my late Mother's will.' William Sadler reported to his fellow executor, James Stuart, that this might be meant 'as a kind of masq'd battery', but it would be 'of small avail against such powerful artillery as we are provided with'. The dispute dragged on, though the point at issue remains obscure. In April 1810 Sadler met Thomas Dent and Mr. Pickard 'at the Cotton Mill meeting'. Pickard, who was presumably Christopher Pickard, one of the mortgagees of 1801, produced evidence of Abraham Dent's mortgages, and Thomas Dent 'candidly confessed . . . that he would have wrote in answer to the first letter sent to him, but could not find such papers as he thought could be of use to him'. It was agreed that Thomas 'should have a further look amongst his papers'. Later in the month Pickard 'returned into Wensleydale' and dined with Sadler and Lupton Topham, 'the attorney'. They discussed 'how it was best to act', and the following day Sadler, Topham and Breare met and examined again the assignments of the property at Kirkby Stephen and Sedbusk which Abraham Dent had made. They concluded, as Sadler reported to James Stuart, that 'neither we, nor Mr. Thomas Dent, or his sister, had anything at all to do with or power over the premises in question'. They agreed, therefore, that they could 'safely make a distribution of the surplus' of Isabel's estate, and this was done in the summer of 1810. Presumably Thomas Dent had had 'a further look amongst his papers' and had found nothing that would support his case. He seems to have thought that he could redeem some of his father's former property by using the equity of redemption. By this device a mortgagor could redeem his property by repaying the mortgagee even after the date at which such payment was due. It is doubtful whether Thomas Dent had a good case; he certainly did not press it.

It would be impossible to write a full biography of Abraham Dent, for little is known of him as a man. His private life remains private. With rare exceptions, his surviving letters are business letters; his surviving accounts do not follow the earlier practice of mixing household and business items, a practice which can be useful to the biographer even if it shocks the accountant. Yet some personal impressions can be derived from such unpromising material. Dent's relations with his successive wives remain obscure. Nothing is known of Elizabeth Grainger, whom he married in 1754, or of the mysterious Ann, who died in 1781. His marriage to Isabel Metcalfe in 1783 was announced in a curiously laconic, almost off-hand way, but there is nothing to suggest that the marriage was not a happy one. It is possible that Isabel had indifferent health; in October 1784 Dent wrote to Samuel Parker hoping that he and Mrs. Parker would 'continue in a perfect state of health', and added 'I should have been glad to have given you account of Mrs. Dent being in the same condition'. Two years later Isabel had been 'very poorly'. She outlived her husband by four years, but she may well have been much younger than he.

Dent's relations with his children seem to show a normal paternal regard. He was clearly fond of his daughter Elizabeth, who married William Dobson. She was his first child to survive infancy, she married young, and she and her husband left the north to live in London, where Dent sent them, in May 1781, '1 flitch bacon, 1 peice string beef, 1 dryd leg mutton'. Dent wrote to his daughter, though his letters have not survived, and sent his 'love to Billy and Bessy' in letters to John Harrison and Thomas Dobson. It is possible that William Dobson's business, whatever it was, did not prosper. On 4 May 1784 Dent wrote to Law and

Holme, 'I have taken the liberty also to inclose my letter of attorney &c. to you on Wm Dobson's account and hopes you will do whats necessary till I can return the favours done'. Six months later he was enquiring anxiously from Law and Holme, 'pray have you heard anything about Wm Dobson's affairs?' It is possible, too, that Dobson's wife returned to the north and lived with her father at Sedbusk. Dent's sons, Thomas and Abraham, remain shadowy figures, but there again the scanty evidence suggests an affectionate relationship with their father, who was concerned with finding a suitable career for 'my son Tom' and who seems to have employed Abraham as an assistant in the hosiery business. No letters between Dent and his sons have survived, even for the period when he was separated from them by living at Sedbusk. It was otherwise with Samuel Parker in London. Dent's letters to 'son Sam' are concerned largely with business matters, but they suggest a deep affection for Samuel and his wife. It was no conventional phrase when Dent signed himself 'thy affectionate Father', but it makes the mystery of Samuel's precise relationship to Dent all the more tantalizing.

Dent's degree of kinship to John Waller is equally uncertain, but Waller, who was a naval purser at Plymouth, left the management of his property at Kirkby Stephen to Dent. It was Dent who paid the taxes on the property, collected the rents and saw to the repairs. It was from the rents of the property that Dent tried to meet Waller's many requests for money. Waller's elder brother Lancelot, who was an excise officer at Sunderland, also had some property at Kirkby Stephen, and this, too, Dent administered in the 1770s. John Waller's letters show that he relied on Dent for news and gossip of Kirkby Stephen, though in a letter of 31 January 1772 Waller complained, 'I am favor'd with your very *long* epistle containing all the news you cou'd think of in the space of ten minutes, the time you certainly allow'd yourself to write it in'. It was through Dent that Waller sent greetings to his friends and relations. Indeed Waller seems to have regarded Dent as a combination of the family patriarch and the family business man, which he may well have been.

Abraham Dent's position in the family was matched by his

position in the local community of Kirkby Stephen. His property qualified him as a voter in the election of M.P.s for the county, and in 1761 he voted for Sir James Lowther and John Upton, the successful candidates.[1] For many years he served on the jury of the manorial court of the manor of Kirkby Stephen, and he was also a churchwarden. In 1767-68 Dent and Thomas Petty were overseers of the poor for the township of Kirkby Stephen, and Dent kept the overseers' accounts in one of his ledgers. If the accounts are complete, they do not suggest that the office of overseer was very onerous or that the poor were very numerous. Only two or three families were receiving relief. Montgomery's family received 9s. 7d. in June 1767, but this did not include 2s. for 'a journey to Starforth[2] on Montgomery's account'. The following month Montgomery's wife received 18s. 1d., and in August and September she was getting 3s. a week. Molly Cumpstone, on the other hand, received only a single payment of 1s.; that was on 30 June 1767, and the following day Mr. Stubbs was paid '12d. for carrying Cumpstone to Sowerby'. Presumably she was being moved to her parish of settlement. Responsibility did not end with death, for the poor had to be decently buried. On 18 August 1767 2s. 6d. was paid for 'a shroud for Caygill', 4s. for church dues, 6s. 6d. for a coffin, and 6s. for 'ale, bread, cheese &c.' The dead had sometimes to be found; on 27 February 1768 William Barnett was paid 1s. 'for searching for J. Holmes' child and going for corroner'. The coffin on this occasion cost 3s. 6d.

Twelve years later, in 1780, Dent shared with John Thompson the surveyorship of highways, but no accounts for their term of office seem to have survived. There is only a list of the 'inhabitants and occupiers of lands and tenements in the township of Kirkby Stephen liable to perform their statute work on the highways'.[3] The statute work had been commuted into a money payment of 6d. in the £ on the 'yearly value each person occupies'. Dent himself was assessed at 6s. on property value £12 p.a., and John Thompson at £1 7s. 6d. on property value £55 p.a., which was

---

[1] Poll Book for 1761 (Westmorland Record Office).
[2] Startforth near Barnard Castle ?
[3] Hallam MSS. (Westmorland Record Office).

the highest figure in the township. The link between property and power was close in the eighteenth century, and so was the link between property and office at all levels of society. Dent filled those public offices which fell to the lot of the propertied tradesman in a country town. They were offices too lowly for the gentry, but at least they reflected some consequence in their holders.

Most men who are neither very rich nor very poor combine together three lives: their private lives, their public lives and their working lives. That was true of Abraham Dent, though little is known of his private and public life. Much more is known of his working life, even if the records are incomplete; at this level business history may simply depend on what the rats have not eaten. The records, many of which seem to be in his own hand, show that Dent was a man of great industry. There is a close attention to detail, whether this is in detecting short measure in the groceries supplied or in fulfilling the orders for stockings. There is the conduct of a number of enterprises simultaneously; hosier, shopkeeper, wine merchant. This involved personal contacts with customers and suppliers in London, which Dent visited fairly regularly. These contacts were personal in another sense. Many of the people in London, with whom Dent had dealings, had local connections with Kirkby Stephen or they were related to Dent. Thus John Law and William Holme had local connections; Samuel Parker, the Dobsons and John Harrison were Dent's relatives. Such personal connections may have been as important in eighteenth-century business life as they were in eighteenth-century politics. Certainly the personal links between provincial merchants and shopkeepers and their London associates would be worth further study. Dent's letters to his London customers and suppliers may be couched in the conventional language of deference, but they do not suggest that the writer was overawed by or subservient to his correspondents. Indeed Dent seems to have moved with easy familiarity among his London associates, just as in his local world he was accepted by men like Charles Kinsey who were his social superiors. Perhaps it was the social snobbery of the Victorians that invented the tradesman's entrance.

There is much of interest in Dent's business activities, but it would be misleading to regard those activities as typical of the small town shopkeeper of the eighteenth century. Dent was too versatile, he combined too many roles, to be typical. Had he been simply a shopkeeper or a hosier or a wine merchant or a brewer he would have been more typical of the small town business man. He was typical only in the sense that small towns often produce an ambitious and energetic man who finds scope for his energies, not by moving to the big city, but by diversifying his interests within the confines of his native place. He prefers to be a big fish in a small pond. He is the urban counterpart of the energetic yeoman who adds farm to farm, or adds farming to corn and cattle dealing and milling. Abraham Dent was this type of man. His interests were not agricultural, but commercial and industrial. He developed those interests within the limits of a small market town, but they drew him into contact with a much wider world extending from Newcastle to London. If more were known about more Abraham Dents, eighteenth-century England might appear less bucolic and less provincial.

Appendices

APPENDIX I

A NOTE ON SOURCES

Dent's business records, upon which this book is largely based, were found under the rafters of a house in Sedbusk in 1952. The house had belonged to the Stuarts for many generations, and the records themselves seem to have lain undisturbed for at least a century. Among them were some fragments of printed material, including a very worm-eaten copy of *An Account of the Charities of the late William Strafford L.L.D.*, printed by James Ashburner of Kendal in 1766 and bearing John Harrison's signature. The business records are as follows:

1. A day book recording the credit sales at the shop from 1762 to 1765. 373 folios ($6\frac{1}{2}$ v. 16 inches), of which the first 23 are missing. Between the folios are a number of loose bills of goods or services supplied to the Dents, the handbill about light gold and the broadsheet advertising Daffy's Elixir.

2. A ledger of purchases recording goods bought for the shop from 1756–77. 177 numbered folios ($6\frac{1}{4}$ v. $15\frac{3}{4}$ inches). It gives the name and usually the address of the supplier and the value of the goods supplied, but rarely the nature of the goods. On the right-hand folios are the receipts for payment signed by the supplier or his agent and comments made by the Dents on the goods supplied. Dent's accounts as overseer of the poor for 1767–68 are on f. 140. Between the folios are loose receipts, letters and inland bills.

3. Ledger of sales covering the years 1767 to 1780. 88 numbered folios ($6\frac{1}{2}$ v. 16 inches). Records the sale of stockings (to 1778) giving the name of the purchaser, the quantity, type and price of the stockings, and the method of payment. Includes also Dent's purchases of stockings from the Nottingham hosiers and from Thomas Fawcett, purchases of wool, malt and some spirits, the bill accounts with Richard Harrison and Law and Holme, and accounts with James Ashburner and John Moore of Kendal and with Lancelot and John Waller.

4. Letter book (8 v. $12\frac{1}{2}$ inches) covering the years 1780–89 (with some gaps from missing folios). It contains copies of the business letters Dent wrote, but not of those he received. At the end are two loose letters from Pearse and Son.

The letters from John Waller to Dent and a small bundle of letters relating to the dispute over Isabel Dent's will were among the papers of my grandfather, Thomas Stuart, who was born and brought up at Sedbusk. This again suggests some connection between Dent and the Stuarts.

All these records are at present in my possession. Some day they will probably go to the Westmorland Record Office in Kendal, which would seem to be their natural home.

Additional material has been found in the following local record offices:

1. Westmorland Record Office (Kendal). The bishops transcripts of the parish registers for Kirkby Stephen; the Kaber census of 1787; the Hallam MSS. (a solicitor's collection as yet unclassified).
2. Cumberland Record Office (Carlisle). Wills among the probate records of the Consistory Court of Carlisle; Lowther MSS., which include the records of the manor of Kirkby Stephen.
3. North Riding Record Office (Northallerton). Land tax returns for the North Riding.
4. Archives Department, Leeds City Library (Sheepscar Library, Leeds). The bishops transcripts of the parish registers of Hawes and Hardraw; wills of the Eastern Deaneries of the Archdeaconry of Richmond.

I could find no relevant wills among the probate records at The Borthwick Institute of Historical Research, York, and only a single Administration among the probate records at the Lancashire Record Office, Preston.

APPENDIX II

The following extracts show the sort of credit sales that were recorded in the day book. In the original the entries are crossed through to show that the account had been settled.

f. 39 Mr James Highmoor of Flittholme

		£	s	d
20 July 1762	1 Ainsworth Dictionary 2 Volls	1	7	0
	1 Second hand Hammond on the test		13	
	1 Stirlings Terence 8to.		5	
	1 Clarks Grotius		5	
	Herveys Meditations 2 Vols		6	
		2	16	0

f. 46 John Williamson in town Glover

		s	d
10 Aug. 1762	2 Dram Silk 3¾		3¾
14	1 lb Sugar 6d. 2 Dram Silk 3¾d. 1 lb Sugar 6d.	1	3¾
4 Sept.	¼ oz Red & blue Silk 7½		7½
20 Oct.	1 lb f. Lint 16	1	4
		3	7

f. 50 James Petty a Labourer in town

		s	d
Sept. 1762	½ Sugar 2½d. Sept. 2 ½ Do 2½		5
Sept 2	1 lb treakle 2¼d. 1 lb treakle 2¼ the 5th		4½
11	Lent 18d. ¼ lb Sugar 1¼ 19th.	1	7¼
26	7 lb flower 11d. Candles 3½ ½ lb Sope 3½	1	6
28	7 lb flower 11d. the 29th 1 lb treakle 2¼	1	1¼
4 Oct	3½ flower 5½d. 2 lb treakle 4½		10
6	2 lb barley 3d. 9th day flower 5½d. Candles 3¼		11¾
10	1 lb treakle 2¼ 1 lb do. 2¼ the 13th flower 5½		10
18	½ lb treakle 1¼d.		1¼
		7	9

f. 55 John Yeats in town

14 Sept. 1762	1 Daffy Bottle 15*d*.	1	3
18	1 Daffy Bottle 15*d*. by maid	1	3
27	1 Do by Daughter	1	3
24 Jan. 1763	¼ Powder 4½*d*. Shott 2*d*. by Grame		6½
26 Feb.	1 Deal plank 4*s*. 6*d*.	4	6
		8	9½

f. 65 Will Ewbank of town Mason

20 Oct. 1762	2½ yds Worsted Shagg	5	10
	flanil 15*d*. buttons 3*d*.	1	6
	twist 2*d*. Harden 4½*d*.		6½
	thred		1½
		8	0

f. 91   John Fothergill of town Innkeeper

Jan. 14 1763	3¾ yd Glazd Lin 10½ ¼ yd Canvis 4½	1	3
	½ yd Shalloon 6*d*. 1 Bottle blue 14*d*.	1	8
Oct. 28	1 Turners Ex. 18	1	6
Nov. 16	1 Grammar 18 1 Inkhorn 2*d*. for Nephew	1	8
30	½ qr paper 5*d*. quils 1*d*.		6
Dec. 12	1 Doz. horn buttons 2*d*. quils 1*d*.		3
6 Jan. 1764	1 qr paper 10*d*. quills 1*d*.		11
27 Mar	1 Lattin Testament 13*d*.	1	1
3 April	1 Kings Heathen Gods 2*s*.	2	
6	1 qr Paper 10*d*.		10
	s d		
16	1 Youngs Dictionary 7*s*. a/d	7	
24	buttons, thred &c. 9*d*. by W. Warcop		9
May 4	1 yd Black Ribbon		8
	June 18th 1764 recd. 17*s*.	17	2

f. 108   Mr Fawcett in town

8 March 1763	5 yds frized Cloth @ 2s. 8d.		13	4
	5 yds Callamanco @ 14d.		5	10
	2½ yds Shallown @ 16d.		3	4
	2¾ yds Bla. worsted Shagg @ 2s. 4d.		6	5
	2¾ yds flannil @ 14d.		3	2½
	harden 9d. Buckram 6d.		1	3
	14 Coat Buttons 9d.			9
	3 Doz. Horn Buttons @ 2d.			6
	thred 6d. Silk & twist 6d. tape 2d.		1	4
		1	15	11½
4 Apl	Buckram 4½			4½
	Apl 14 Received the Contents per Mr Fawcett	1	16	4

f. 151   Mr Leonard Barnett in town

July 5 1763	7 lb Sugar 2s. 9d.		2	9
26	3½ lb Sugar @ 6 1 oz Green tea 8		2	5
Aug 15	1 oz Hy. tea 13½ 1 oz Souc. tea 8½d.		1	10
	1 Spelling Dictionary 12d. 7 lb Sugar 3s. 5d.		4	5
16	1 Sugar Lofe 24½ lb @ 9d.		18	4½
29	½ Stone Sugar 2s. 7d.		2	7
Sept 10	A stone flower 2s. by Maid		2	
18	4 lb Soft & Hard Sope @ 6½		2	2
26	1 lb Hard Sope 6½			6½
	1 lb Stone blue 22d. 1 lb Powder 18d.		3	4
	5/2 oz Starch @ 6d.		2	6¾
30	1½ lb Sugar @ 5½d. 5½ lb do the 17th		3	2½
Oct 15	2 lb Hard Sope & 2 Soft Sope		2	2
Dec 16	Raysins Currans &c.		4	
		2	12	4¼

f. 208   Mr John Ewbank at Hartley

Feb 9 1764	1 lb tobacco 14*d*. by Se [? Servant]		1	2
Mar 5	1 lb tobacco 14*d*. Lent cash 12*d*.		2	2
19	Cash 12*d*. 1 lb tobacco 14*d*. March 24th		2	2
Apl 16	Cash 12*d*. 1 lb tobacco 14*d*.		2	2
24	Cash 2*s*.		2	
May 1	Cash 1*s*. 1 lb tobacco 14*d*.		2	2
8	Cash 3*s*. 19th 1 lb tobacco 14*d*. Cash 5*s*.		9	2
June 4	Cash 2*s*. 1 lb tobacco 14*d*. the 7th		3	2
14	Cash 3*s*. 1 lb tobacco 14*d*. the 22nd		4	2
27	Cash 21*s*.	1	1	0
		2	9	4
30	Cash	5	10	8
		8	0	0
30	Same time received a Bill Vallue	8	0	0

f. 232   Doctor Wilson at Redgill

April 16 1764	2 lb L. Sugar @ 8*d*.		1	4
	½ lb Bla. peper 10*d*.			10
	12½ lb treakle @ 2¼*d*. Sealing wax 1½		2	5½
30	1 lb L. Sugar 8*d*. by Se [? Servant]			8
May 26	1 Stone flower 2*s*. 2*d*. per Epm Jackson		2	2
31	2½ yds Everlasting @ 2*s*. 8*d*.		6	8
	Buckram & Canvis 3½*d*. Shallown 4*d*.			7½
	Buttons 4*d*. twist & thred 3½*d*.			7½
	ferritt 3*d*. tape 1*d*.			4
	Sent a Note May 31st.		15	8

f. 281   The Revd Mr Richardson of Huddersfeild

5 Oct 1764	3¼ yds Superfine Cloth @ 16*s*.	2	12	0
	5½ yds Shallown @ 16*d*.		7	4
	1¾ yds Dimothy @ 12*d*.		1	9
	1 yd Buckram 12*d*. Canvis 2¼*d*.		1	2¼
	1⅛ yd Pocket fustian @ 10*d*.			11¼
	1 Doz. Coat buttons 8*d*. 1 Doz. breast buttons 4*d*.		1	
	twist 6*d*. thred 4½*d*. Silke & tape 2*d*.		1	8½
		3	5	11

f. 284   Miss Bird of Crosby

11 Oct 1764	quils 2*d*. by man		2
	1 pr. bla. Stockins 2*s*. by Miss Nelson	2	0
19	1 Stone flower 21*d*. 1 lb barley 1½*d*.	1	10½
29	1 oz Nutmegs 8*d*. ½ oz Cinnamon 8*d*.	1	4
	1 stone flower 21*d*.	1	9
30	1 Gross Corks 14*d*. 1 lb Hops 18*d*.	2	8
	¼ Green tea 2*s*. 6*d*. 2 oz Sou. tea 16½*d*.	3	10½
		13	8

f. 288   George Harker & Co. at Awgill

3 Nov 1764	6 lb powder @ 12½*d*. per Jas Harker	6	3
18	4 lb powder @ 12½ per Geo. Harker	4	2
1 Dec	8 lb Powder @ 12½ by Jas Harker	8	4
8	4 lb Do @ 12½*d*. Jas Harker	4	2
16	4 lb Do @ 12½*d*. by Geo. Harker	4	2
6 Jan 1765	4 lb Do @ 12½ by Jas Do	4	2
13	4 lb Do @ 12½ by Jas Do	4	2
20	4 lb Do @ 12½ by Geo. Harker	4	2
	38	1 19	7

received in full Feb. 27 1765

f. 298   Thomas Rudd of Warcop by Wife

21 Dec 1764	14 lb Raysins & 14 Currants 13*s*. 6*d*.	13	6
	6 L. Sugar @ 7½*d*.	3	9
	2 lb B. Pepper @ 21*d*.	3	6
	2 lb C. Pepper @ 10*d*.	1	8
	1 lb Candy 10½		10½
	¼ lb Nutmegs 2*s*. 6*d*.	2	6
	1 lb thred 2*s*. 9*d*.	2	9
	3 lb Prunes 10*d*.		10
		1 9	4½

June 24th received £1   9   4½

APPENDIX III

In the original the debit and credit entries are opposite each other.

f. 2v.   Mr Nichs. Pearse   Dr.
  Clothier in Lothbury; goods to be sent to Mr. Colburn
     Packer in Coleman Street.

1770

25 Janry	To 4 Packs cont. 200 Dozn. Marching			
	Regiments at 12*s.*	120		
Do	To 8 Dozn. Serjeants at 31*s.*	12	8	
22 March	To 100 Dozn. Marching Regiments at 12*s.*	60		
	To 6 Hams 97 lb at $6\frac{1}{4}d$ £2 10 6			
	Carriage of 9 stone 11 lb 0 13 3	3	3	9
19 Apl	To 10 Dn. Serjeants at 31*s.*	15	10	
		211	1	9
30 Augt	To 1 Dozn mens fine Ribbed worsted	2	17	
	To 1 Dozn Do Do yarn	1	1	
		214	19	9
	By not charged above			
22 March	To 8 Dozn Serjeants @ 31*s.*	12	8	0
		227	7	9

f. 2r.   per Contra   Cr.

1770

18 Apl	By a Bill payable to M. Fenwick	30		
21 May	By a Bill payable to Mr Geo. Bell	20		
19 June	By a Bill payable to Mr Jas. Fawcett	30		
24 Augt	By a Bill payable to Mr J. Waller	30		
12 Sept	By a Bill payable to Mr J. Waller	30		
20 Nov.	By a Bill payable to Abm. Dent	40		

1771

1 Jan.	By a Bill payable to Mr Abm Dent for Bunyan			
	Nottingham	34	19	9
		214	19	9
Apl 15	By Bill to A. Dent	12	8	0
		227	7	9

f. 7v.   The Honourable Thos. Harley & John Hillman   Dr
          Merchants in Craven Street goods to be sent Mr Wm Worsfold
          packer in Mark Lane.[1]

1770
15 Feby   To 2 Packs Marching Regiments qt. 100 Dn at
                                              12s.   60
               To 8 Dozen of Serjeants at 31s.   12   8
22 March   To 100 Dozn. Marching Regiments at 12   60
               To 578 lb Hams at $6\frac{1}{4}d$ £15   1   0
               Carriage of 2 packs & 5 stone   18   10
                  at 26s. 6d. a pack   2 19 10
               To 8 Dozen Serjeants at 31s.   12   8
19 Apl   To 2 Pks marching Regiments 100 Dn. at 12s. 60
               To 78 Dn. Guards at 15s. 6d.   60   9
29   To 6 Dozn. Serjeants at 31s.   9   6
10 May   To 7   Do   Do   at 31s.   10   17
15 June   To 4 pr Mens ribbed worsted Hose at 5s.   1   0   0
               & 2 pr I think sent by Mr Waller before   10
                                                        ____
                                                        304 18   10

f. 7r.
                    Per Contra   Cr.

1770
30 March   By a Bill to Abm. Dent   18   10
9 October   By a Bill to Mr Wm. Monkhouse   30
23 Octr.   By a Bill to Mr Waller   40
3 Decr.   By a Bill to Abm. Dent   20
27 Decr.   By a Bill to Wm Todd   20

1771
1 Jany.   By a Bill to Abm Dent for Killer,
                                   Nottingham   26   9   0
10   By a Bill to Martin Fenwick   30
               By 8 Dozn Serjeants sent by mistake to
                                   Mr Pearse   12   8   0
16 March   By a Bill to Abm. Dent   50
22   Do   By a Bill to Abm. Dent sent to Martin
                                   Fenwick   58   1   0
                                                        ____
                                                        304 18   10

[1] Messrs Burfoot and Son Packers has been crossed out.

f. 12v.   Messrs Bunyan Hosiers at Nottingham   Dr.

1771

Jany. 1st.   By a bill sent you on Mr Thomas Elton

London	40	2	0

f. 12r.   Per Contra Cr.

1770

31 Jany.	By 8 Dozn Rolls at 26s. 6d.			10	13	0
9 Apl	By 10 Do Do			13	6
29	By 6 Do Do			8
28 May	By 6 Doz. 1 pr. 2d. Stout w^t Long hose				
	@ 26s. 6d.			8	3	11½
				40	2	11½

f. 23v.   Mr Martin Fenwick   Dr.

1771

Jany 18	By Bill sent you on Messrs Harley & Hillman	30	0	0
March 22	By Do	Do	58	1	0
Augt 10	By 3 Bank notes		30
			118	1	0

f. 23r.

Per Contra Cr.

1770

Nov 10	1 pack fine Sheep 14st. @ 11s. 18 lb to the stone	7	14	0
16	2 Do 2^d Lamb 28 st. @ 10s. 6d. Do	14	14	0
Dec. 14	1 Do fine Sheep 14 @ 11s. Do	7	14	0
Do	1 Do 2^d Lamb 14 @ 10s. 6d. Do	7	7	0
Do 28	1 Do 2 Lamb 14 @ 10s. 6d. Do	7	7	0

1771

Jany 4	3 Do 2 Lamb 42 @ 10s. 6d. Do	22	1	0
Feb. 15	1 Do fine Lamb @ 13s. 14 @ 13 Do	9	2	0

The above chargd to Mr Barnett & below to A. Dent   75 19 0

			£	s	d
28	1 pack fine Sheep 14 @ 11s.	Do	7	14	0
March 22	2 packs 2^d Lamb		14	14	0
24	5 Stone fine Sheep @ 11s.		2	15	0
	9 Stone 2^d Ditto @ 9s. 6d...		4	5	6
30	9 Stone 2^d Ditto @ 9s. 6d.		4	5	6
June 27	14 Stone Do @ 9s. 6d.		6	13	0
Augt. 10	By Ballance received of John Robinson		1	15	0
			118	1	0

f. 29v.   Richard Harrison Esqr Charing Cross London   Dr.

1772		£	s	d
Sept 24	One promissory note on Eliz^a Davis London	66	0	0
	1 Do on Wm Nutt London	140	0	0
	Intrest of Do from Jany 12 1772 to	4	0	2
Octr 14	By Bill on Messrs Harley & Hillman at Thirty days	55	18	0
Nov 17	By Bill on Messrs Henry Boldero & Comp. at one Month dated Octr. 20	50	0	0
Decr. 13	1 York Bank note on Boldero Kendale &c at fourteen days sight	10	0	0
Do	By Bill on Harley & Hillman at six weeks	50	0	0

1773				
Jany 4	By 3 Notes on Henry Kendall Geo Addey & John Kendall Henry Boldero on Demand dated 16 Dec. 1772 20 each	60	0	0
	4 Notes on Do Do Do 10 each	40	0	0
	1 Bill Williamson & Waller on Henry Hand. Norris London past due dates from Hutt Dec. 2nd 1772	9	17	8
22	By Cash paid Mr John Raytton at Ewbanke	20	0	0
Do	By Bill on Harley & Hillman six weeks	53	15	0
25	Michael Dent's receipt	12	0	0
Feb. 20	By Bill on Mr. Nichs. Pearse	57	10	10
23	By Do Danl. Prince on Robt. Child & Co.	50	0	0
		679	1	8
	By Ballance Feby. 23rd. 1773	26	8	10
		705	10	6

f. 29r.   Per Contra   Cr.

Sept 24	By Bill to J. Harrison at Settbusk at one month	35	0	0
30	By 1 Bill £30 1 Do £10 at one month to Mr. Richd. Mather	40	0	0
Oct. 7	By Bill to Monkhouse & Hopper at six weeks	111	0	0
14	By Bill to Mr. John Law at sight	79	18	0
Novr 12	By Do at sixty days to H. Hargreaves	30	0	0
16	By Do to Mr Kinsey at one Month	6	0	0
28	By Do to Wm Green Esqr at one Month	20	0	0
Decr. 1	By Do to John Mason at 60 days	16	13	0
Do				
Do	By Do to Robt. Monkhouse at 60 Days	30	0	0
Decr. 7	By Bill to Mr Geo. Brown @ 1 Month	12	0	0
Do	By Bill to Mr Geo. Brown at 1 Month	15	3	0
8	By Bill to Thos Cleasby at Six weeks	16	15	6
1773				
Jany 4	By Do to Mr John Neal at Six weeks	66	0	0
14	By Do to Wm Green Esqr at one month	30	0	0
19	By Do to Mr Thos. Strickland Six weeks	10	0	0
23	By Do to Mr Robt. Wilson, Appleby, at one month	60	0	0
26	By Do to Mr Geo. Bunyan at 6 weeks	44	17	6
Feb. 1	By Do to Mr Thos Clawson at one Month	22	0	0
2	By Do to Mr Thos Breaks at one Month	10	3	6
16	By Do to Mr Robt. Islip at one Month	20	0	0
20	By Do to Mr John Mason at Six weeks	30	0	0
		705	10	6

f. 31v.   Dr. To Mr John Law near St Pauls Wharf London

1773				
Augt 31	1 Bill to R. Aspinwall @ 6 weeks	16	11	0
Sepr 16	Do to Geo. Pickup @ 50 Days	6	1	0
Do 18	Do to R. Islip @ 30 Days	20	0	0
25	Do to Mr Chas. Kinsey @ 6 weeks	11	0	0
27	Do by Bill to Messrs Eskridge & Gardner Six weeks	10	0	0
Octr 1	Do to Ed. Clark @ 40 days	50	0	0
Do Do	Do to Jas. Clarkson @ 6 weeks advised of	20	0	0
Do 5	Do to Thos. Baldwin @ 30 days	6	10	0
7	Do to Hugh Davis @ 6 weeks	16	18	6

8	Do to Mr Richd. Bustard @ 6 weeks	20	0	0
9	Do to Mr Ricd. Pedder @ 6 weeks	11	10	0
11	Do to Mr. Geo. Brown @ 30 Days	43	0	0
14	Do to Mr Thos. Rawson @ 6 weeks	43	5	0
18	Do to Mr John Shutt @ 6 weeks	20	16	0
27	Do to Mr Geo. Brown @ 6 weeks	10	0	0
Novr 15	Do to Thos. Rudd Sowerby @ 30 Days	50	0	0
16	Do to J. Ashburner @ 30 Days	30	0	0
19	Do to Messrs Thos. & Anth. Whittwell 60 Days advised of	16	13	0
		402	4	6

f. 31r.   Cr. by Bills To Abm Dent   Cr.

1773

Sept 3	1 Bill John Baker on D. Baynes & Co 1 month	13	10	0
Do Do	Do Thos Atkinson on Tobias Atkinson 6 weeks	20	0	0
Octr 1	My own Draft on N. Pearse Oct 1 advised of the above	109	4	0
Octr 16	Bradberry on Bradberry 6 weeks	60	0	0
Novr 5	Bradberry on Bradberry one Month	60	0	0
Do Do	J. Ripley on Barnabas Camble one month	20	0	0
Octr 30	David & Daniel Dyson on Wm Webster, Lond. 6 weeks	20	0	0
Novr 19	Do self on Harley & Hillman 60 days advised of	100	0	0
		£402	14	0

f. 34v.   To Thomas Hutton at Soulby

1774

Augt 29	2 Load malt	3	0	0
Sepr 14	4 Load Do	6	0	0
Oct 15	6 Do	9	0	0
Decr 12	8 Do	12	0	0

1775

Jan 30	2 Do	3	2	0
May 1	2 Do	3	2	0
29	4 Do	6	4	0
June 24	4 Do	6	4	0
Sept 13	3 Load malt	4	13	0
25	3 Load Do	4	13	0
Oct 8	4 Do	6	4	0
12	4 Do	6	4	0
		70	6	0

f. 34r.

1775	Cash	10	10	0
Mar 14	By Bill on Law and Holme	10	0	0
Do	Cash	4	4	0
	Cash by Martin Schoolmaster	1	4	0
June 26	Cash	10	0	0
Do	By Bill on Law and Holme	20	0	0
Nov 18	By receipt for Ballance	14	8	0
		70	6	0

f. 35v.

Cr.   To Mr John Law near St Pauls Wharf No. 28 London

1774

Mar 28	117 Galls Gin @ L/A	43	17	6
Do	1 Hdd Vinigar No. 10 £2 10s. puncheon 10s.			
	Suff [erance] warfage &c. for vinigar 1s.	3	1	0
April 25	120 Do Jamaica old Rum	48	0	0
Augt 4	43 Stg Melloss Brandy @ IX	19	7	0
	12½ Annaseed @ D/D	2	14	2
	12½ Cinn[amon] @ A/A	4	1	3
	14 Doz W paper @ I^s	5	12	0
	Box and Casks		14	0
	Yeatts Wine Licence	2	4	0½
		129	10	11½

f. 35r.

    To Abm Dent   Dr

1775

July 18th	Received Bill on Wright	10	15	
	do on Harley	94	15	
	do on Borgrave	3		
	do Cash	21		
	Abated			11½
	Wm Holme[1]	129	10	11½

[1] The signature is autograph.

APPENDIX IV

JOHN WALLER

There were many Wallers in and around Kirkby Stephen in the eighteenth century and, as with the Dents, it is now almost impossible to disentangle them. It would, for example, be interesting to know more about Robert Waller, a wine merchant of Tower Street, London, who owned property in Kirkby Stephen and who, in 1786, leased from Thomas Monkhouse of Winton his fourth or furthest pew in the East Gallery of Kirkby Stephen parish church. Waller paid £10 for the lease and was to pay a peppercorn rent for the residue of a period of 1,000 years from 4 March 1740. The gallery had been made by Richard Waller, late of Kirkby Stephen, deceased, who had let the pew to Joseph Thornton in 1740.[1] John Waller, Abraham Dent's kinsman, was the son of John Waller, a wright or carpenter of Kirkby Stephen, who died in 1774 aged 82. The eldest surviving son of John Waller, senior, seems to have been Lancelot Waller, who was baptized on 2 March 1727 and who married an unidentified Elizabeth. In 1752 Lancelot was described as a joiner,[2] but some time later he became an excise officer at 'Sunderland by the sea'. He owned a little property in Kirkby Stephen, which Abraham Dent administered for him in the 1770s. Dent recorded the payment of small sums for Lancelot's land tax, poor cess, church cess, highway tax, and 'Lord Thanet's rent'; there were also small payments for repairs.

Lancelot seems always to have kept a house at Kirkby Stephen, and his elder sons were baptised there. Smithson, born in 1752, became a purser in the Navy. He served in the *Brunswick* in 1801–2 when Lieutenant Gardner described him as 'a glorious fellow for keeping it up; and after taking his full share of Madeira would then turn to upon rum and water, and about two or three in the morning would give his last toast, "a bloody war and a sickly season!" and then retire in a happy state'.[3] Two other sons, John born in 1755 and Lancelot junior born in 1757, both died young. Two further sons, another John and a Robert, and two daughters, Elizabeth and Frances, survived their childhoods and

[1] Hallam MSS. (Westmorland Record Office).
[2] Ibid.
[3] *Recollections of James Anthony Gardner*, eds. Sir R. V. Hamilton and J. K. Laughton, Navy Records Society, xxxi (1906) pp. 241, 248.

married. Lancelot retired to Kirkby Stephen, where he was a church-warden in 1791, and was buried there on his death in 1804. By his will he left his stock of provisions and liquors to his wife Elizabeth; perhaps they represented the fruits of his career as an excise officer. Elizabeth had also a life interest, with reversion to a son Robert, in any goods she wished to keep; ready money, securities for money, and the produce of goods sold were to go to Robert in trust to pay interest to Elizabeth for life. Finally the will declared that certain furniture in the house at Kirkby Stephen was the property of Lancelot's grandson, John Burn, an infant who lived with him.[1] John Burn was the son of Lancelot's daughter Frances by her marriage to William Burn, master of a trading vessel at Sunderland.

Lancelot Waller's younger brother, John, was baptized on 6 February 1729. His early career remains obscure. He may have had some con-nection with the stocking trade, and even retained that connection after he became a naval purser. On 10 January 1769 his brother-in-law, John Barnett, received from John Waller 'the sum of twenty pounds for the profit of my one hundred pounds in trade, which sum is all at present between us'. This may be connected with the fragment of an account on the same page in Dent's ledger, which deals with transactions in which Waller was concerned. It gives some payments for stockings and wool, and includes the interesting items: 'In the knitters' hands 2 packs £14', and 'paid sope for 80 dozen in the knitters' hands £1 10s.' The fragment is not easy to interpret, for it is dated 1770 and at that time Waller was in the Navy, but it does imply that he had some in-terest in the manufacture of stockings under a domestic system in which the knitters were supplied with wool by the hosiers.

Whatever his sources of income may have been, Waller was cer-tainly a man of some property. In 1766 he bought an inn at Kirkby Stephen called the Mitre and in 1769 he paid £150 for Bilbow or Bilboa Croft of 3½ acres.[2] He also owned a house in Kirkby Stephen and other property which he referred to as his 'two estates'. The house was a 'large, genteel, fash'd, blue-slated dwelling house' in the Market Place of Kirkby Stephen, with a bowling green, a garden and a summer house which commanded 'a variety of beautiful and romantic prospects'. It was subject to the 'yearly ten-penny fine certain rent of 2s. 5d.', and was let, in 1776, to George Brown, linen draper. The two estates were

---

[1] The will is in the Cumberland Record Office.
[2] Lowther MSS., Manor of Kirkby Stephen, Verdicts (Cumberland Record Office); Hallam MSS. (Westmorland Record Office).

Coat Gill and Light Trees. The former was in Langdale in the parish of Orton and comprised two dwelling houses, about 150 acres of land, and rights of common. It adjoined the River Lune, which abounded 'with fine trout', and was let for 40 guineas a year. Much of Coat Gill was freehold, subject to a rent of 4d. p.a., but the rest was customary, paying a fine certain rent of £1 10s. 6d. p.a., except for two small parcels which paid an arbitrary rent of 3¾d. to Sir James Lowther. Light Trees was in Stainmoredale in the parish of Brough; it comprised two houses and about 100 acres of land which, in the timeless language of the farm advertisement, was 'well fenced and watered'. There was unlimited right of common on Stainmore and great prospects of improvement, 'there being plenty of coal and limestone in the premises'. Light Trees was let for 60 guineas a year; it was a customary estate of inheritance, subject to the payment of an unspecified fine certain rent to the Earl of Thanet.[1]

Abraham Dent administered this property for Waller, who seems to have sold much of it in 1776, but he did not sell the inn until 1805,[2] and he bought some houses in Kirkby Stephen in 1788 for £120.[3] It is impossible to tell how Waller acquired this property. He was not an eldest son, and in any case his father was alive until 1774. His father was a carpenter; it was possible to be a prosperous carpenter, but Waller's letters to Dent show that his parents were in straitened circumstances. He may have inherited property, or invested the profits of his naval career in it, or acquired it by marriage. On 20 September 1763 he married Isabella Barnett of Kirkby Stephen. The Barnetts were as thick on the ground as the Dents and the Wallers. Isabella was probably the daughter of Edward Barnett, a local butcher who died about the end of 1765 and whose will shows that he was a man of some substance.[4] Waller had only one child by the marriage, a son John, the 'Do' of the letters, who was born in 1765 and died in 1773. Isabella died three years later.

John Waller seems to have entered the Navy as purser of the *Blenheim* in December 1762.[5] He later transferred, by exchange, to the *Somerset*.[6] The purser was a warrant officer of ward-room rank; the pay

[1] These particulars are taken from the advertisement of sale in *The Newcastle Chronicle*, 22 June 1776.

[2] Lowther MSS., Manor of Kirkby Stephen, Manor Court Book, 1778–1810, f. 314 (Cumberland Record Office).

[3] Hallam MSS. (Westmorland Record Office).

[4] The will is in the Cumberland Record Office.

[5] Admiralty. Ships' Musters, Series I 5112.   [6] Ibid., 7894.

was small,[1] but the perquisites could be large, for the purser was entitled to a commission on the provisions issued and on the slop clothing that passed through his hands. He had to provide sureties, either from himself or his friends, before entering on his pursery.[2] It may have been mere coincidence that Waller sold two houses and a garden in October 1762,[3] but the sale may have been to raise money to equip himself for his naval career. That career involved residence in the south, and Waller never returned to live at Kirkby Stephen. In 1788 he was living at Park in Cornwall, and in 1805, when he sold the Mitre inn, he was described as 'of Park in Cornwall, esquire'.[4] He continued to live at Park in the parish of Landulph until his death in 1808.

Waller's will was made on 30 July 1808 and proved in London on 22 December of the same year.[5] It reveals, not only Waller's wealth, but also his attitude towards his nephews, which is hinted at in his letters. Waller made bequests amounting to about £2,455 in cash and £14,700 in 4 per cent Consols, which were to be administered by two trustees in Cornwall, who were to sell his property there, and three trustees in Westmorland. The Cornish trustees, William Dansey, an attorney of Cullington and James Gilbard of Boxhill, Devon, were to get £100 each for their pains; the Westmorland trustees, The Rev. John Waller of Appleby, The Rev. Lancelot Bellas of Brough and John Jackson of Kirkby Stephen, were to have 100 guineas each and 5 guineas for a ring. If any of the Westmorland trustees declined to act or died, the others could appoint a new trustee, who was not, however, to be one of Waller's nephews. The Devon bequests included £800 of 4 per cent Consols and some furniture and plate to Waller's housekeeper, Ann Susannah Collings, in consideration of her long service, care and fidelity, and £20 to each of his two servants. The Devon and Exeter Hospital received 20 guineas, the Plymouth Dispensary 10 guineas, and the Patriotic Society of London £300 for the benefit of poor widows and children of naval officers and seamen. Finally the rector, churchwardens and overseers of the parish of Landulph were left a sum for the poor, which Waller surprisingly failed to specify.

The Westmorland bequests were larger and more interesting.

---

[1] Between 10 March and 30 September 1777 Waller's 'neat wages' as purser came to £24 5s. 4d. (Admiralty, Ships' Pay Books, Treasurer's Series II 84).

[2] M. Lewis, *A social History of the Navy, 1793–1815*, pp. 235, 240, 246–50. Mr. Lewis gives John Waller as an example of a purser who prospered.

[3] Lowther MSS., Manor of Kirkby Stephen, Verdicts (Cumberland Record Office).   [4] Ibid., Manor Court Book, 1778–1810, f. 314.

[5] Prerogative Court of Canterbury, Ely 1002 (1808).

Waller's three nephews, Smithson, John and Robert Waller, were left the proverbial shilling, but John's children were to have £700 of 4 per cent Consols equally divided between them, and Robert's children, born or to be born to his present wife, were to share £6,000 of 4 per cent Consols at the age of 21 or at marriage. Out of this £6,000 Robert Waller's mother was to receive an annuity of £60 for life. Similarly Thomas Attlay, the only son of Waller's late niece Elizabeth Attlay, was left 1s., but his children received £700. Finally John Burn, the orphaned son of Lancelot Waller's daughter Frances, received £6,000 of 4 per cent Consols, from the interest of which some small annuities were to be paid, including £20 p.a. to Edward Barnett, the brother of Waller's late wife, as an affectionate remembrance. No doubt these bequests disappointed Waller's nephews, for some of them had anticipated his death by borrowing £300 from John Robson of Brough at a high rate of interest. This sum and the interest were to be paid on Waller's death. Though Waller disapproved of this usurious transaction, 'from humanity' he bequeathed that sum with interest to Robson. The money was to be provided by the sale of his house at Kirkby Stephen immediately after the death of his sister-in law[1] who inhabited it, for the house had long been a place of resort and rendezvous 'for idle relatives'.

Waller clearly disapproved of his nephews, one of whom, probably Smithson, he denounced as a scoundrel in 1777. There is little doubt that he sold his copyhold estate in 1776 partly to prevent it from being inherited by Smithson on his death. The grounds of this disapproval, especially in the case of John and Robert, are not apparent. Though Waller disapproved of his nephews, he retained an affection for their and his native place. He had a 'respect and veneration' for Kirkby Stephen, 'altho in a manner forbidden from it', and showed that respect in his will. He left £1,000 of 4 per cent Consols to the vicar, churchwardens and overseers of the poor of the parish of Kirkby Stephen, the interest from which was to be distributed among the poor every half year. He also left £200 of 4 per cent Consols to trustees 'for the erection of piazzas against the church wall of the said parish as a shelter for the people going to and returning from church in rainy weather also for the benefit of the market people'. The piazzas, or cloisters as they are called, were built in a classical style and were opened in 1810. It is still possible to shelter in them and to wonder where the money really came from.

Waller's letters to Abraham Dent deal largely with his property, his

---

[1] Lancelot Waller's widow.

financial worries and his family cares. They do not say much about the Royal Navy or about national concerns. They throw some light on both Waller and Dent and on the circle of their friends and relations in Kirkby Stephen. They are best left to speak for themselves.

THE LETTERS

John Waller, ?Plymouth, to Abraham Dent, Kirkby Stephen, 19 Oct. 1770.

Kirkby Stephen,[1] 19 Oct. 1770

Dear Sir[2]

I am favour'd with yours, giving an account of the things sent us, which I cou'd wish was here, as I have taken a little house, bought a few usefull things and only want what you have forwarded. Bedding I have borrow'd till my own arrives. An amazing number of little usefull things, tho' necessary only for a small house, you know runs away with money, insomuch that I am now in debt for some of them, therefore must beg for a remittance as soon as possible, for ready money is the word here.

Matters in regard to peace or war still remains doubtfull, and in my opinion will do so till the Parliament meets, which is the 13th of next month—many think a war unavoidable.[3] However, as things turn'd out and now remains, I think it was lucky we were not sett out for the North, because I might perhaps been oblig'd to return again into the West this winter, which wou'd have been very disagreeable. Merrill's affair I think you have done for the best. Is the note of hand to be discharg'd at any particular time? Let Sandwath as you think best. We are very sorry to hear of poor Miss Rudd's death[4]—these things will happen. Tell Holmes that I wou'd not have him to think of going to sea till there is a certainty of a war, I mean a declaration of it, and then a word from Colonel Robinson to a friend at the Admiralty will get him into a fine 74. Poor Kinsey, I am sorry for him, as I believe his gloomy letter proceeds from the loss of poor Miss R-dd. I think he has done right in making a visit to Mr. Moor, who is a very worthy man. We are

[1] Clearly a mistake; the contents of the letter suggest that it was written from Plymouth.

[2] Waller usually addressed Dent as 'Dear Dent'.

[3] War with Spain over the Falkland Islands was in fact avoided when England and Spain reached agreement on the Islands in 1771.

[4] Isabella, daughter of Thomas Rudd, apothecary, was buried on 4 October 1770.

sorry to find the bad harvest you have had; it was rather backward here, but has been well got and plenty of it. As to the hop affair; they I find have had a rise, but will certainly be cheap, and wou'd not have you think of me now, as I am in a very unsettled state. God knows how things will turn out. The account between me and Mr. Barnett[1] which you have sent, I have look'd over and beleive to be right, but I would have Mr. Barnett satisfied that it is so. The carriage you have left a blank, for the goods sent, till I went away. You may easily make a charge for it from the last leaf or two on the leidger. I wrote you a letter about a fortnight since, but I do not find that you have received it. I have a particular friend here just now with me, who I wish I cou'd furnish with a firkin of butter more or half a one might do. If you can procure it, please to do so, and I shall be oblig'd to you. At Martinmas you will please to settle with my tenants and put down as you'll see in the estate book of disbursements, Coatgill for 1 year's rent, but there will be a deduction of the usual taxes and about £19 for walling; but mind to charge them in future for the interest of that sum, and they owe me 5s. 3d. for half of the lease drawn out by Mr. Fawcett.[2] Johny Eubank and Henry Longrigg will settle with you before this month is out for Whitsuntide rent, Tom Moss for half a year's rent up town, Mr. Tunstall for interest of £100 at £4 4s. 0d.[3] due at Martinmas, and Robert Bell is to pay you £20.

I think I told you in my last letter that I found your account to be very right, and how to dispose of any liquor in the cellar, sugar hanging up and tea in the kitchen corner cupboard, but I fear you did not receive the said letter, as you do not mention it. The ballance of your account in my favour is £54 9s. 0d. Please to send me a draught for £40[4] and the remainder will serve for matters that you may disburse for me, and as soon as Mr. Barnett can send me a bill for £40 not £50 to pay Mr. Toulmin, I will be oblig'd to him. Bell is very well. Do[5] had the other day a touch of last autumn's complaint, but I hope is going off again. Tell Father, Mother and Aunt to be as happy as possible, as I hope all will turn out well, and we all join in duty and respects to them, yours, Mr. Barnett and all friends in general, being very truly, Dear Sir,

Yours Affectionately
J. Waller

[1] Presumably his brother-in-law, John Barnett.
[2] Presumably James Fawcett, the attorney.
[3] In 1777 Mrs. Tunstall was paying the interest.
[4] This was done on 23 Oct. by a bill for £40 on Harley & Hillman.
[5] The pet name for his son John.

P.S. When I last wrote to Dr. Chaytor[1] I wrote to you also. In my last letter I begged you would have the register at Kendal search'd for the age of Thomas Richardson, son of Edward and Dorothy Richardson, who he beleives was baptiz'd in December 1707. Please to write to Peder or get young Tommy Pearson to do it and pay the expence, which you will let me know and I shall get here.

P.S. Compliments to Mrs. and Dr. Rudd and would be glad to know how they are. How is Isbel?[2] Sarah[3] sends her love.

John Waller, Plymouth, to Abraham Dent, Kirkby Stephen, 29 Jan. 1770 [1771][4]

I am just now favour'd with yours, and am glad to find you are all so well. I make no doubt how much trouble the loss of Lanty[5] has occasion'd to my Father, Mother and Aunt, but alas, we must all submit to the dispensations of providence. I assure you I never felt so much on any occasion before. On the otherside, you have a prescription for my poor Mother from Dr. Musgrave.[6] I wish it may be of service, but you know my Mother's old age, and nature will wear out, however I pray God she may receive benefit from it and 'ere long perhaps I may chance to see her. I am now glad you have not let the house, as my stay longer here than till September next is very uncertain, because you must have heard 'ere this of the sudden stroke made by our famous M——y; peace with Spain, I fear (with too much reason) a most disgracefull one, at the expence of two or three millions, and all for having a barren rock restor'd to us. Matters were come to such a crisis that war or peace was the word—but the most sensible think it is only a poor paltry patch'd up thing, and therefore won't last above a twelve month, however by September we shall know, and then be able to judge what to do. The *Queen* was order'd to fit and indeed is still fitting out, but I suppose will soon be put a stop to, otherwise I was to have exchang'd into her. This being the case dear Dent, do not make yourself uneasy about the money, because if I shou'd want it I will make a shift till Robert Moss pays you, or perhaps I may not then want it. You see how

[1] Henry Chaytor, Ll.D., vicar of Kirkby Stephen.
[2] Probably Isabel Dent, Dent's maid servant.
[3] The Wallers' maid servant.
[4] The reference to peace with Spain shows that the letter should be dated 1771.
[5] Presumably Lancelot, the son of Lancelot Waller; he was baptised on 18 Dec. 1757, but he does not seem to have been buried at Kirkby Stephen.
[6] The prescription has been cut out of the letter.

precarious the times are. Remember on the 1st of March to make Mr. Kinsey's account out, and send me on the half of a sheet of paper, for my enclosing to Sir Charles putting over the top Disburs'd by Mr. Waller for Mr. Kinsey; and at the bottom Receiv'd the above, by Charles Kinsey.[1] This will be the sum I shall want for some time.

Please do send my spurs and stockings as soon as you can to my brother, who I wrote to this day and sent a parcel of tobacco for my Father and Mother and a lump of fine Castile soap from Mrs. Waller for my Aunt to wash her hands with. My love to Betty Moreland[2] and tell her I shall not forget her. Please my compliments to Mr. Brathwaite and Doctor Chaytor's family. I am glad to hear the latter has so good a prospect. He is now in the best channel of preferment in England. Tunstall I beleive is appointed to the *Orford* and if so, she is going to the East Indies with several other ships under the command of Admiral Harland.[3] I suppose at the end of three years I may have my money or else be admitted tenant, otherwise how and when can I get my cash, pray enquire into the mystery of this. On Candlemas day we purpose to drink all your healths, not having thought of the 21st instant, so that I fancy we shall celebrate our birth day at the very same time. I am glad to find my godson so good a boy, Tom will behave better by and by. Poor Betty I hope will get thro' her complaints. Do grows a fine cunning lad, says he hopes his dear Uncle, Grandfather, Grandmother, Aunt, and Mr. Dent's family are well. He prays every night for you all and longs to see you. I have enclos'd two recommendatory letters in a packet for my brother, for my Uncle Joseph,[4] which I have desir'd my brother will forward to him as soon as possible at Croglin, so wou'd have my Aunt to acquaint him of it immediately. If I shou'd go to sea, which is now very uncertain, Mrs. Waller and Do intend to come and see my Mother and you all, as it is her desire. I hope she will keep up her spirits and I will do everything I can for her. Mrs. Waller and Do joins in duty to Father, Mother, and Aunt, love to Mr. Barnett, you and your family, Ann, Kinsey, and all friends.

[1] There is no evidence on the nature of this account or on the identity of Sir Charles.

[2] In 1776–7 both Lancelot and John Waller were making regular payments to Betty Morland, who may have been a relative. In 1764 a John Morland married an Isabel Waller.

[3] Sir Robert Harland (?1715–84); he went out to the East Indies as commander-in-chief in March 1771.

[4] Perhaps Joseph Barnett, the brother of Edward Barnett.

Fragment of a letter from John Waller to Abraham Dent endorsed 'Answered April 23 1771'.

Thank God we are all exceeding well. Do grows and promises to be a very fine boy. He longs for Easter Sunday that he may be breech'd; a sett of shirts are making, and he is to appear in green on that day, but he thinks it will never come. I put into a parcell for my Aunt a letter for Mr. Brathwaite and another for Mr. Kinsey, by way of a *How do ye*, which is gone in a vessel for Sunderland, but I fear they will not get them as soon as I cou'd have wish'd, the wind being easterly, indeed Mr. Brathwaite's was only half finished. I hope he is better of the gout; pray my compliments to him and all friends. You say nothing how Mr. Kinsey goes on. I have mentioned to Sir Charles that I have heard nothing but very well. When you write again, have this letter before you. On mature consideration, as my return into the north is uncertain, and the house is now suffering from want of being . . .[1]

My best respects to Doctor Chaytor and family and all friends in general. Smithson[2] turns out a promising young man. I think, of the allowance to the old folks, you must take off 20s. a year for drink money to my Father. Whats the matter that Dr. Barnett &c. has left Wy[3] Barnetts? I thank Mrs. Dent for the hint given to my Aunt about Dr. D-y; I shou'd be glad to know what it is. Sarah and all of us desires to be remember'd to Isbel and Ann.

John Waller, Plymouth, to Abraham Dent, Kirkby Stephen, 16 April 1771.

This day I have received a letter from my old friend Captain Hughes, who commanded the *Blenheim*,[4] but now the *Somerset* a 70 gun ship, telling me that he will be glad of my company as Purser on board that ship, which is now fitting out at Blackstakes, or as some calls it, Sheerness, which I have accepted of till war shou'd happen. The Purser of her and me are only to exchange duties, so that I shall still retain the *Blenheim* for a further occasion, but am to enjoy the sole emoluments of the *Somerset* without giving a farthing, which being new, and Captain Hughes one of the oldest Captains, there is a very great probability of her being one of the Guardships at Chatham, which will be a very fine

---

[1] The rest of the sentence is cut away.   [2] Lancelot Waller's son.
[3] Willy?
[4] Edward Hughes was Captain of the *Blenheim* in 1762 when Waller succeeded Samuel More as Purser of the ship (Admiralty, Ships' Musters, Series I. 5112).

thing, as it's thought they will be upon a more respectable footing than ever before, I mean in the number of men kept on board &c., but indeed my greatest inducement of going, is on account of the worthy commander. Tomorrow I set out for London to go thro' the customary forms on such an occasion, then proceed to Chatham to fit out. It's said she with several others at that place and the Nore will soon go and join the fleet at Spithead, where the whole will be review'd, muster'd &c., and then those that are to be Guardships will be order'd to their respective ports. Bell &c. are to remain here till we know how the *Somerset* is to be destin'd, and then act accordingly, which we shall certainly know in about 6 or 7 weeks. We are all pretty well, thank God.

Now, Dear Dent, the above being how I stand circumstanc'd, and the necessity I shall be under of laying out a great deal of cash, may I beg the favour of your letting me have what cash you can conveniently spare, which I hope you will be able to do, as you say you are to receive a sum on May Day. I need not tell you how sorry I am to request this, as I fear it will put you to an inconvenience, however, shall leave it to your own management. You have heard me often say that the fitting out a ship is attended with a great expence, and therefore hope you'll excuse my troubling you. On recollecting, perhaps I may have the pleasure of seeing you, as you say you'll be in Town the beginning of May. I wish I may have that pleasure. If you can make any remittances, please to send them to Mr. Harrison, Charing Cross, or to my agent Mr. Toulmin, Crutched Fryars, and you may direct for me at the latter place, who will forward it immediately. As matters seem now to be settled between us and our enemies, I hope my Father, Mother and Aunt will make themselves easy, especially as I am going to do for the best. I hope I shall hear soon how they are, and that my Aunt will send a letter very soon here for Bell directed as usual. Do is breech'd, proves tall, pretty and genteel, and promises to be a good boy.

Please my best respects to all your family, friends and relations.

P.S. I wish you may meet with a tenant for the house.

John Waller, London, to Abraham Dent, Kirkby Stephen, 25 April 1771.

What think you of the uncertainty of human affairs? I had only just got to Town and receiv'd another letter from my worthy Captain Hughes, but a courier arrives from France and Spain, giving an account that their armaments were reducing and that all disputes were finally settled between us and them; whereupon 13 Sail of the Line and some frigates were order'd immediately to be paid off, among which is the *Somerset*, so that it was very lucky indeed that I was not got on board her or had commenc'd the least connection with her. I have just seen my friends, and intend setting out this night by the coach for Plymouth, so that what I wrote to you about, you need not be under any concern about, except, if you receive your money of Moss and shou'd come to Town, you will please to leave with Mr. Harrison 40 or £50, who I owe a part of that sum to. Please to tell my Father and family that Smithson is with Captain Graham and I hope will do very well. How he likes it, I shall not know till my return. I shall now employ myself in my little garden, read and walk about. Bell and the boy I hope will bathe.

Write soon, pray, and let us know how you all are. I hope Mr. Brathwaite has had no further complaints with the gout. I have nothing further to add than that I expect a long letter very soon, and beg you will present my best duties, love and services to where due, and accept my best wishes.

John Waller, London, to Abraham Dent, Kirkby Stephen, 14 May 1771.

I was duly favour'd with yours, for which I thank you, and am glad to hear of my friend Brathwaites alliance to your family,[1] on which I congratulate you and all.

The whole of my affairs I shall leave entirely to your management, as I know you will do the best you can and therefore shall be satisfied with it.

Mrs. Waller, Do and myself arriv'd here last night. Do has been a good deal troubled with a worm fever; he has got quit of one very large, and is now recovering with his journey, besides the shews here are very pleasing indeed. Mrs. Waller talks of bringing him down. But I must go on board the *Somerset*, being sent for again, and in a few days I expect to be on board her. She is to be a Guardship at Plymouth, with 300 men, so that it will be no bad thing. I am sorry for Mr. Brathwaite's ship the *Prince of Wales* being order'd to be paid off. A week will determine whether Mrs. Waller, Do and Sarah are to go into the North.

I am sorry in being oblig'd to desire what remittances you can make, to send them as soon as convenient to my friend Harrison, and it will much oblige me. I wish I may be so happy as to see you at Chatham, but I fear the *Somerset* will be sail'd for Plymouth before then.

[1] I have not been able to trace this alliance.

We are all glad to find you, yours and my relations and friends so very well, to whom pray our duty and best respects.

P.S. Please to mention what you think you can muster up conveniently, because I shall want a great deal of cash to fit out the ship.

John Waller, Plymouth, to Mrs. Setree, Kirkby Stephen, 6 Sept. 1771.
Dear Aunt

Mr. Dent wou'd receive a letter from me three days before this will reach you, which wou'd inform you of my safe arrival and health. Indeed I was never better in my life, but Bell had suffer'd a good deal in my absence, what with fretting about our being parted, and what with the trouble she had with the sailor Captain Hughes left with her as a guard, who immediately on our sailing fell ill with a fever, which frighten'd her and the boy into the country for a fortnight. They then return'd and the man relaps'd, so that he was ill till I came, when I sent him to the hospital, and Bell is now I hope recovering fast. As to Do, he has got quit of a great number of worms since my arrival and seems now to thrive apace. I shall be glad to hear how you all are. I am very sensible of your situation, Dear Aunt, and I scarcely know what to say on the occasion except that of my being very sensible how much I am oblig'd to you for the regard you have to my poor Mother, which I make no doubt the Lord will requite you for, and you and them shall always have my sincere prayers to the last. Pray my duty to them.

Do not fail to beg Mr. Dent will as soon as possible speak to our friends at Coatgill for 4 firkins of butter and 4 from Johny Eubank to be well work'd and such as they can recommend, one of the best to be directed to Captain Hughes in Craven Street, Strand, the rest to come here; of which if they are particularly recommended, let them have a mark. This I shall have a great dependence upon. If you can send half a firkin in addition to the above the better. Butter will be very dear here this winter.

I hope 'ere this the house is let and the sale over, and cou'd wish I had some cash, the ship affairs requiring a great deal, which I hope will answer very well. If the settee is not sold Bell desires it may be kept. Write soon and let us know all you can. Is Mrs. Barnett returned to Brough? Mr. Bailiff is hereabouts, but in no business, nor indeed can I do anything more for him. How he subsists, God knows. I am really very sorry for him. Please our love to Betty Moreland, Mr. Barnett, Mr. Dent's family, Ann, Sarah, Isbel and all friends, not forgetting

Doctor Chaytor, Doctor Rudd and Mr. Barnett's families, Mr. Kinsey, Holmes and all your neighbours, being very truly Dear Aunt

Yours affectionately
J. Waller

P.S. Tell Mr. Barnett that Bell is bravely to-day.

John Waller, Plymouth Dock, to Abraham Dent, Kirkby Stephen, Oct. 1771.[1]

I am favour'd with yours, which I can assure you gives me a great concern, because I fear you are in the same situation as myself, namely, in want of money; and I am very sorry likewise at the dismal account you give of K. Stephen, its decline in point of business and the neighbours not being agreeable to each other. In short, as you seem to lose all relish of the place and cou'd wish to be more agreeably situated, I can only say, how happy I shou'd be to assist you in a more eligible one: but in fact the times are now very bad and nothing in view that I can least depend upon, for many trades people here have fail'd of late. A war might do something, but when that will happen God knows. What you observe about going into company I think is quite right for the less it is the better, and indeed nothing but oeconomy will answer in these very hard times.

As to Doctor Barnett's looking shy, mind it not, nor follow him on my account. He has no reason to be so to us that I know of. I want nothing of him. If Haygarth will make the alterations and commence tenant at Martinmas, he may have it at £14 a year, giving security for the rent. If not, let Isbel or any poor person that is careful live in it till something offer, and as for selling it under £350 I am not willing.

I have been thinking that God knows how uncertain it is whether I shall ever live again in the North, especially as I am launch'd again into a sea life, which is so precarious, and my little boy being tender, made me ask Mr. Dan. Robinson's advice about my affairs, for after our deaths, Smithson wou'd come in for all my copyhold estates, to the predjudice of his brothers and sisters. Mr. Robinson gave me such a disagreeable an account as wou'd almost puzzle anyone, tho' I am sensible quite consistent with the customs of the manors, which are so disadvantageous to families, as almost persuades me to dispose of everything I have in the north, and place the produce in the funds, which wou'd bring me in a better interest and enable me to leave the cash as I

---

[1] Endorsed 'Answered Nov. 17 1771'.

thought best. What think you wou'd they sell well at present or not? Coatgill can dispose of when I will. Stanmore is tenanted by a tack note for a term, but I fancy it is not binding. But pray keep this at present to yourself.

I shall write this day to Mr. Brathwaite about his money, to know if he shall want it, also to my friend Harrison, on which will depend my wanting the money of you. Pray lose no time in sending me a bill, and collect the sale money without loss of time, for I am really moneyless and almost asham'd at not paying the debts I have contracted.

Between this and Martinmas you will have the rents of Coatgill, Stanmore, Tom Moss's (for a year), Tunstall's, Merril's house (and I hope £20 he promis'd) and for the hay &c. to receive, all which you must send me as soon as you can. As to the coals my Mother mentions, I know nothing of. Poor woman she must be certainly doating. But send her in a dozen load. I shall be oblig'd to you to send the butter when ready and not make a mistake again, for I paid for one firkin more than I received.

You say in a letter about Sarah as follows, '*Sarah supposes that she has had* 13 *or* 14 *guineas (but what ever you fix it at it will be very agreeable) when she was at K. Stephen*'. I wish that book had been found to have been certain about it, but if the above is right as you say that she says it is, there is only 4 guineas to be added to it, what she has had here, and the same to be subtracted from £30, six years wages.

What raisin wine there is, or the made sort, let the old folks have.

Best respects attend your family

[P.S.] I have sent a couple of handkerchiefs for my Father and Mother by way of Sunderland.

Does not Kinsey owe you something? As Tunstall's mortgage expires this time twelve months, pray can I call in my money, or must I be set tenant? I now find that I have not time to write to Mr. Brathwaite. Tell him that the *Dublin* is appointed in the room of the *Fame*, and ask him about the money I owe him.

John Waller, Plymouth Dock, to Abraham Dent, Kirkby Stephen, 20 Nov. 1771.

I shou'd certainly have wrote to you before this, but for waiting till Martinmas was over, which might enable you to send me something, for in fact since the time I can first remember, I never knew the want of money so much as at present, and I am really quite asham'd to shew myself amongst my friends at Plymouth, where I am in debt to several of the tradesmen, who I must at all events soon satisfy or else my credit will be greatly wounded. I am now living upon what little credit I can muster both as to the expences of my family and the ship, which requires no little, therefore what you can do [?for][1] me, let it be immediately. If you had [ ] wrote me, I shou'd been more satisfied [ ] sake. Why shou'd Sir Charles have so much credit, as he does not require it? You certainly had money due the 1st of Sept. last to the amount of half a years disbursements to Mr. Kinsey, who Sir Charles expected to hear of from me before this, and I in duty bound have only been waiting for your account. In short I fear Sir Charles will attribute this to neglect and may be of some disservice to me. Never, never my friend was I in such a situation as at present for want of money, which gives me much trouble. I owe my friend Harrison £100, Toulmin £80, Mr. Brathwaite £150, and £70 to the people here, and having nothing to carry on housekeeping, you may easily judge the disagreeable situation I am in, such indeed as I never before was acquainted with. Do collect all you can for me and write immediately.[2] [ ] I shall not be disappointed in the butter [ ] and that it will come soon. When you [?make] out Mr. Kinsey's account, please to do it in the same manner as usual and send it to me.

We are all pretty well and join and [sic] love and best respects to Father, Mother, Aunt, Mr. Barnett, your good family and all friends.

John Waller, Plymouth Dock, to Abraham Dent, Kirkby Stephen, 31 Jan. 1772.[3]

I am favour'd with your very *long* epistle containing all the news you cou'd think of in the space of ten minutes, the time you certainly allow'd yourself to write it in; however, in earnest you have our thanks for it, especially as we are so glad to hear that all friends are well.

I am sorry you have been so often and so greatly disappointed in the money you expected from Moss, which being you say uncertain when you will get, I therefore must beg you will settle with Mr. Brathwaite for the £150 and interest if it's not inconvenient to you, and Mr. Brathwaite is agreeable to it, as God knows when I [?shall have][4] an

[1] The square brackets show where the MS. has been torn away.
[2] On 21 November Dent remitted £120 to Waller by a bill on Harley and Hillman.
[3] Endorsed 'Answered March 6th.'
[4] The square brackets show where the MS. has been torn away.

opportunity of doing it myself, and [?it will] help something towards reducing my [?debts .On] the other hand when you have an opportunity [?of] applying to Mrs. Tunstall or to her father [ ] next time of holding Court, about the mortgage, as I cou'd wish to have it in October Court, being then due, and wou'd be more agreeable to me than being set tenant of the land, as I want to pay that sum to Harrison. The sale bill, please to send it to my brother, which he can forward any week, and with it if you please Mr. Brathwaite's note; and the account warrant by the post, with a list of those things and where put, if it is not too much trouble, all which may be of service sometime or other. In short what is so, do not dispose of. I have look'd over the butter account and found it right. The firkin of this year sent up to Captain Hughes's lady proves so bad that she can't make use of it. All ours is tollerable but not so good as that of last year. It runs very high this year. I wish you had mention'd what Granger has for carrying a firkin to Sunderland.

When you shou'd go to Coatgill or that road in the spring, give a look to the land damag'd there and hold a parley with Geordy and Bryan about securing it and know what they will do it for.

I am glad to find you have got such good tenants into my house, who I make no doubt [?will take] care of it and the garden, and I rejoice to find [ ] stand with your father-in-law Mr. Granger [ ] he has certainly done right, and I am glad [ ] him so prettily situated in the great room and [ ] you. Our best compliments to them both.

I was in hopes of writing myself to Mr. Brathwaite to tell him there was a great probability of the *Prince of Wales* being put into commission, which was talk'd of, instead of the *Intrepid* Guardship now fitting out for the East Indies, but instead of her it is the *Bellisle*, so that there is no present appearance. Tom Thomas is expected here next week in his return from Cornwall to Downton, when I expect him to dine with me, and then we shall drink his health.

We are all very well, thank God, and presents our duty to Father and Mother, and love to Aunt and all friends.

P.S. When you can conveniently raise any cash for me, do.

John Waller, Plymouth Dock, to Abraham Dent, Kirkby Stephen 15 March 1772.

I have your very kind favor inclosing Mr. Brathwaite's note for the money he lent me, who I have by this very post wrote to.

The cash between you and me never gave me the least uneasiness, farther than the great want I was in to fit out the ship, and it is very dis-agreeable to be in debt to an agent and pay 5 per cent for it. Now if this had not been the case, I am sure you had been welcome to it as long as you pleas'd. I have look'd over the account and beleive all is right. I perceive you have not got any rent or interest from Jackson or Merril yet, in which do the best you can. And as for Tunstall's money I must get you to prevail on Mr. Robinson at the May Court to pay in the £100 at the next one in October. I wonder the meaning of his wanting to see the deed.

As you seem to hint that you will be able to pay the ballance soon (*if I chuse it*), I can only say that if you shou'd get Moss's money or any other to enable you to do it, and it is not inconvenient, I will be much oblig'd to you for it, to pay what I owe. As to the interest of £278 I think you must calculate it from January 1771 to January 1772, that is one year at 10*d*.[1] As to the little remaining time of three months never mind it, for I am sure you have had trouble enough on my account, which I am much oblig'd to you for. My Aunt tells me how bad my poor Father and Mother are, who I have wrote to and desired they may want for nothing necessary. What few things are left, please to keep, except the copper, which you had best dispose of to the best advantage. It is certainly right for me to employ Geordy and Bryant upon the land lately damag'd by the floods, but at the same time I shou'd be glad to know upon what footing. I think I must get your Uncle Robert Atkin-son to inspect over them whilst upon it, and allow them what he thinks right between man and man. This certainly will be the best way.

We have been all pretty well this winter till an easterly wind came, which has affected us all, but I hope as soon as the wind changes we shall be better.

We all join in best respects to you, yours and all friends in general.

P.S. Remember us properly to Father, Mother and Aunt.

John Waller, Plymouth, to Abraham Dent, Kirkby Stephen, 10 July 1772.

I am favor'd with yours enclosing a bill for £42 7*s*. and am truly sorry to find my Mother so very feeble, to whom, my Father and Aunt, please to present my duty and love. You astonish us in regard to Miss Nelson's affairs, but we hope there is still a good chance for Doctor

---

[1] This unusual way of giving the rate of interest meant 10*d*. in the £, or a rate of $4\frac{1}{6}$ per cent.

Rudd's getting what we think he is entitled to, otherwise it will be hard indeed.

Mrs. Waller and Do still talk of coming to Kirby, that he may have schooling, which I fear must be the case, as he only gets a lesson now and then here, tho' a parting from them wou'd hurt me very much.

I have a peice of silk for Miss Dent,[1] which wou'd have been sent 'ere this but for wanting an opportunity by a collier; there is one now unloading and you may expect it 'ere long. You must give her a kiss for me with it.

I am exceeding uneasy about an education for Do, who wou'd I dare say learn very well, but here indeed we are badly off, some way or other he is frightened at the school here, and only gets a lesson when the boys are out of it.

Mrs. Waller is sorry she has not a cap she is now in hand with ready for her God daughter, which she will send as soon as done. I hope Mr. and Mrs. Brathwaite and little girl are well, who you will please to present our best respects to, and we hope Mrs. Dent, you, Father and family will accept them from Dear Dent, Yours affectionately J. Waller.
P.S. I shall always be glad you will remember us respectfully to Doctor Chaytor, Messrs. Fawcett, Doctor Rudd's and Fletcher Hill's families, also Mr. Holme, and of course brothers John and Ned. Mrs. Waller will write very soon to Mr. Barnett.
Mr. Harrison tells me he comes down next month with Mr. Marshall. You say I shall be sett tenant of Tunstall's land in October Court, but my brother says not till May next. Pray how is it?

John Waller, Plymouth, to Abraham Dent, Kirkby Stephen, 8 Aug. 1772.
I have sent a hogshead of cyder for Mr. Dan. Robinson by the *Venus* Captain Dickinson for Sunderland and desir'd my brother to take care of it as usual: at the same time a parcel directed for you containing a peice of silk for a gown for Miss Dent which I hope she will accept of with kisses from Mrs. Waller, me and Do, also a work'd cap for Miss Brathwaite and another for Miss Nelly Rudd, Mrs. Waller's god daughters; kisses also accompanies them.

When my brother was at Kirkby he mention'd that I was to be set tenant of Mr. Tunstall's house &c. next May; pray shou'd it not be in October? I hope so. The deed does not expire till the 11th of November

[1] Presumably Dent's daughter Betty, then aged 11.

next; now is that the reason it can't be done till the Court after? Do ask Mr. Jackson or Mr. Fawcett. If it can be the next Court, let it be so.

Do remember us to all enquiring friends, particularly those at Warcop and your own family.

Isabella Waller to Abraham Dent[1]
Der Brother

I am glad to hear you are so whall but very sorey to hear of my der Mother Waller's bead state of halth; pray go often and do evey thing to comfort her. I thank God I ham beter and intend to see you.

                              I am your afectenet Sister
                                        Ia Waller

Do sends his duty to Grand Father, Grand Mother, Aunt Setree, Uncle John and all friends.[2]

John Waller, Portsmouth, to Abraham Dent, Kirkby Stephen, 19 May 1773.

As I find we shall stay here for some little time, I must beg the favour you will be so good as send me so soon as you have received the Whitsuntide rents from Coat Gill a bill, taking care to pay John Eubank out of the arrears due to me for what work he does, agreeable to my letter dated the beginning of April, relating to the raising of cash for building &c.

Mrs. Waller and my little boy are now at Clapham for the benefit of his schooling and being more agreeable to them during my absence in case of going abroad, which seems uncertain. In short the times are ticklish, and by the last accounts it's thought that Sir Charles Saunders will at last go to the Mediterranean.[3] We have orders one day and countermanded next. Various inconsistent things have happen'd to us of late more than ever was known since the memory of man, which shews the instability of the news received from abroad, for our enemies are sometimes arming and then pretend to disarm. However it is, I want to have a bill sent every half year to Clapham or else to Mr. Toulmin my agent, which I think will be the better way, as then Mrs. Waller being so near can soon get cash.

---

[1] Written at the foot of the preceding letter.
[2] Apparently in Do's handwriting.
[3] Sir Charles Saunders (?1713–1775) was nominated to the command in the Mediterranean on 23 April 1773, but he did not take up the command.

Do write me soon and let me hear how my Father and Mother are and Aunt. I shall write to them 'ere long.

I have just now received a line from Clapham saying they are all very well. How does Mr. Brathwaite? What does he intend in case of a war? Many think it will break out 'ere long, but my sentiments are not so. Remember me affectionately up town, best respects to your fireside and all friends.

P.S. Its beleiv'd His Majesty will be here very soon to see the Fleet. My Aunt mentions that Smithson is settled at Barnard Castle. I have wrote to him this post. Pray how goes he on?
By the inclos'd you will see what Mr. Robinson says.

John Waller, Plymouth, to Abraham Dent, Kirkby Stephen, 6 Aug. 1773.

On the situation of affairs being very peaceable and likely to continue, together with Mrs. Waller and John's not chusing to part from each other, on account of his going to school, I sent for them here, where they arriv'd the day before yesterday very well but much fatigu'd. I expected you wou'd have wrote before this, but now hope to have that pleasure very soon. Both join in love to Mr. Barnett, respects to you and yours, Mr. Brathwaite &c., and please to tell him that I have been at Fowey to see Tom Thomas, who is very well and intends to write him soon.

P.S. Please to send the enclos'd to my Aunt.

John Waller, Plymouth, to Abraham Dent, Kirkby Stephen, 22 Aug. 1773.

I wrote to you about three weeks since in a frank and inclos'd a letter for my Aunt, who tells me by a letter yesterday that she has not had a line for some months, neither from me or Bell, so that I must suppose the letter miscarried. Bell and John has been here three weeks, and thank God are both with me very well. I am sorry you have not now and then mention'd how Mr. Kinsey is, as sometimes I have been asked by Sir Charles's friends how he is, but you have never been so good as say anything, so that I have been quite at a loss in that respect. In fact it looks as if I had quite disclaim'd Mr. Kinsey and Sir Charles. I wrote to you twice on this head, but you never answer things. Indeed I am afraid you have so much business of your own to manage, that mine must

N

interfere with it, and if so, beg you will let me take it out of your hands.
I know you have a great deal of trouble on my account and I also know
you have a very great deal of your own, so that mine in some measure
must take up more of your attention than you can conveniently
spare.

Bell and John joins in best respects to you and Mrs. Dent, Mr. Dent,
your family and all friends, those at Warcop in particular.

P.S. Our love to Mr. Barnett, are glad to hear he is well. Compliments
to Ann. Mrs. Waller saw Mr. Wright in Town who was very well. You
never told me if you gave John Taylor a drink. In short I may as well
not write at all.

John Waller, Plymouth, to Abraham Dent, Kirkby Stephen, 26 Sept.
1773.

I have received your letter and find that Mr. Harrison has paid to Mr.
Toulmin a ballance of £14 odd.[1] And now as the last account you sent
me makes me no further acquainted with my affairs than Martinmas
1771, must beg you will not fail to send it at Martinmas next, so soon as
you have collected the rents and settled with John Eubank for the house
&c., who I now enclose a line to for that purpose and have desir'd him
to pay in course with those at Coat Gill &c. for the future, so I make no
doubt the house will be paid for with the Whitsuntide and Martinmas
rents, and from Martinmas he must pay 40s. a year more for interest, if it
amounts to £40, but I hope it will be far less. He has had the whole
management of it to himself, but I confide much in his honesty, and I
hope everything is done in a proper and workmanlike manner.

I have also enclosed a line for George Harrison about the cart house,
which I shou'd be glad your uncle wou'd be so good as look at, as I
have no objection to its being properly secur'd, tho' I am quite tir'd of
repairs. As I shall expect some money the latter end of November so I
must get you to spur up those that are indebted to me, for I am really in
great want of cash. If you remember, I enclos'd you a note from Mr.
Dan Robinson, saying that I might have the letting of Tunstall's house
and land, so as to pay myself and the remainder pay to Mrs. Tunstall,
but if she pays the four guineas a year regularly I have no objection
to her management, tho' in strictness, as I am tenant, so I can do as I
please.

[1] In July 1773 Richard Harrison paid £14 8s. 2d. to Toulmin, part of which
was noted as paid to Mrs. Waller.

The total of the last account between us is thus, which you sent me.

Mr. Waller Dr.			Cr.		
£317 7s. 5½d.			402	8	2
By interest of £278 at 10d.			11	11	8
			413	19	10
			317	7	5½
Ballance due Mr. Waller			97	12	4½

Mrs. Waller and John are both in tollerable health and join with me in most affectionate duty and love to Father, Mother and Aunt.

You say you have forgot many things that you intended to say. I say I am not now a bit disappointed in that respect, for you never answer one thing I write about, however you have all our best wishes for all your good healths and welfare, best compliments to Doctor Chaytor, who I am much oblig'd to for his kind letter, Mr. Brathwaite and all enquiring friends.

[P.S.] I shall write a line 'ere long to Doctor Chaytor. Mrs. Waller writes a line to Mr. Barnet on the frank and returns thanks with compliments to Ann and all friends.

John Waller, Kensington, to Abraham Dent, Kirkby Stephen, 7 Dec. 1773.

I have just now received the favour of yours and am very unhappy to hear of my poor Father's being so ill. I now am so involv'd in the bitterest affliction that I am prepar'd for any other that may come, so that I pray to God to have mercy on the poor old folks, and make them resign'd to him, whenever he shou'd think fit to call them, and yet, tho' they have liv'd to an extraordinary age, a parting from so strong a tye of blood is truly affecting. I now experience it in truth by my late dreadfull loss.[1] Pray God send us both strength and comfort to bear the shock.

I find that Mr. Dennison's land has sold well, which I am glad of for the family sake. In regard to my own, I shall not think about disposing of it till there is a good opportunity. When there is I shall be ready to do so, and if anything shou'd offer in regard to the house I shall have no objection to sell it. Between you and me, Mr. Fawcett has apply'd about it, but I have reason to think he wants it for far below the value,

---

[1] The death of his son John.

so that it shall remain as it is, till their [*sic*] is a chearful bidder, or I come to end my days at Kirby.

Our best respects to Doctor Chaytor and his lady, who we most sincerely congratulate on his promotion.

As to coming into the North, I fear it will not be in my power for some time, and if it was now so, I shou'd only add greif to a very great one on my parting with the old folks. As I think I shall never be more happy again in this world, I sometimes am inclin'd to come and end my days with you, at others, that the giving up of my views in the Navy wou'd be absurd and ridiculous, so that I am all inconsistency, owing a great deal I beleive to the unhappiness I labour under.

As I dare say you will see John Eubank and George to settle, be so good as to send me my account and let me know the state of my affairs. John Eubank is to settle for a whole year against the house he has built, and please to collect all in you can.

Tell my Aunt that I have been to wait on Mr. Raincock today, who was not in Town, so that I shall see him tomorrow. I am sorry for her case, as the above gentleman does not bear the best of characters, however I shall do the best I can for her. It must be done as moving and gentle as possible.

I am sorry to find our friends at Warcop in so weak a condition, but hope now are better. I shall present your respects to Mr. Harrison who I din'd with and Joseph Fothergill the other day. Joseph's law affair is over and he tells me is ended as well as he expected.

Remember us dutifully to Father and Mother, love to Aunt, Mr. Barnett, your family and friends.

P.S. Mr. Wright lives close to Kensington. We dined with him today. He lives cleverly and desires to have his Father the usual quantity of hams, and that you will send to H. Eubank a ten gallon cask of ale for Christmas. Do the same for me to the good old folks.

John Waller, Plymouth, to Abraham Dent, Kirkby Stephen, 21 Jan. 1774.

Your letter to Kensington I have this moment received. We came from thence the 4th as I told my Aunt we shou'd do, and have been here this fortnight. I am now again plung'd into grief at the account you give of the situation of my Father, who I fear by this is no more, if so, I shall not fail to pray to God he may have a happy change. Alas of late how much I have felt of the most poignant sorrow, and now no likely of any alleviation, but a continuation of it. But if my poor Father is still alive as I hope he is, I cou'd wish whenever the Lord shall please to take him, that his funeral be perform'd decently with hatbands and gloves to the bearers as customary and in such manner as my Mother, Aunt and you shall judge proper. I hope my poor Mother[1] and Aunt are well and will take care of themselves, especially on the change that is likely to happen.

Mrs. Waller has been very ill in a cold, is now better, but with me fretts and grieves much, for our dear loving boy has left such everlasting remembrances, that nothing can efface them, so that a great deal of philosophy, at least as much as we can muster, is put to the tryal to alleviate our distress. Good God what unhappy mortals mankind are.

I hope you are 'ere this better of your cold and that Mrs. Dent and all the family are well. Nothing but colds all over Europe, with fevers, sore throats &c., which has carried many off.

Inclosed you have a letter for my Aunt in regard to her affair with Mr. Raincock, and beg you will present.

Mrs. Waller and my best respects to Mrs. Dent, family and friends.

P.S. In your next be so good as tell me what the tenants say, and what the Langdale folks have done about Orton Moor.

John Waller, Plymouth, to Abraham Dent, Kirkby Stephen, 25 Feb. 1774.

I am just now favour'd with a letter from my brother telling me of his having been at Kirby and the sorrowful situation he found my poor Father in, which with the account of their parting has greatly affected me. Alas poor old man how I feel for him, and I pray God will please to assist and releive him from such pain and distress.

I have given an invitation to my poor Aunt to live with us as long as she pleases, and in case she shou'd not dare to undertake so long a journey and shou'd chuse to live with her sister, who my brother says intends to move to Kirby in April, I have offer'd them Bilbow Croft to keep a couple of cows, as I find it is their plan to have some, which they are wellcome to for nothing.

What think you of the *Somerset* and another ship having orders to prepare for sea with all expedition, which we are now very busy about? It is suppos'd we are intended for Boston in North America, on account of the inhabitants there being very troublesome, but however some

---

[1] His mother was buried at Kirkby Stephen on 6 February 1774; she was 85 years old.

think we shall not get away, or if we do, there is no doubt we shall get back before winter.

My brother tells me that he has wrote to Mr. Ed. Dixon to pay off some money that was due to my Father, in order to pay the funeral expences, and that he has wrote to you about it. Will you be so good as to let me hear from you by return of the post letting me know how my poor Father[1] is, lest we shou'd leave England, sending at the same time the account between us, because I want to leave my affairs as clear as possible, so beg you will not fail; and I shall take it as a favour you will ask Doctor Rudd, Mr. Holmes, Mr. Leonard Barnett or any other you think likely, that has any of my books, particularly the three volumes of the Universal History, which are wanting out of the twenty I had at Kirby. I wonder you did not miss them when they were pack'd up.

Please to present our best respects to all friends in general.

John Waller, Plymouth, to Abraham Dent, Kirkby Stephen, 8 April 1774.

I beg the favour you will be so good as forward the enclos'd.

We have now got orders to remain in England here and as a Guardship as before, the Ministry thinking, we fancy, that smaller ships will do the business in America, so that my Aunt may be a little satisfied on that account; and as I suppose you both imagin'd we were sail'd, I thought it proper to give you a line that I shall be glad to hear from both of you, and that you will let me know if what I wrote last is right. We are both tollerable well thank God, but still grieving much. Pray make our best love and respects to Mrs. Dent, family, Aunt and all our friends.

P.S. Love to Mr. Barnett and compliments to Ann.
I wish my Aunt wou'd send us a couple of looking glasses, and there is a very small picture of the Crucifixion of our Saviour which I want to get fram'd.
Mrs. Waller begs the favour you will make for her a cag of cowslip wine and send to Sunderland and make a charge.

John Waller, Plymouth, to Abraham Dent, Kirkby Stephen, 15 May 1774.

This day I received a letter from my Aunt and beg you will be so good

---

[1] His father was buried at Kirkby Stephen on the day this letter was written, 25 Feb. 1774; he was 82 years old.

as send the enclos'd answer, as well as those which accompanies it. I received your last letter dated the 10th April and really cannot at present flatter myself in the least with the pleasure of seeing you in the North, nor do I know when I shall have that happiness. I do not know why the Stanmore tenants shou'd not pay as well as those at Coat Gill as the tack notes are the same, at least they do not pay agreeable to the promise made in them, so that they have no right of being so exact, and sooner than their doing so, wou'd oblige them to give up their farms. I can scarcely beleive them, because I fancy they may give them up any year they please, if they did not answer their purpose. Surely Johnny Eubank did not give himself that *air* in saying so, because I have often befriended him. As to my being concern'd in Chancery with all those that subscrib'd in the Town, I must beg to be excus'd as I do not chuse to have any concern in it, nor was I ever spoke to about it.[1]

My Aunt tells me you are building a brewery in the Market Place, which I think you wou'd not do if the business did not answer. I heartily wish it may and everything that is good to you. I hope Mr. Brathwaite and Dr. Rudd are both better than when you wrote last and their families are well. Please our best respects to Mrs. Dent and all yours, friends and relations in general. Mr. Barnett in particular. How does your hosiery go? I hope very well.

Mrs. Waller joins in best respects.

P.S. Does the woodwork of the house without want painting? I think it shou'd be done immediately by Tommy Atkinson, who you will perceive is in my debt by a note of hand you have in your hands amongst my papers.

Mrs. Waller begs to have a box of such pills as he us'd to take himself at night, and please to pay for them. Mr. Nelson's family here desires their compliments to you and their uncle's family.

John Waller, Liverpool, to Abraham Dent, Kirkby Stephen, 23 Feb. 1775.[2]

I wrote some time ago to my Aunt Citry but have had no answer which makes me afraid she is not well. I shou'd be glad to hear from you and that you wou'd be so good as forward me all the letters that

---

[1] This seems to have been a tithe case between the local landowners and Henry Chaytor, vicar of Kirkby Stephen (Hallam MSS. Westmorland Record Office).

[2] Neither the signature nor the rest of the letter appears to be in Waller's handwriting.

come for me from abroad. Pray how are Mrs. Dixon, Dr. Barnett and Miss Rudd? Pray give my compliments to Mrs. Dent and all friends and love to relations.

P.S. Must beg you to forward me immediately a barrel of raisin wine.

John Waller, Plymouth, to Abraham Dent, Kirkby Stephen, 7 April 1776.

I propose with Mrs. Waller to set off for London this day week, where I shall tarry about ten days, and as you seem'd to hint that you shou'd soon be there and desirous to have a meeting, so I shall hope for that pleasure. I did intend to write sooner, but one thing or another entirely prevented me, however I hope my Aunt or Mr. Fawcett has inform'd you 'ere this of my intentions to be there about the middle of this month, which I hope will be a means of your contriving to be there about the same time.

That you let Light Trees in the best manner you cou'd and as for yourself, I never the least doubted. As Smithson has behav'd so very ill, I am come to a resolution of disposing of both estates, and I was afraid it cou'd not be so well done as you had let it for three years. My mentioning that you had no right to do so, without my power of attorney, was not in contempt of what you had done, but in order, that in case Bousfield had not taken possession[1], to make him desist from it, and so not be prevented from disposing of it this summer.

Please to inform yourself in everything how I had best act upon this occasion and then we can talk it over in Town.

Mrs. Waller joins in best respects to you, Mrs. Dent, family and all friends.

John Waller, London, to Abraham Dent, Kirkby Stephen, 14 May 1776.

I am favour'd with yours and shall leave you to judge for the best respecting Light Trees, and you may tell Henry Longrigg that I am sorry matters have so happen'd as to send him from thence, but please to enquire what is best to be done.

I am glad to find that there is a liklihood of a sale for the two estates and house, for I find some in London have been enquiring about the

---

[1] He appears to have taken possession, for John Bousfield was paying rent for Light Trees in 1776–7.

premisses, so that if it is possible I will get down at the sales. I wrote to
Mr. Fawcett to have an advertizement prepar'd and put in the New
Castle papers, to be inserted once or twice a month till the time of the
sale in August which I think will do with advertizements put up in all
the neighbouring towns.[1] When the days are fixt upon for the sale,
which I wou'd only have about a day or two asunder, I shou'd be glad
to know them that I may (if possible) be there. I have just now received
a letter from Geo. Harrison, who with some other wants to purchase
Coat Gill and to know if he can have his lease out, all which I have
answer'd in a letter to Mr. Fawcett; that is, in order to give him a chance
for the upper estate, it will be tried for that purpose; but as to the remaining part of the lease, it possibly cannot be in their possession, considering they have had 8 years and was liable from the nature of it to be
sold every year since that time, so that they must excuse the circumstances of my being oblig'd to dispose of it. I am sure, everything in my
power that is reasonable I shou'd be glad to favour them in, but a publick sale I propose for everything.

I must beg the favour you will acquaint Mr. Wm. Greer on the
receipt of this, that I shou'd have answered his letter before now, if I had
not been out of Town, and that I think it a very extra-ordinary one, to
demand of me for his neice £14 10s. 11d., which happen'd near twenty
years ago, and which, if he had any right of claiming, why did he not
demand it of her father, as he says it was sometime before his death. By
his account he demands 7 months board; Mrs. Waller says she was on a
visit about three months, absolutely denies borrowing any money, and
says she brought in return for the above visit, home to Kirby, his two
sons, Billy and Jacky, where they had learning and the former liv'd
with her father two years, so that she thinks his demand very extraordinary indeed. For my own part I know nothing of it and think that
if anything had been due to Mr. Greer, he shou'd have settled with old
Mr. Barnett, as being an affair of his, not mine; besides I think it very
extraordinary he shou'd not when at Kirby, if he had anything to
demand of me, not to do it then, when Mrs. Waller and me saw him
every day. In short let him know that his menacing letter I defy, at the
same time no person is more willing to do justice than myself.

As soon as there is an advertizement in the N. Castle papers, please
to cut it out and send me. I suppose about the middle of August will be
the time of sale. We propose setting out for Plymouth in four days, so

[1] James Ashburner of Kendal charged 6s. 6d. for these sale bills. The sale was
advertised in *The Newcastle Chronicle* of 22 June, 6 and 27 July 1776.

that you may direct for me as usual. Please my best respects to Mrs. Dent and family, my Aunt, Mr. Fawcett &c. &c.

[P.S.] Mrs. Waller says you are a fine man not to mention whether we are likely to have a servant or not from Kirby. We wrote to my Aunt but she never answer'd my letter. We have no servant. Memo.[1] In the advertizement of Light Trees, 'the small estate of it, to be enter'd upon at mid-April next', this should be inserted.

John Waller, Plymouth, to Abraham Dent, Kirkby Stephen, 4 June 1776.

We are just return'd from Town quite fatigu'd, with empty pockets, running deeply into debt and no signs of being able to pay God knows when; therefore must beg you will releive me in such distress.

Being a good deal fatigu'd I can only present Mrs. Waller's compliments with mine to you and yours.

Abraham Dent, Kirkby Stephen, to John Waller, 2 July 1776.[2]

Kirkby Stephen, July 2nd 1776

Dear Waller

I received yours of the 4th June; am glad to hear you are safe arrived at Plymouth. I hope by this time you are both recovered of the fatigue of the journey and will be able to undertake a trip to Westmorland at the time of the sale of your estates. I shall be very happy to see you. I am very sorry I cannot at this time inclose you a draft as I cou'd have wished but shall be able to do the whole in August for you, as I wou'd not willingly draw on my friends in London but at the usual credit. I hope you received mine of the 4th June. Inclosed you have an advertisement which I cut from the N C paper as you desired. Betty Fothergill, Dick's daughter, has been about 10 days at Sunderland and your brother says he hopes their [sic] will be a ship sailing for Plymouth very soon. I gave her on your account $2\frac{1}{2}$ guineas to pay for her passage &c. Mrs. Seetry desires her love and expects a line from you soon. Its said Mr. Kinsey and Miss Rudd is going to be marryed in London.[3] Mr. and Mrs.

---

[1] Written at the head of the letter, below the address.

[2] A draft or copy written on the back of the preceding letter.

[3] Charles Kinsey of St. Pancras, Middlesex, gentleman, aged 26 married Elizabeth Rudd, aged 24, on 21 December 1776 at Kirkby Stephen. Dent was a witness.

Fawcett desire their compliments. Accept the same from me and my family.

I am Dear Waller
Yours affectionately
A. Dent

John Waller, Plymouth, to Abraham Dent, Kirkby Stephen, 23 July 1776.

Before this, you will have heard of the loss of my poor Mrs. Waller, which melancholy event has thrown me into the deepest and bitterest affliction, and therefore hope you will excuse my entering into particulars so disagreeable to relate; but indeed you may principally inform yourself by a letter I sent her brother Mr. John Barnett the last post.

I certainly did intend to be at the sale, if poor Mrs. Waller's bad state of health had not prevented it, who urg'd it much, but alas she is no more. I am strongly advised by Mr. Nelson and more of my friends to go down with him by way of a change, but really at present I do not know whether my present situation of affairs will permit it. If I come, we shall set out about the 2nd of next month. But if prevented, then I make no doubt you with my friends will do all in your power for me, and that I wou'd have you consult together for the best. I do not mean to undervalue those sales, as it is not absolutely from want, and if they do not answer what you think they are worth, we need not dispose of them.

I am really involv'd in debt, and therefore in case I do not come down, beg you will send by Mr. Nelson my account with a bill for what you can raise.

My best compliments attend on you, family and friends.

P.S. Remember me affectionately to Mr. Barnett, Mr. Leonard and family, Dr. Barnett and all friends.
I write this post to Mr. Rd. Harrison, our friend, who will be with you about the time this letter gets to you.

John Waller, Plymouth, to Abraham Dent, Kirkby Stephen, 17 Sept. 1776.

We arriv'd here safe and well after an agreeable journey and without the least accident about fourteen days ago. I shou'd have wrote you sooner but for waiting the coming of the horse which was only last night, being kept in London three or four days by way of a rest. The man that brought him gives a good character of him in point of being good natur'd, and indeed he is in better order than I expect'd and without the least accident, so that I hope he will answer very well.

As soon as you have an opportunity of sending the £10 to Dr. Langhorne's sister, do it, and tell her to write immediately to the Doctor. We staid with the Doctor two nights, and he is to be here the 1st week in November. When you see Mrs Thompson or any of the family, do present my compliments and let her know that her granddaughter is one of the finest little girls in the world.

I still remain in debt to Mr. Fawcett for the horse and likewise for the business relating to the sale of the estates. When you can clear off that matter be so good; and in case Mr. K——y shou'd settle with you (as I think you have a good chance for it) I shall take it as a favour you'll send me a bill for what you can spare, as I am really run out.

I continued ill for some time after I left Kirby, but now thank God am better. Mr. Brathwaite I think will soon leave you, who I write to this post. My best wishes attend you and family. Remember me kindly to my Aunt and tell her that I am well, compliments to Mr. Thos. Nelson and Mrs. Fothergill, say that Mr. Nelson and sister are both so. I am just going to take pot luck with them. God bless you.

[P.S.] Remember me to your back neighbour affectionately &c &c.

John Waller, Plymouth, to Abraham Dent, Kirkby Stephen, 5 Nov. 1776.

I have only just to acknowledge the receipt of the deed, which I have returned to Mr. Fawcett and given directions about the security, as the purchaser I am an entire stranger to.

I beleive we shall not leave England yet as affairs I fancy has alter'd the system of things. All the twenty guardships are fitting, victualling and storing as we are, and the *P. of Wales* is order'd to be got ready for Capt. Barrington, a brother of the Lords of that name,[1] so that the last post I wrote to Mr. Brathwaite to come here immediately to settle for the best and to his own liking, which I think he shou'd do. If I go to Fayal, or any of my friends, which is not uncommon, I shall write a line to your relation.

When you have an opportunity of speaking to Jon. Merill, get a note by some means or other, for I left with Mr. Fawcett an account what it was. I will not give it up by any means. I wish I had known of Mr. J.

---

[1] Samuel Barrington (1729–1800), fifth son of John, first Viscount Barrington.

Dent's being at Fayal about a month ago, I had an excellent opportunity of writing a line by one of our men of war that is gone there and will be here in about six weeks. Please my best respects to Mrs. Dent &c. &c.

John Waller, Plymouth, to Abraham Dent, Kirkby Stephen, 9 Sept. 1777.

I have receiv'd your letter which has no little disappointed me indeed,[1] and I am sorry to say is like the rest of your former promises. What from my brother's family, the long arrears due from government and the insincerity of mankind, together with the large sums I have been drawing and running in debt for, I am at length wore out of all patience. As to Mr. Wright, I have assign'd over his note to Mr. Toulmin (who I had promis'd that money to in part for what I owe him) to use what means he pleases, so that unless he pays it on or before Michaelmas next, I am persuaded he will not be spar'd, nor indeed does he deserve it, considering his not answering my letter and the several times he has fix'd for the payment of the note to Mr. Toulmin, who declares he is only made a fool of.

I have look'd over the account and find that John Bousfield is in arrears for half a year to Whitsuntide last and Mrs. Tunstall 2 years at Martinmas. Concerning the last I shall write to Mr. Fawcett about. But pray how comes J. Bousfield to charge £6 7s. 5d. for the sesses of half a year? This must be some mistake and exceeds everything of the kind before, as well as reducing the rent, which is now far less than I ever receiv'd from J. Eubank who had the land cheaper. Another mistake is, that you have charg'd me with four guineas you have paid my Aunt, which I desir'd might be paid out of the rents of the field and house, at the rate of £4 a year to my Aunt and £2 to B. Moreland, so that I am not only giving up those rents to my brother, but am saddled with more charges which shou'd have been taken from the rents. I am sure I have more than I can manage with his sons, one of whom a scoundrel[2] has drawn for no less than £60 in one year. Now putting all these things together and being so pinch'd, I must insist upon your immediately sending me a sixty pound bill, therefore don't disappoint me any longer. It grieves me to write in this stile, but why shou'd I have such sufficient

---

[1] Dent had sent a statement of account to Waller on 3 September which showed a balance of £263 16s. 6d. in Waller's favour.

[2] Probably Lancelot Waller's son, Smithson, who as a naval purser was 'a very generous fellow, but kept it up too much' (*Recollections of James Anthony Gardner*, op. cit., p. 248).

reasons for it? If I am pressed for money, money must be got, and to have it and meet with such difficulties in coming at it, is enough to throw any man out of humour.

Please my best respects to Mrs. Dent and family, Mr. and Mrs. Brathwaite &c. &c.

Abraham Dent, Kirkby Stephen, to John Waller, 20 Sept. 1777.[1]

I received yours of the 9th of September and to your request have enclosed you a bill on Law and Holme for £60, and wish it had been in my power at present to have sent you more as I find I am not the only person that disappoints you. However, as I mention'd to you in my last that my endeavours shall not be wanting in getting you the whole as soon as possible. My disappointments is from particular acquaintances or it wou'd have been done before this. I wrote to Mr. Wright last week and mention'd that you had had no answers to your letters to him. As to the £4 4s. I paid Mrs. Seetree on your account December 6th., I have not yet got clear'd up but doubts not but it will be set right as I have her receipt mentioning by Mr. J. Waller's order, but shall say more on that when I write again. As to John Bousfield it's for a year sesses as they was not collected when J. Ewbanke left Lighttrees, but if any mistake in that or anything, shall rectifie. My family all joyne in good wishes.

John Waller, Plymouth, to Abraham Dent, Kirkby Stephen, 27 July 1783.

As I have not heard a word from Kirby since I saw you in Town, I have inclos'd this in a frank to Mr. Fawcett, with one to me, whenever you will be pleas'd to favor me with a line.

Is it true that you are married to the lady you once hinted to me; if so, I most sincerely congratulate you on the occasion, wishing you both health and happiness. I only heard an oblique report of this and hope it's true. At the same time something was said about my brother Jack's death, but as I had not heard from any of my friends at Kirby, so I did not absolutely give credit to it, for I thought if such an event had happen'd, that surely some of my freinds wou'd have wrote upon the occasion.

My Uncle Joseph who lives not far from Sunderland writes that he is in great distress; will you be so good as send him a couple of guineas and place to my account, and pray send me 4, 5 or 6 pair of stockings against winter, which I wrote to you about last year.

[1] A draft or copy on a blank part of the preceding letter.

I am with best respects to Mrs. Dent, family and all my friends and connections, Dear Dent, Your affectionate humble servant

John Waller

P.S. Remember me kindly to Mr. Brathwaite and family.

Index